The NOLO *News*—

Our free magazine devoted to everyday legal & consumer issues

To thank you for sending in the postage-paid feedback card in the back of this book, you'll receive a free two-year subscription to the **NOLO** *News*—our quarterly magazine of legal, small business and consumer information. With each issue you get updates on important legal changes that affect you, helpful articles on everyday law, answers to your legal questions in Auntie Nolo's advice column, a complete Nolo catalog and, of course, our famous lawyer jokes.

Legal information online–24 hours a day

Get instant access to the legal information you need 24 hours a day.

Visit a Nolo online self-help law center and you'll find:

- hundreds of helpful articles on a wide variety of topics
- selected chapters from Nolo books
- online seminars with our lawyer authors and other experts
- downloadable demos of Nolo software
- frequently asked questons about key legal issues
- our complete catalog and online ordering info
- our ever popular lawyer jokes and more.

Here's how to find us:

America Online Just use the key word Nolo.

On the **Internet** our World Wide Web address (URL) is: http://www.nolo.com.

Prodigy/CompuServe Use the Web Browsers on CompuServe or Prodigy to access Nolo's Web site on the Internet.

NOLO PRESS
YEARS
LAW FOR ALL

SECOND EDITION

Make Your Own LIVING TRUST

by Attorney Denis Clifford

Edited by Mary Randolph

Illustrated by Mari Stein

NOLO PRESS BERKELEY

Please Read This

Your responsibility when using a self-help law book

We've done our best to give you useful and accurate information in this book. But laws and procedures change frequently and are subject to differing interpretations. If you want legal advice backed by a guarantee, see a lawyer. If you use this book, it's your responsibility to make sure that the facts and general advice contained in it are applicable to your situation.

Keeping up to date

To keep its books up to date, Nolo Press issues new printings and new editions periodically. New printings reflect minor legal changes and technical corrections. New editions contain major legal changes, major text additions or major reorganizations. To find out if a later printing or edition of any Nolo book is available, call Nolo Press at 510-549-1976 or check the catalog in the *Nolo News,* our quarterly newspaper.

To stay current, follow the "Update" service in the *Nolo News.* You can get a free two-year subscription by sending us the registration card in the back of the book. In another effort to help you use Nolo's latest materials, we offer a 25% discount off the purchase of the new edition of your Nolo book when you turn in the cover of an earlier edition. (See the "Recycle Offer" in the back of the book.)

This book was last revised in: **APRIL 1996.**

SECOND EDITION	April 1996
PRODUCTION	Stephanie Harolde
ILLUSTRATIONS	Mari Stein
BOOK DESIGN	Jackie Mancuso
COVER DESIGN	Toni Ihara
PROOFREADING	Robert Wells
INDEX	Jane Meyerhofer
PRINTING	Delta Lithograph

Clifford, Denis.
    Make your own living trust / by Denis Clifford ; edited by Mary
Randolph ; illustrated by Mari Stein. -- 2nd ed.
      p. cm.
    Includes index.
    ISBN 0-87337-305-7
      1. Living trusts--United States--Popular works. I. Randolph,
Mary. II. Title.
KF734.Z9C57 1996
346.7305'2--dc20
[347.30629]   95-39116
                                      CIP

Quantity sales: For information on bulk purchases or corporate premium sales, please contact the Special Sales department. For academic sales or textbook adoptions, ask for Academic Sales. 800-955-4775, Nolo Press, Inc., 950 Parker St., Berkeley, CA, 94710.

Dedication

Once again, to Naomi.

Acknowledgements

My thanks to all those friends who helped me with this book, both putting it together and over the years:

First, to two friends at Nolo Press, without whose aid this book would never have come into existence: Mary Randolph, a superb editor and writer, and organizer extraordinaire, and Stephanie Harolde, who prepared so many drafts of the book so well and did much fine editing, too.

Second, to Mark Peery, of Greenbrae, California, a superb estate planning lawyer (and great friend), and Marilyn Putnam, of San Francisco, another estate planning wizard.

Third, to Jake Warner, for his brilliant editing and assistance on this book and all his help through the years.

Fourth, to Toni Ihara, a spirit forever joyous—thanks again for getting me into all this.

Fifth, to all my other friends and colleagues at Nolo Press. In the past, I listed everyone, but now we have 70 or more employees, plus more outside writers and an employee manual. Still, Nolo retains the relaxed, friendly atmosphere that makes it such a pleasant (as well as productive) place to work.

Sixth, to Attorney Magdalen Gaynor, of White Plains and New York City, New York, an excellent estate planning lawyer who gave me information generously and cheerfully.

Seventh, to other friends who helped me with this book: Linda Moody, of Mill Valley, California, a law school friend who's become another superb estate planning lawyer; Ken Fisher, of Pleasant Hill, California, a fine insurance agent, and the many, many other people who helped with this book and over the years, with earlier materials I've written about living trusts.

And finally, my heartfelt thanks to my clients from past years, from whom I learned so much reality I could never have learned in books or school (sure never did in law school), and also to the many readers of earlier books of mine that discussed living trusts, who wrote me with suggestions, comments, corrections and other thoughts that contributed greatly to this book.

Contents

4

WHAT TYPE OF TRUST DO YOU NEED?

5

THE TAX-SAVING AB TRUST

6

CHOOSING WHAT PROPERTY TO PUT IN YOUR LIVING TRUST

7

TRUSTEES

8

CHOOSING YOUR BENEFICIARIES

9

PROPERTY LEFT TO MINOR CHILDREN OR YOUNG ADULTS

10

PREPARING YOUR LIVING TRUST DOCUMENT

11

TRANSFERRING PROPERTY TO YOUR TRUST

12

COPYING, STORING AND REGISTERING YOUR TRUST DOCUMENT

13

LIVING WITH YOUR LIVING TRUST

14

AFTER A GRANTOR DIES

15

A LIVING TRUST AS PART OF YOUR ESTATE PLAN

16

WILLS

17

IF YOU NEED EXPERT HELP

Glossary

Appendix

Introduction

How to Use This Book

Whether you are single or a member of a couple, this book lets you prepare your own basic living trust. A basic living trust enables people with small or moderate estates—in estate tax terms, those with a net worth of less than $625,000 to $750,000, depending upon the year of death—to transfer their property after their death to whomever they want to have it, without any attorneys or court involvement. The people who inherit your property can avoid probate—that expensive, lawyer-ridden process required of most wills.

This book also enables more prosperous couples with a combined estate worth over $625,000 to create a living trust that both avoids probate and saves on estate taxes. I call this type of trust an AB trust or occasionally a "living trust with marital life estate." As you read through the book, you'll learn whether or not it's wise for you to create this type of trust with the forms in this book.

Any intelligent person can create a valid, effective living trust. You don't have to be a nuclear physicist—or an attorney. Indeed, with the aid of this book, most people can safely create their living trusts themselves, without any need for a lawyer.

Louisiana residents. This book is designed for residents of all states except Louisiana, which has a legal system based on the Napoleonic Code, different from all other states.

Many books or so-called authorities on living trusts assert that it is foolish to try to do your own living trust. They maintain you must hire a lawyer or even a "team of experts" (lawyer, accountant, financial planner)—they'll see to it you don't have much of an estate left. Some even argue that doing your own living trust is like trying to do your own brain surgery. This is ridiculous. For most people, there is nothing difficult about preparing a living trust. After all, most people simply want to transfer their own property after their death to those they want to have it, without involving lawyers and courts. There is nothing inherently complex about that. For most people, there's no reason to hire a lawyer to accomplish this goal.

As you read the book, you'll learn exactly how living trusts work and what form is right for you. Some readers, particularly those with net estates worth more than $625,000 to $750,000, may decide they want a lawyer's assistance to prepare their final living trust. This book doesn't claim to present definitive advice on all aspects of living trusts. There are volumes of books on the topic in any good-sized law library. As you'll see, in some situations I urge you to consult a lawyer or other expert. When I do so, I also use an identifying symbol (see "Icons Used in This Book," below), so you can readily see that an expert is recommended.

Even if you decide to get an expert's help in preparing your living trust, you'll benefit greatly by comprehending the basic issues and objectives involved. The information you gain by reading this book will enable you to deal with a professional to get the help you really need, for a reasonable fee.

Keep in mind that creating a living trust has important, long-term consequences for your family and their finances. You can do it yourself, in most cases, but you must do it right, which means educating yourself about your options so you can make well-informed decisions.

The trust forms in this book have been carefully prepared to be both clear and fully acceptable in the real world. There is no "standard" living trust. Anyone (or any book) who asserts that trusts must be written in "legalese" (language that is peculiar to the legal profession) is flat-out wrong. A living trust functions just fine if it covers the basics, such as what property is in the trust, who gets it and who manages the trust after you die. And although no legalese is mandated, it is prudent to have a trust form that, like the ones in this book, is sufficiently traditional that it looks familiar to institutions that may be presented with it—such as banks, title companies or stock brokerage companies. ❦

ICONS USED IN THIS BOOK

whenever there is a general warning.

when you need to consult a lawyer or other legal expert. Although quite a few of these symbols appear throughout the book, most readers won't be affected by them.

when form instructions apply only to marital living trusts.

when I want to refer you to other resources.

Make Your Own Living Trust is a workbook, not a treasure to cherish unmarked. Its purpose, after all, is to help you understand and prepare your own living trust. While reading this book, take notes, record information about your own situation, use the worksheets to the extent you find them helpful and then decide how you want your trust to work. Finally, use one of the trust forms provided in the Appendix to draft your own living trust.

Before you actually start to prepare a living trust, read through the book once. You need to know how a living trust really works and how it fits in with your overall estate plan. Also, obviously, you need to resolve basic personal issues, such as what property to transfer to your trust and who your beneficiaries are (who gets what).

Chapter 1

An Overview of Living Trusts

$\mathcal{L}$iving trusts are an efficient and effective way to transfer property, at your death, to the relatives, friends or charities you've chosen. Essentially, a living trust performs the same function as a will, with the important difference that property left by a will must go through the probate court process. In probate, a deceased person's will is proved valid in court, the person's debts are paid and, usually after about a year, the remaining property is finally distributed to the beneficiaries. In the vast majority of instances, these probate court proceedings are an utter waste of time and money.

By contrast, property left by a living trust can go promptly and directly to your inheritors. They don't have to bother with a probate court proceeding. That means they won't have to spend any of your hard-earned money (at least, I presume it was hard-earned) to pay for court and lawyer fees.

Some paperwork is necessary to establish a probate-avoidance living trust and transfer property to it, but there are no serious drawbacks or risks involved in creating or maintaining the trust. You don't even need to maintain separate trust tax records. While you live, all transactions that are technically made by your living trust are reported on your personal income tax return.

These trusts are called "living" or sometimes "inter vivos" (Latin for "among the living") because they're created while you're alive. They're called "revocable" because you can revoke or change them at any time, for any reason, before you die.

While you live, you effectively keep ownership of all property that you've technically transferred to your living trust. You can do whatever you want to with any trust property, including selling it, spending it or giving it away. Basically, a revocable living trust is merely a piece of paper that becomes operational at your death. At that point, it allows your trust property to be transferred, privately and outside of probate, to the people or organizations you name as beneficiaries of the trust.

A. Living Trusts Explained

A trust can seem like a mysterious creature, dreamed up by lawyers and wrapped in legal jargon. Trusts were an invention of medieval England, used as a method to evade restrictions on ownership and inheritance of land. Don't let the word "trust" scare you. True, the word can have an impressive, slightly ominous sound. Historically, monopolists used trusts to dominate entire industries (for example, the Standard Oil Trust in the era of Teddy Roosevelt's "trust-busting"). And trusts have traditionally been used by the very wealthy to preserve their riches from generation to generation. (Indeed, isn't one version of the American dream to be the beneficiary of your very own trust fund?) But happily, the types of living trusts this book covers aren't complicated or beyond the reach of ordinary folks. Here are the basics.

1. The Concept of a Trust

A trust, like a corporation, is an intangible legal entity ("legal fiction" might be a more accurate term) that is capable of owning property. You can't see a trust, or touch it, but it does exist. The first step in creating a working trust is to prepare and sign a document called a *Declaration of Trust.*

Once you create and sign the Declaration of Trust, the trust exists, and you can transfer property to it. The trust becomes the legal owner of the property. There must, however, be a flesh-and-blood person actually in charge of this property; that person is called the *trustee.* With traditional trusts, the trustee manages the property on the behalf of someone else, called the *beneficiary.* However, with a living trust, you, the person who creates the trust, can be the trustee and also, in effect, the beneficiary, until you die. Only after your death do the trust beneficiaries you've named in the Declaration of Trust have any rights to your trust property.

2. Creating a Living Trust

When you create a living trust document, you must identify:

- Yourself, as the *grantor* (or, for a couple, the grantors). The grantor is the person who creates a trust.

- The *trustee*, who manages the trust property. This is normally the person (or persons) who establishes the trust—as long as she, or one of them, lives.

- The *successor trustee*, who takes over after the grantor(s) dies. This successor trustee turns the trust property over to the trust beneficiaries and performs any other task required by the trust.

- The *trust beneficiary* or beneficiaries, those who are entitled to receive the trust property at the grantor's death.

- The *property* that is subject to the trust.

Normally, a Declaration of Trust also includes other basic terms, such as the authority of the grantor to amend or revoke it at any time, and the authority of the trustee.

3. How a Living Trust Works

The key to a living trust established to avoid probate is that the grantor (remember, that's you, the person who sets up the trust) isn't locked into anything. You can revise, amend or revoke the trust for any (or no) reason, any time before your death, as long as you're legally competent. And because you appoint yourself as the initial trustee, you can control and use the property as you see fit.

WHAT IS COMPETENCE?

"Competent" means having the mental capacity to make and understand decisions regarding your property. A person can become legally "incompetent" if declared so in a court proceeding, such as a custodianship or guardianship proceeding. If a person tries to make or revoke or amend a living trust and someone challenges her mental capacity, or competence, to do so, the matter can end up in a nasty court battle. Fortunately, such court disputes are quite rare.

And now for the legal magic of the living trust device. Although a living trust is really only a legal fiction during your life, it assumes a very real presence for a brief period after your death. When you die, the living trust can no longer be revoked or altered. It is now irrevocable. The trust really does own the property now.

With a trust for a single person, after you die, the person you named in your trust document to be successor trustee takes over. He or she is in charge of transferring the trust property to the family, friends or charities you named as your trust beneficiaries.

With a trust for a married couple, the surviving spouse manages the trust. A successor trustee takes over after both spouses die, or become incapacitated.

There is no court or governmental supervision to insure that your successor trustee complies with the terms of your living trust. That means that a vital element of an effective living trust is having someone you fully trust be your successor trustee. If there is no person you trust sufficiently to name as successor trustee, a living trust probably isn't for you. You can name a bank, trust company or other financial institution as successor trustee, but that has serious drawbacks. (See Chapter 7, "Trustees," Section C.)

After the trust grantor dies, some paperwork is necessary to transfer the trust property to the beneficiaries, such as preparing new ownership documents and paying any death taxes assessed against the estate. (See Chapter 14, "After a Grantor Dies.") But because no probate is necessary for property that was transferred to the living trust, the whole thing can generally be handled within a few weeks, in most cases without a lawyer. No court proceedings or papers are required to terminate the trust. Once the job of getting the property to the beneficiaries is accomplished, the trust just evaporates, by its own terms. No formal documents need be filed to end the trust.

Some types of living trusts, however, are designed to last much longer. First, the living trust forms in this book include provisions for creating what's called a "child's subtrust" (discussed in Chapter 9, Section C). This type of subtrust is for property you leave to a minor or young adult beneficiary. These trusts are managed by your successor trustee and can last for years, until the young beneficiary reaches the age you specified in your Declaration of Trust. Then the beneficiary receives the trust property, and the subtrust ends.

If you and your spouse create an AB living trust (discussed in Chapters 4 and 5) designed both to avoid probate and save on estate taxes after one spouse dies, that spouse's trust keeps going until the second spouse dies.

Other types of living trusts, not set out in this book, can also continue for years. These trusts may be desirable for one of many reasons: to protect assets for a disadvantaged child; to be sure assets in a second or subsequent marriage left to one spouse are substantially preserved for children from earlier marriage; to save on estate taxes beyond the method provided by Nolo's AB living trust. These types of trusts are discussed in Chapter 15, Section F.

A MINI-GLOSSARY OF LIVING TRUST TERMS

Although I've already used and defined some of these terms, I want to give you a summary of all basic trust terms that are essential when preparing or understanding a living trust. Unfortunately, you can't escape legal jargon entirely when you deal with living trusts.

- The person who sets up the living trust (that's you, or you and your spouse) is called a **grantor(s)**, **trustor(s)** or **settlor(s)**. These terms mean the same thing and are used interchangeably. I use the term **grantor** in this book.
- All the property you own at death, whether in your living trust or owned in some other form, is your **estate**.
- The market value of your property at your death, less all debts and liabilities on that property, is your net or **taxable estate**. Technically, the IRS allows your successor trustee to choose market value at your death or six months later.
- The property you transfer to the trust is called, collectively, the **trust property, trust principal** or **trust estate**. (And, of course, there's a Latin version: the trust corpus.)
- The person who has power over the trust property is called the **trustee**.
- The person the grantor names to take over as trustee after the grantor's death (or, with a trust made jointly by a couple, after the death of both spouses) is called the **successor trustee**.
- The people or organizations who get the trust property when the grantor dies are called the **beneficiaries** of the trust. (While the grantors are alive, technically they themselves are the beneficiaries of the trust.)

B. Probate and Why You Want to Avoid It

If you're reading this book, you probably already know that you want to avoid probate. If you still need any persuasion that avoiding probate is desirable, here's a brief look at how the process actually works.

Probate is the legal process that includes:

- Filing the deceased person's will with the local probate court (called "surrogate" or "chancery" court in some places)
- Inventorying the deceased person's property
- Having that property appraised
- Paying legal debts, including death taxes
- Proving the will valid in court, and
- Eventually distributing what's left as the will directs.

If the deceased person didn't leave a will, or a will isn't valid, the estate must still undergo probate. The process is called an "intestacy" proceeding, and the property is distributed to the closest relatives as state law dictates.

People who defend the probate system (mostly lawyers, which is surely no surprise) assert that probate prevents fraud in transferring a deceased person's property. In addition, they claim it protects inheritors by promptly resolving claims creditors have against a deceased person's property. In truth, however, most property is transferred within a close circle of family and friends, and very few estates have problems with creditors' claims. In short, most people have no need of these so-called benefits, so probate usually amounts to a lot of time-wasting, expensive mumbo-jumbo of aid to no one but the lawyers involved.

The actual probate functions are essentially clerical and administrative. In the vast majority of probate cases, there's no conflict, no contesting parties—none of the normal reasons for court proceedings or lawyers' adversarial skills. Likewise, probate doesn't usually call for legal research or lawyers' drafting abilities. Instead, in the normal, uneventful probate proceeding, the family or other heirs of the deceased person provide a copy of the will and other financial information. The attorney's secretary then fills in a small mound of forms and keeps track of filing deadlines and other procedural technicalities. Some lawyers hire probate form preparation companies to do all the real work. In most instances, the existence of these freelance paralegal companies is not disclosed to clients, who assume that lawyers' offices at least do the routine paperwork they are paid so well for. In some states, the attorney makes a couple of routine court appearances; in others, normally the whole procedure is handled by mail.

Because of the complicated paperwork and waiting periods imposed by law, a typical probate takes up to a year or more, often much more. (I once worked in a law office that was profitably entering its seventh year of handling a probate estate—and a very wealthy estate it was.) During probate, the beneficiaries generally get nothing unless the judge allows the decedent's immediate family a "family allowance." In some states, this allowance is a pittance—only a few hundred dollars. In others, it can amount to thousands.

Probate usually requires both an "executor" (called a "personal representative" in some states) and someone familiar with probate procedures, normally a probate attorney. The executor is a person appointed in the will who is responsible for supervising the estate, which means making sure that the will is followed. If the person died without a will, the court appoints an "administrator" (whose main qualification may sometimes be that he's a crony of the judge) to serve the same function. The executor, who is usually the spouse or a friend of the deceased, hires a probate lawyer to do the paperwork. The executor often hires the decedent's lawyer (who may even have possession of the will), but this is not required. Then the executor does little more than sign where the lawyer directs, wondering why the whole business is taking so long. For these services, the lawyer and the executor are each entitled to a hefty fee from the probate estate. Some lawyers even persuade (or dupe) clients into naming them as executors, enabling the lawyers to hire themselves as probate attorneys and collect two fees—one as executor, one as probate attorney. By contrast, many executors do not take the fee, especially if he or she is a substantial inheritor.

Probate can evoke exaggerated images of greedy lawyers consuming most of an estate in fees, while churning out reams of gobbledygook-filled paper as slowly as possible. While there is truth in these images (far more than lawyers care to admit), lawyer fees rarely actually devour the entire estate. In many states, the fees are what a court approves as "reasonable." In a few states, the fees are based on a percentage of the estate subject to probate. Either way, probate attorney fees for a "routine" estate with a gross value of $400,000 (these days, in many urban areas, this may be little more than a home, some savings and a car) can amount to $10,000 or more. Fees based on the "gross" probate estate means that debts on property are not deducted to determine value. Thus, if a house has a market value of $200,000 with a mortgage balance of $160,000 (net equity of $40,000), the gross value of the house is $200,000.

In addition, there are court costs, appraiser's fees and other possible expenses. Moreover, if the basic fee is set by statute and there are any "extraordinary" services performed for the estate, the attorney or executor can often ask the court for additional fees.

EXTREME PROBATE FEES

Marilyn Monroe's estate offers an extreme example of how outrageous probate fees can be. She died in debt in 1962, but over the next 18 years, her estate received income, mostly from movie royalties, in excess of $1,600,000. When her estate was settled in 1980, her executor announced that debts of $372,136 had been paid, and $101,229 was left for inheritors. Well over $1 million of Monroe's estate was consumed by probate fees.

Even England—the source of our antiquated probate laws—abolished its elaborate probate system years ago. It survives in this country because it is so lucrative for lawyers.

C. Avoiding Probate

The most popular probate-avoidance method is, undoubtedly, the living trust. However, there are a number of other methods.

1. Informal Probate Avoidance

You may wonder why surviving relatives and friends can't just divide up your property as your will directs (or as you said you wanted, if you never got around to writing a will), and ignore the laws requiring probate. Some small estates are undoubtedly disposed of this way, directly and informally by family members.

For example, an older man lives his last few years in a nursing home. After his death, his children meet and divide the personal items their father had kept over the years. What little savings he has have long since been put into a joint account with the children anyway, so there's no need for formalities there.

For this type of informal procedure to work, the family must be able to gain possession of all of the deceased's property, agree on how to distribute it and pay all the creditors. Gaining possession of property isn't difficult when the only property left is personal effects and household items. However, if real estate, securities, bank accounts, cars, boats or other property bearing legal title papers are involved, informal family property distribution can't work. Title to a house, for example, can't be changed on the say-so of the next of kin. Someone with legal authority must prepare, sign and record a deed transferring title to the house to the new owners, the inheritors.

One good rule is that whenever outsiders are involved with a deceased's property, do-it-yourself division by inheritors is not feasible. For instance, creditors can be an obstacle; a creditor concerned about being paid can usually file a court action to compel a probate proceeding.

Another stumbling block for an informal family property disposition is disagreement among family members on how to divide the deceased's possessions. All inheritors must agree to the property distribution if probate is bypassed. Any inheritor who is unhappy with the result can, like creditors, file for a formal probate. If there's a will, the family will probably follow its provisions. If there is no will, the family may look up and agree to abide by the inheritance rules established by the law of the state where the deceased person lived. Or, in either case, the family may simply agree on their own settlement. For example, if, despite a will provision to the contrary, one sibling wants the furniture and the other wants the tools, they can simply trade.

In sum, informal probate avoidance, even for a small estate, isn't something you can count on. Realistically, probate avoidance must be planned in advance.

2. Other Probate-Avoidance Methods

Besides the living trust, these are the most popular probate-avoidance methods:

- joint tenancy
- informal bank account trusts, also called "pay-on-death accounts" or revocable trust accounts
- life insurance
- state laws that exempt certain (small) amounts of property left by will from probate
- gifts made while you are alive.

These methods are discussed briefly in Chapter 15, "A Living Trust as Part of Your Estate Plan," Section B.

Other probat- avoidance techniques are discussed in detail in *Plan Your Estate* (Nolo Press).

While I'm a fan of living trusts, I don't believe they are always the best probate-avoidance device for all property of all people in all situations. It's up to you to determine if a living trust is the best way for you to avoid probate for all your property, or if you want to use other methods. In rare cases, you may even want to use other methods exclusively. (See Chapter 3, "Common Questions About Living Trusts," Section A, and Chapter 15, "A Living Trust as Part of Your Estate Plan.")

D. Saving on Estate Taxes

A basic probate-avoidance living trust, either for a single person or a couple, does not, by itself, reduce federal or state estate taxes. The taxing authorities don't care whether or not your property goes through probate; all they care about is how much you owned at your death. Property you leave in a revocable living trust is definitely considered part of your estate for federal estate tax purposes. If your net estate is worth more than a certain amount—$625,000 in 1996—it will be subject to federal estate tax unless the property is left to your spouse or a charity.

Some specialized kinds of living trusts, however, can save on estate taxes. This book contains one such tax-saving trust, called an "AB" trust or "living trust with marital life estate."

If you are a member of a couple with combined property worth over $650,000, you can save your inheritors substantial federal estate taxes by using an AB trust. Couples can use the AB trust in this book if they have a combined estate worth up to $1,250,000 to $1,500,000 (perhaps more after 2001), depending upon when a spouse dies.

These trusts take advantage of the fact that federal law exempts a certain amount of property from estate taxes. Congress recently increased the value of property that is exempt from tax. The exempt amount depends upon the year of death, as shown below.

Federal Estate Tax Exemptions

If you die in	you can leave this much tax-free	
1996	$625,000	
1997	$650,000	
1998	$675,000	
1999	$700,000	
2000	$725,000	
2001	$750,000	
After 2001	$750,000	*plus an annual cost of living adjustment rounded to the nearest $10,000*

Basically, this book's AB trust allows each member of a couple to use a separate estate tax exemption (that is, use two exemptions in total) while leaving one spouse's property for the use of the surviving spouse. How these trusts work is explained in Chapter 4, "What Type of Trust Do You Need?" and Chapter 5, "The Tax-Saving AB Trust."

Estate tax uncertainty. As of the printing of this second edition of this book, Congress and the President had not resolved their budget struggle. The estate tax exemptions listed above are contained in the Congressional budget bill, and it seems very likely that these exemptions will eventually become law. But until the budget conflict is resolved, the current estate tax law remains in effect. Under this current law, property worth up to $600,000 is exempt from federal tax, no matter what the year of death.

When you read this, you'll probably know whether or not the budget conflict has been resolved, and may well also have learned what happened to the proposed estate tax exemption increases. But if you need to find

out if the proposed exemptions have become law, Nolo Press offers you the following assistance:

- The status of the proposed estate tax exemptions will be reported in our quarterly newspaper, the *Nolo News*. To get a free subscription, just send in the registration card in the back of this book.

- The status of the estate tax revisions will also be posted on Nolo's on-line Self-Help Law Centers. Our World Wide Web address is http://www.nolo.com/ For America Online use the keyword Nolo to get to our AOL site.

- You can call Nolo Press at (800) 728-3555.

If the combined value of your and your spouse's estates exceeds $1,250,000 to $1,500,000, you'll need estate tax planning help that's beyond the scope of this book, although an AB trust will likely be a key component of your final plan.

E. Other Advantages of a Living Trust

As you know, the main reason for setting up a revocable living trust is to save your family time and money by avoiding probate and perhaps estate taxes as well. But there are other advantages as well. Here is a brief rundown of the other major positive features of a living trust.

1. Out-of-State Real Estate Doesn't Have to Be Probated in That State

The only thing worse than regular probate is out-of-state probate. Usually, an estate is probated in the probate court of the county where the decedent was living before he or she died. But if the decedent owned real estate in more than one state, it's usually necessary to have a whole separate probate proceeding in each one. That means the surviving relatives must find and hire a lawyer in each state, and pay for multiple probate proceedings.

With a living trust, out-of-state property can normally be transferred to the beneficiaries without probate in that state.

2. You Can Avoid the Need for a Conservatorship

A living trust can be useful if the person who created it (the grantor) becomes incapable, because of physical or mental illness, of taking care of his or her financial affairs. The person named in the living trust document to take over as trustee at the grantor's death (the successor trustee) can also take over management of the trust if the grantor becomes incapacitated. (If you use this book's trust forms, the grantor's incapacity must be certified in writing by a physician.) When a couple sets up a trust, if one person becomes incapacitated, the other takes sole responsibility. If both members of the couple are incapacitated, their successor trustee takes over. The person who takes over has authority to manage all property in the trust, and to use it for the grantor or grantors' benefit.

Example

Wei creates a revocable living trust, appointing herself as trustee. The trust document states that if she becomes incapacitated, and a physician signs a statement saying she no longer can manage her own affairs, her daughter Li-Shan will replace her as trustee, and manage the trust property for Wei's benefit.

If there is no living trust and no other arrangements have been made for someone to take over property management if you become incapacitated, someone must get legal authority, from a court, to take over. Typically, the spouse or adult child of the person seeks this authority and is called a "conservator" or "guardian." Conservatorship proceedings are intrusive and often expensive, and they get a court involved in your personal finances on a continuing basis.

DURABLE POWER OF ATTORNEY

You should also give your successor trustee (or spouse) the authority to manage property that has not been transferred the trust if you become incapacitated. The best way to do that is to prepare and sign a document called a "Durable Power of Attorney for Financial Management." (See Chapter 15, "A Living Trust as Part of Your Estate Plan," Section E.)

Your successor trustee has no power to make health care decisions for you if you become incapacitated. If your preference is to die a natural death without the unauthorized use of life support systems, you'll want to prepare and sign some other documents. (This is discussed in Chapter 15, Section E.)

3. Your Estate Plan Remains Confidential

When your will is filed with the probate court after you die, it becomes a matter of public record. A living trust, on the other hand, is a private document. Because the living trust document is never filed with a court or other government entity, what you leave, and to whom, remains private. There is one exception: Records of real estate transfers are always public, so if your successor trustee transfers real estate to a beneficiary after your death, there will be a public record of it.

A few states do require that you register your living trust with the local court, but there are no legal consequences or penalties if you don't. (Registration is explained in Chapter 12, "Copying, Storing and Registering Your Trust Document.") Also, registration of a living trust normally requires that you just file a paper stating the existence of the trust and the main players—you don't file the document itself, so the terms aren't part of the public record.

The only way the terms of a living trust might become public is if—and this is very unlikely—after your death someone filed a lawsuit to challenge the trust or collect a court judgment you owed them.

4. You Can Change Your Mind at Any Time

You have complete control over your revocable living trust and all the property you transfer to it. You can:

- sell, mortgage or give away property in the trust
- put ownership of trust property back in your own name
- add property to the trust
- change the beneficiaries
- name a different successor trustee (the person who distributes trust property after your death)
- revoke the trust completely.

If you and your spouse create the trust together, both spouses must consent to changes, although either of you can revoke the trust entirely. (See Chapter 13, "Living With Your Living Trust.")

5. No Trust Recordkeeping Is Required While You Are Alive

Even after you create a valid trust that will avoid probate after your death, you do not have to maintain separate trust records. This means you do not have to keep a separate trust bank account, maintain trust financial records or spend any time on trust paperwork.

As long as you remain the trustee of your trust, the IRS does not require that a separate trust income tax return be filed. (IRS Reg. § 1.671-4.) You do not have to obtain a trust taxpayer ID number. You report all trust transactions on your regular income tax returns. In sum, for tax purposes, living trusts don't exist while you live.

6. You Can Name Someone to Manage Trust Property for Young Beneficiaries

If there's a possibility that any of your beneficiaries will inherit trust property while still young (not yet 35), you may want to arrange to have someone manage that property for them until they're older. If they might inherit before they're legally adults (18, in most all states), you should definitely arrange for management. Minors are not allowed to legally control significant amounts of property, and if you haven't provided someone to do it, a court will have to appoint a property guardian.

When you create a living trust with this book, you can arrange for someone to manage property for a young beneficiary. In most states, you have two options:

- Have your successor trustee (or your spouse, if you created a living trust together) manage the property in a "child's subtrust" until the child reaches an age you designate.
- In most states, you can appoint someone as a "custodian" to manage the property until the child reaches an age specified by your state's Uniform Transfers to Minors Act (18 in a few states, 21 in most, but up to 25 in California, Alaska and Nevada).

Both methods are explained in Chapter 9, "Property Left to Minor Children or Young Adults."

7. No Lawyer Intrudes Into Distributing Your Property

With a living trust, the person you named as your successor trustee has total control over how the property is transferred to the beneficiaries you named in the trust document. With a will, technically the person in charge of the property that passes under the terms of the will is the executor you named in the will, but the probate lawyer usually runs the show. This can be the personal show as well as the silly court show. I've heard of a lawyer calling a family in for a "reading" of the deceased's will immediately after the funeral service, which some family members found highly insensitive. There's much less chance of this type of crassness if only close personal relations are involved in the transfer of the property.

F. Possible Drawbacks of a Living Trust

A basic living trust, which serves just to avoid probate, can have some drawbacks. They aren't significant to most people, but you should be aware of them before you create a living trust. Aside from the problems discussed below, an AB living trust, which is designed to save on estate taxes as well as avoid probate, has a whole set of its own potential problems and drawbacks, which are covered in Chapter 4.

1. Initial Paperwork

Setting up a living trust obviously requires some paperwork. The first step is to use this book to create a trust document, which you must sign in front of a notary public. So far, the amount of work required is no more than writing a will.

There is, however, one more essential step to make your living trust effective. You must make sure that ownership of all the property you listed in the trust document is legally transferred to the living trust. (Chapter 11, "Transferring Property to Your Trust," explains this process in detail.) Transferring property into your trust is simply a matter of doing the paperwork correctly. What you have to do depends on the kind of property you're putting in the trust.

- If an item of property doesn't have a title (ownership) document, listing it in the trust document is enough to transfer it. So, for example, no additional paperwork is legally required for most books, furniture, electronics, jewelry, appliances, musical instruments, paintings and many other kinds of property.

- If an item has a title document—real estate, stocks, mutual funds, bonds, money market accounts or vehicles, for example—you must change the title document to show that the property is owned by your living trust (technically, by the trustee of the trust). For

example, if you want to put your house into your living trust, you must prepare and sign a new deed, transferring ownership from you to your living trust.

After the trust is created, you must keep written records sufficient to identify what's in and out of the trust, whenever you transfer property to or from the trust. This isn't burdensome unless you're frequently transferring property in and out, which is rare.

Example

Misha and David Feldman put their house in a living trust to avoid probate, but later decide to sell it. In the real estate contract and deed transferring ownership to the new owners, Misha and David sign their names "as trustees of the Misha and David Feldman Revocable Living Trust, dated March 18, 1993."

2. Transfer Taxes

In most all states, including California, New York, Florida and Texas, transfers of real estate to revocable living trusts are exempt from transfer taxes usually imposed on real estate transfers. Washington, D.C., used to tax transfers of real estate to living trusts, but repealed those laws.

To learn if there will be any transfer tax imposed on transfer of your real estate to your trust, contact your county tax assessor. Your county land records office (County Recorder's office or Registry of Deeds) may also be able to provide you with this information. If the tax is minor, it may impose no serious burden on creating your trust. If the tax is substantial, you may decide it's too costly to place your real estate in a trust.

3. Difficulty Refinancing Trust Real Estate

Because legal title to trust real estate is held in the name of the trustee of the living trust—not your name—some banks, and especially title companies, may balk if you want to refinance it. They should be sufficiently reassured if you show them a copy of your trust document, which specifically gives you, as trustee, the power to borrow against trust property.

In the unlikely event you can't convince an uncooperative lender to deal with you in your capacity as trustee, you'll have to find another lender (which shouldn't be hard) or simply transfer the property out of the trust and back into your name. Later, after your refinance, you can transfer it back into the living trust. A silly process, but one that does work.

4. No Cutoff of Creditors' Claims

Most people don't have to worry that after their death creditors will try to collect large debts from property in their estate. In most situations, there are no massive debts. Those that exist, such as outstanding bills, taxes and last illness and funeral expenses, can be readily paid from the deceased's property. But if you are concerned about the possibility of large claims, you may want to let your property go through probate instead of a living trust.

If your property goes through probate, creditors have only a set amount of time to file claims against your estate. A creditor who was properly notified of the probate court proceeding cannot file a claim after the period—about six months, in most states—expires.

Example

Elaine is a real estate investor with a good-sized portfolio of property. She has many creditors and is involved in a couple of lawsuits. It's sensible for her to have her estate transferred by a probate court procedure, which allows creditors to present claims, resolves conflicts, cuts off the claims of creditors who are notified of the probate proceeding but don't present timely claims.

On the other hand, when property isn't probated, creditors still have the right to be paid (if the debt is valid) from that property. In most states, there is no formal claim procedure. (California has enacted a statutory scheme for creditors to get at property transferred by living trust.) The creditor may not know who inherited the deceased debtor's property, and once the property is found, the creditor may have to file a lawsuit, which may not be worth the time and expense.

If you want to take advantage of probate's creditor cutoff, you must let all your property pass through probate. If not, there's a good chance the creditor could still sue (even after the probate claim cutoff) and try to collect from the property that didn't go through probate and passed instead through your living trust. ❦

chapter 2

HUMAN EMOTIONS AND LIVING TRUSTS

*B*efore plunging deeper into the mechanics of creating your own living trust, I want to switch gears and acknowledge the underlying reality we're talking about here: death, and the transfer of one's property after a death. Although property concerns can be minor indeed in the face of the overwhelming force and mystery of death, these deep imponderables are beyond the scope of this book and are appropriately left to poets, philosophers, clergy and—ultimately—to you.

Even when the focus shifts to property, this is basically a technical how-to-do-it book. Yet clearly, planning for the transfer of property on your death can raise deep emotional concerns, problems or potential conflicts. No matter how well you deal with the legal technicalities, your living trust won't achieve what you want unless you take human concerns into account.

For many people—probably most—no serious personal problems arise when preparing their living trust. They know to whom they want to give their property. They have no difficulty deciding who to name as successor trustee. They do not foresee conflict among their beneficiaries or threat of a lawsuit by someone angry at not being named a beneficiary. On the human level, these people can, happily, focus on the satisfactions they expect their gifts to bring.

Other people's situations are not so clear and straightforward. They must deal with more difficult human dynamics, such as possibilities of family conflicts, dividing property unequally between children, providing care for minor children or handling complexities arising from second or subsequent marriages.

Before beginning the work of preparing your living trust, it's vital that you assess your personal circumstances and resolve any potential human problems regarding distribution of your property. If you're sure you don't face any such problems, wonderful. If, however, you think you might face complications—or if you're not sure what kinds of problems can come up—try to identify and resolve those problems now, or as you go along. After all, you surely don't want the distribution of your property to result in bitterness, family feuds or fights between former friends.

A self-evident truth about a living trust is that it transfers property—money or things that can be converted into money. Money, as most of us have learned, is strange stuff indeed. It has power to do good in a number of material ways, and can alleviate anxiety and provide security. Unfortunately, however, human flaws and fears are sometimes unleashed when substantial sums of money are involved; meanness, greed and dishonesty have certainly been known to surface. Naturally, in making your gifts, you don't want to unnecessarily stir up negative feelings or emotions. What about your beneficiaries? Are they clearheaded enough to accept your gifts in the spirit in which you give them, or are some of them likely to create their own brand of trouble? Sadly, bitterness, strife and lawsuits are far from unheard of upon distribution of property after one's death. This chapter discusses a number of human concerns, based on examples drawn from my living trust legal practice.

A. Leaving Unequal Amounts of Property to Children

Most parents feel it's very important to treat their children equally regarding the distribution of property, to avoid giving the impression that they value one child more than another. However, in some family situations, parents sensibly conclude that the abstract goal of equal division of property isn't the fairest or wisest solution for their children. The most important issue here, I suggest, is to explain your reasoning to your children.

Example

A widower with three grown children feels that one, a struggling pianist, needs far more financial support than his other two, who have more conventional and well-paying jobs. He wants to give the pianist the bulk of his money, but worries this might cause problems among his children. So he writes a letter explaining that he loves all three children equally and that his decision to give the pianist more is a reflection of need, not preference. He attaches the letter to his living trust. He also leaves most family heirlooms, which are emotionally but not monetarily valuable, to the other two children to emphasize how much he cares for them.

Example

An elderly couple owns a much-loved summer home in the Poconos. Only one of their four children, Skip, cares about the home as much as they do, and they plan to give it to him. But they question whether they should reduce his portion of the rest of their estate by the value of the home, or divide the rest of their estate equally among their four children, and on top of this, give the summer home to Skip.

As the family is a close one, they discuss the problem with the kids. One of them doesn't think their last alternative is fair. Skip doesn't think so either. The parents decide to give Skip less than one-fourth of the rest of their estate, but not to reduce his share by the full value of the summer home. They explain their decision to the others on the basis that Skip helped maintain the summer home for many years, and that his work should be recognized. It is, and the plan is accepted in good grace by all.

B. Second or Subsequent Marriages

People who marry more than once may face problems reconciling their desires for their present spouse (and family) with their wishes for children from prior marriages. Individual situations vary greatly here, and you must work carefully through your needs and desires. How much of one spouse's property might a surviving spouse need? How much property does each spouse want to leave

to his or her own children? Sometimes, spouses can readily resolve such concerns and use a basic living trust to leave their property.

Other couples find they want more control than a basic living trust offers. Many couples with substantial assets create a trust leaving one's property to the surviving spouse for his or her life, with specific, limiting controls over how that property can be spent for that spouse. Then, when that spouse dies, the trust property goes to children from the other spouse's prior marriage(s). These types of "life estate" trusts are briefly discussed in Chapter 15, "A Living Trust as Part of Your Estate Plan," Section F. (They are discussed in detail in *Plan Your Estate* (Nolo Press).) You need a lawyer to draft this kind of a trust.

Example

Ellen and Alex, a married couple, each have children from prior marriages. Both spouses want to eventually leave their property to their own children, but both also want to protect the interest of the survivor. They own a house, with each spouse owning half. If the first spouse to die leaves half directly to his or her children, they may want to sell it or use it before the other spouse dies. At best, the surviving spouse will be insecure and, at worst, may be thrown out of the house. Neither spouse wants to risk that.

They decide to each leave the other what's called a "life estate" in their one-half of the house, specifying that the other spouse cannot sell the house. If Alex dies first, Ellen can live in the house during her lifetime, but when she dies, Alex's share automatically goes to his children. Because Ellen's share will go to her kids, the house will probably be sold, and the proceeds divided, when she dies.

C. Disinheriting a Child

Sometimes, people are troubled by deciding how much, if any, property to leave to a child. Legally, you can disinherit anyone you want, with the exception, in many states, of your spouse. (See Chapter 6, "Choosing What Property to Put in Your Living Trust," Section D.) But deciding to disinherit a child is often not easy to do emotionally. An explicit disinheritance clause may legally be required. Many people decide that something less harsh than disinheritance is desirable. Rather than completely cutting off a child by direct words, they decide that it's wiser to leave some small, lesser amount to this out-of-favor child.

Example

Toshiro and Miya have three daughters and a substantial estate. They are very close to two of the daughters, but are bitterly on the outs with the third, Kimiko. Toshiro and Miya had originally intended to leave most of their property to the surviving spouse, with some to the two daughters they're close to. Then, when the surviving spouse dies, the remaining property is to be divided between these two daughters.

But they have second thoughts. Do they really want to cut Kimiko out entirely? If they do, aren't they creating an incentive for her to sue and try to invalidate their estate plan? They decide that good hearts and prudence both dictate the same decision. Each will leave Kimiko $25,000 in their living trust and include a "no-contest" clause in both their wills and trusts. This clause states that if any beneficiary challenges a will or trust, she gets nothing if her challenge is unsuccessful. The parents expect Kimiko to take the certain $50,000 rather than risk an expensive lawsuit she's very likely to lose. Also, Toshiro and Miya are relieved that they haven't had to formally disinherit one of their own children.

No-contest clauses. The trust and will forms in this book do not contain "no contest" clauses. These clauses are not, technically, hard to draft. But the reason to include a no-contest clause in a living trust or will isn't a simple, technical matter. It indicates a serious problem and conflict with a family member. If you think you need a no-contest clause, you should see a lawyer to be sure you've done all you can to discourage a lawsuit against your trust or will.

If you do decide to leave one child a lesser amount than your other children, you can use the trust forms in this book to achieve your goals.

Example

Ben and Estelle met in the 1970s, as teachers in an alternative school. They fell in love, ran away to Oregon to live in a commune, and had two daughters. What a long, strange trip it was; they wound up, to their considerable surprise, owning a prosperous business in San Francisco. Now that it is time to draw up their living trust, Ben and Estelle are in complete accord about how to distribute their property, with one exception—Ben's daughter Susan (now age 23) from his first marriage. Ben wants to leave her a substantial part of his estate; he suggests 20%. Estelle thinks that is outrageous, since his daughter has long treated him terribly, and is a wastrel with money besides. Estelle says it's too late to try to buy her love. Ben insists he feels a duty to his child no matter how she treats him.

Fortunately, both Ben and Estelle recognize signs of trouble and understand they're talking about a lot more than property here. What, if anything, does Ben owe his child? Will his ex-wife get involved if his daughter inherits money? If so, so what? Ben and Estelle discuss these problems themselves and with a therapist they see from time to time.

Eventually, they reach a compromise. Ben will leave some property to Susan, but not a percentage of his total estate. He and Estelle agree on a figure of $40,000. The money will be left in a child's subtrust (see Chapter 9, "Property Left to Minor Children or Young Adults"), managed by Estelle. Susan won't receive the money outright until she's 35. Susan may well not be happy with a subtrust managed by Estelle, but Ben and Estelle don't see who else could manage the trust. And realistically, since Ben and Estelle are only in their early 50s, it's likely Ben will live long enough so no child's subtrust will be needed for Susan, and she'll be old enough at Ben's death to receive her gift outright.

D. Special Concerns of Unmarried Couples

Unlike married couples, unmarried couples have no automatic legal right to inherit any of each other's property. A central concern of most unmarried couples—whether lesbian, gay or heterosexual—is to ensure that each will inherit property from the other. Happily, people have the right to leave their property by living trust to whomever they want, as long as they're mentally competent. As a general rule, a person must be very far gone, mentally, before a court will declare him incompetent. In case of serious threat by hostile family members, a couple may take action to establish by clear proof that they were competent when they prepared their trusts.

Example

Ernesto and Teresa have lived together for several years. Aside from a few small gifts to friends or family, each wants to leave all their property to the other after death. They're concerned with efficiency and economy, but above all they want to be sure that their estate plan can't be successfully attacked by several close relatives who have long been hostile to their lifestyle. Ernesto and Teresa discuss their situation with a sympathetic lawyer. Each then prepares a living trust leaving their property as they desire. They videotape their signing and the notarization of this document to provide additional proof they were both mentally competent and not under duress.

E. Communicating Your Decisions to Family and Friends

Most of the examples in this chapter demonstrate my belief that talking can help resolve many potential difficulties with family and friends. But talking is not invariably a panacea. Certainly, there are times when someone doesn't want to listen or talk, or times when communication reveals only a deep and unbridgeable gulf. Still, most of the people I've worked with have been aided by talking openly about what they want to accomplish with their living trusts. If you have a personal problem or two, something to work out on the human level, it can require a good deal of thought, understanding and judgment. For these problems, two or more heads do seem better than one. ❧

chapter 3

COMMON QUESTIONS ABOUT LIVING TRUSTS

$\mathcal{C}$omplexities and doubts can certainly arise even when preparing a living trust, so before you dive into the actual preparation of your trust, look through this chapter. It answers a number of questions about living trusts I've been asked over the years, both by clients and by readers of my estate planning books.

A. Does Everyone Need a Living Trust?

For those who want to arrange now to avoid probate— the elderly, the seriously ill, as well as anyone who is cautious and doesn't want any risk of subjecting property to probate—living trusts are usually the best probate-avoid-

ance device. Indeed, most people who plan their estates ultimately choose a living trust to transfer their property, at least their big-ticket assets—house, stocks and bonds and other valuable items.

Given the advantages of avoiding probate that a living trust confers, shouldn't every prudent person use one for all his or her property? Norman Dacey, in his pioneering work *How to Avoid Probate* (Macmillan), essentially asserts that living trusts should be used by all people in all situations. A number of lawyers now make the same claim in advertisements and seminars. These sweeping claims are too extreme. First, some people don't really need to plan now to avoid probate. Second, other probate-avoidance methods may fit an individual's needs better, at least for certain types of property.

Generally, you may conclude that you don't need a living trust, at least not right now, if:

- **You are young and healthy.** Your primary goals probably are to be sure your property will be distributed as you want, and to provide financial resources and arrange for someone to care for your minor children. A will (perhaps coupled with life insurance) often achieves these goals more easily than a living trust.

  Here's why: A will is simpler to prepare than a living trust. While using a will usually means property goes through probate, probate occurs only after death. As long as you are alive, the fact that probate will be avoided is obviously of no benefit. Because very few healthy younger people die without any warning (and because they often don't yet own enough property that probate fees would amount to that much anyway), it can make good sense to use a will for a number of years. Later in life, when the prospect of death is more imminent and you have accumulated more property, you can create a revocable living trust to avoid probate.

- **You can more sensibly transfer your assets, or at least some of them, by other probate-avoidance devices.** Other easy ways to avoid probate include joint tenancy, informal bank trusts ("pay-on-death" accounts), life insurance and gifts. In addition, the laws in some states allow certain amounts or types of property (and occasionally all property left to certain classes of beneficiaries, such as a surviving spouse) to be transferred without probate even if a will is used. None of these devices has the breadth of a living trust, which can be used to transfer virtually all types of assets. However, each can be easier to use, and equally efficient, in particular circumstances. It's best to understand all probate-avoidance methods and then to decide which ones will work best for you. (See Chapter 15, "A Living Trust as Part of Your Estate Plan," Section B.)

- **You have complex debt problems.** As I've discussed, if you have a serious debt problem, such as a business that has many creditors, probate provides an absolute cut-off time for notified creditors to file claims. If they don't do so in the time permitted (a few months, in most states), your inheritors can take your property

free of concern that these creditors will surface later and claim a share. A living trust normally doesn't create any such cut-off period, which means your property could be subject to creditors' claims for a much longer time.

- **Your primary goal is to name a personal guardian to care for your minor children.** Generally, a living trust can't be used for this purpose.

NAMING A GUARDIAN IN A LIVING TRUST

Some states' laws, such as California, can be read to allow the appointment of your minor children's personal or property guardian in your living trust. However, this is most definitely not common practice. A judge must confirm the appointment of any acting personal or property guardian. It's unwise to present judges with novel legal documents about matters you care about.

A will can always be used to name a personal guardian for your minor children. (See Chapter 16, "Wills.") Of course, if you have a great deal of valuable property, you will probably create a living trust (or other probate-avoidance device) to transfer it and name a personal guardian for your minor children in a "back-up" will.

- **Your state has streamlined probate procedures.** In a very few states, probate law has been simplified sufficiently so that people may not need to worry about avoiding probate. One example is Wisconsin, which lets married couples avoid probate altogether for their marital property by using a written agreement. For Wisconsin couples who don't want a tax-saving AB trust, this procedure could work fine. In Texas, probate is not very complicated, but property still must go through court, and a lawyer take fees. The process will probably be more costly than using a do-it-yourself living trust.

- **You own little property.** If you don't have a lot of assets, there isn't much point in bothering with a living trust and probate avoidance, because probate won't cost that much. Often parents in this situation provide money for their young children, in case of a parent's death, by purchasing life insurance. (Insurance proceeds do not go through probate.) However, if the policy is fairly large, you might want to establish a child's trust (as part of a will) and name the trust, not the child, as beneficiary of the policy. The reason for this is that the insurance proceeds cannot legally be turned over to children under 18. And you may well not want to risk turning over large sums of money (insurance proceeds) to young adults. By leaving the proceeds in a child's trust, that money will be managed by a responsible adult until your child becomes old enough to handle the money.

How large should your estate be before you need to concern yourself with avoiding probate? There's no mathematical rule here. Even a relatively small estate—say $50,000—might cost $1,000 or more to transfer by probate. One sensible approach for smaller estates is to check out the dollar amount of property your state allows to be transferred by a will without formal probate. This varies widely from state to state. California, one of the more generous states, allows you to transfer up to $60,000 by will free of probate. (A state-by-state list of each state's rules regarding exemption from normal probate is in Nolo's *Plan Your Estate.*)

B. If I Prepare a Living Trust, Do I Need a Will?

Yes. Even if you arrange to transfer all your property by a living trust, you should always prepare a "back-up" will. The purpose of a back-up will is to ensure that any of your property that didn't make it into your trust—for example, a last-minute inheritance or lottery winnings—goes to who you want to have it. Also, just in case you haven't properly transferred some item of property to your trust, you want to control who receives that property, by use of your will.

Finally, a living trust won't work for property you don't presently own, but expect to receive, like an inheritance from someone else, or property in a trust that you haven't actually yet obtained. A living trust works to transfer only property you currently own. If you've been left property by someone's will that is still in probate, or you expect to get money from a lawsuit settlement, only a will can transfer that property.

(Back-up wills are covered in Chapter 16, "Wills." Tear-out will forms are included in the Appendix.)

C. How Can I Leave Trust Property to Children and Young Adults?

Using living trusts to leave property to minor children or young adults is covered in depth in Chapter 9, "Property Left to Minor Children or Young Adults." Here I cover some basic, preliminary questions.

1. Providing for Minor Children

You can leave property to minor children (those under 18) in your living trust and name an adult to manage that trust property.

If any of your living trust property is left to a beneficiary who's a minor when you die, an adult must manage that property for the minor. Minors cannot own any substantial amount of property outright.

WHAT YOUR LIVING TRUST CAN'T DO FOR CHILDREN

You cannot name a personal guardian (someone responsible for raising your children if you die) for your own minor child or children in your living trust. Similarly, you cannot name a general property guardian, responsible for managing all property owned by your minor children, in a living trust document. You must use your will for those purposes.

Various legal devices can be used to leave property to minors:

- **Small gifts for children's benefit.** If your estate is relatively modest and there is a trusted person to care for the child (usually the other parent), it's often easiest simply to leave property directly to the adult who will care for the child.

- **Larger gifts.** If the gift is larger—as a rough rule, say up to $50,000—it can be desirable to name a "custodian" in your living trust to manage the property. To do that, your state must have passed a law called the Uniform Transfers to Minors Act. (See Chapter 9, Section D.)

- **Very large gifts.** The best way to leave even larger gifts to minor children is through your living trust by what is called a "child's subtrust," which allows you to designate the age at which the child will receive the property. Your successor trustee manages the subtrust property for the child's benefit. (See Chapter 9, Section C.)

The trust forms in this book allow you to use the Uniform Transfers to Minors Act if your state has it. The trusts also allow you to create a child's subtrust as a part of your revocable living trust. If you die before a minor beneficiary has reached the age you've chosen, that child's trust property is held in a child's subtrust. If you don't specify an age, the trust form provides that the property remains in the child's subtrust until that child becomes age 35. This subtrust is irrevocable after your death. If the child has already reached that age when you die, she receives her property outright, and no child's subtrust is created for her.

Example

One of the beneficiaries of Edward's living trust is Abigail, age 17. Edward establishes a child's subtrust for her, as part of his living trust. She is to receive her trust property when she becomes 35. Edward dies when Abigail is 26. Her property is maintained in the subtrust until she becomes 35.

While a child's subtrust is operational, the trustee (the successor trustee of your living trust) has broad powers to spend any of that trust's income or principal for the child's health, support, maintenance or education. When the child reaches the age you specified for her to receive her property outright (or age 35, if you didn't specify an age), the successor trustee turns the trust property over to her.

2. Young Adult Beneficiaries Who Can't Handle Money Responsibly Now

A child's subtrust does not have to be used solely for minors. You can leave a gift in a child's subtrust for any beneficiary who is under 35 when you create your trust.

Example

Julio's son Enrique is 22. Julio wants to leave Enrique a large amount of property, worth over $100,000. Julio worries (sadly, with good reason) that Enrique isn't mature enough to handle this money responsibly if he happens to inherit it soon. So Julio creates a child's subtrust for this gift to Enrique, and provides that Enrique will receive the gift outright at age 35.

D. Will My Living Trust Reduce Estate Taxes?

When some people hear the word "trust, they feel it must mean "tax savings." But it depends on which trust you use. A basic trust for a single person, or a basic shared living trust for a couple, will not reduce federal estate taxes. These trusts are designed solely to avoid probate.

By contrast, an AB living trust (the other kind of trust in this book) can achieve substantial federal estate tax savings for a couple with a combined estate between $625,000 to $750,000 and $1,250,000 to $1,500,000. (See Chapter 4, "What Type of Trust Do You Need?," Section C, and Chapter 5, "The Tax-Saving AB Trust.")

E. Will I Have to Pay Gift Taxes?

Some people worry that by creating a living trust, they'll become enmeshed in gift taxes. Not to worry.

No gift tax is assessed when you transfer property to your living trust. Legally, to make a taxable gift you must relinquish all control over the property. Since you keep complete control over property in your living trust (and

you can revoke the trust at any time before you die), you don't make a gift simply by transferring property to the trust. (See Chapter 15, "A Living Trust as Part of Your Estate Plan," Section C, for a discussion of gifts and gift taxes.)

F. Will a Living Trust Shield My Property From Creditors?

Some people think that a living trust can protect their assets from creditors. No such luck.

1. While You're Alive

Property in a revocable living trust is not immune from attack by your creditors while you're alive. Some "authorities" have inaccurately stated that property in a revocable living trust can't be grabbed by the grantor's creditors, because for collection purposes a revocable living trust is legally distinct from its creator. I know of no law or court ruling that supports this position. It's most unlikely that any judge would accept it, because during your life you have complete and exclusive power over the trust property.

On the other hand, if property is put in an irrevocable trust—and you no longer have any control over it—it's a different legal matter. Property transferred to a bona fide irrevocable trust is immune from your creditors. The key words here are "bona fide." If an irrevocable trust is set up to defraud creditors, it's not bona fide. This book does not include irrevocable trusts.

Keeping creditors away from your property. If you're concerned about protecting your assets from creditors, see a lawyer.

2. After Your Death

A living trust won't shield your assets from your creditors after your death either, even after the property has been turned over to your beneficiaries.

One "advantage" claimed for probate is that it ensures that one's debts and taxes are paid before property is distributed to inheritors. If duly notified creditors don't make their claims within an allotted time, they're simply cut off. Does that mean you should worry about how your debts, including death taxes, get paid if there's no probate and no probate court supervision? In most all cases—no.

Many people leave no significant debts, and even if they do, they normally leave sufficient assets to pay them. The most common kinds of large debts—mortgages on real estate or loans on cars—don't have to be paid off when the owner dies. Normally, these kinds of debts are transferred with the asset to an inheritor, who then becomes liable for the mortgage or loan. In other words, mortgages or car loans pass with the property and don't need to be paid off separately.

Your successor trustee (who should also be named as executor of your will—see Chapter 7, "Trustees," Section C, and Chapter 16, "Wills," Section C) has the legal responsibility of paying your debts. If no probate occurs to cut off creditors' claims, all your property, including all property that was in the living trust, remains liable for your debts. This is true even after the property is transferred to inheritors. If only one person inherits from you, that person will wind up paying your debts and any death taxes from the inherited property.

If there are several inheritors, who will pay your last debts and taxes might cause more confusion. You can eliminate this problem by designating a specific trust asset—often a bank account or stock market account—to be used to pay your debts. If you don't have a suitable asset available to do this, consider purchasing insurance to provide quick cash to pay debts. (Providing in your trust for payment of your debts is covered in Chapter 10, "Preparing Your Living Trust Document," Section D.)

G. Do I Need a "Catastrophic Illness Clause" in My Trust?

The term "catastrophic illness clause" is commonly used to mean a clause that, hopefully, preserves assets from being used for the costs of a major illness that strikes oneself or one's spouse. More particularly, many people are concerned with becoming eligible for Medicaid or Medicare without having to use up all (or even any) of their assets; they don't want their assets counted when eligibility for government aid is determined. Married couples want to protect at least the assets owned by the healthier spouse.

A catastrophic illness clause certainly sounds like a good idea. But unfortunately, no simple clause can protect your assets. Simply put, the law doesn't allow people to easily retain their assets and still become eligible for federal aid. There are various, more complex, ways of protecting some of your assets if you're faced with huge medical bills: making gifts, paying children for services, using certain complex types of trusts.

Methods of hanging onto your assets are discussed in *Beat the Nursing Home Trap,* by Joseph Matthews (Nolo Press).

If you want to take concrete actions to protect your assets from possible medical costs, see a lawyer knowledgeable in this distinct legal area. To help you, a lawyer must be up to date on relevant federal and state statutes and regulations, which can change fast.

H. How Does Where I Live Affect My Living Trust?

Living trusts are valid under the laws of every state. Still, a number of questions can arise about living trusts and where you live.

1. Determining Your Legal Residence

In your trust document, you'll include the state where you live; that state's laws govern the document. If you live in one state but work in another, it's the state where you live whose laws apply. You must also sign appropriate documents to transfer property to your trust in that state. (See Chapter 11, "Transferring Property to Your Trust.")

For most people, determining what state they reside in (in legalese, their "domicile") is self-evident. But for others, it can be more complex.

If during the course of a year you live in more than one state, your residence is the state with which you have the most significant contacts—where you vote, register vehicles, own valuable property, have bank accounts or run a business.

If you might be justified in claiming more than one state as your legal residence, you may want to arrange your affairs so that your legal residence is in the state with the most advantageous state death tax laws. Some states (such as New York) impose stiff inheritance taxes; others (California and Florida, for example) essentially have no inheritance tax.

Example

Carlo and Sophia, a couple in their 60s, spend about half the year in Florida and the other half in New York. They have bank accounts and real estate in both states. To take advantage of Florida's lack of a state inheritance tax, they register their car in Florida, vote there and move their bank accounts there. This leaves them owning nothing in New York but a condominium near where their son lives. They decide to sell him the condo and lease it back six months of every year, severing their last important property ownership contact with New York.

If you have significant contacts with more than one state and a substantial estate, it may be worthwhile to have a lawyer with tax and estate planning experience advise you.

2. If You Live Out of the Country

If you are living outside the United States, your residence is the state you still have contacts with and expect to return to.

If you don't maintain ties with any particular state and have a large estate, see a lawyer to discuss what state you should declare as your residence.

If you are in the Armed Forces and living out of the country temporarily, your legal residence is the state you declared as your Home of Record—the state you lived in before going overseas, or where your spouse or parents live.

If you acquire property in a foreign country, such as real estate, you must check out that country's laws regarding transfer of real estate on death.

3. If You Move to Another State or Country

Revocable living trusts are valid and used in every state, and your trust stays valid if you move to a different state. However, if you're married and you move from a community property state to a common law state, or vice versa, you may want to check the marital property ownership laws of your new state. (See Chapter 6, "Choosing What Property to Put in Your Living Trust," Section D.) Also, if you moved from a state that allows gifts to be made under the Uniform Transfers to Minors Act (see Chapter 9,

"Property Left to Minor Children or Young Adults," Section D) to a state that has not adopted the Act, and you made a gift using that Act, you'll have to amend this portion of your trust. (See Chapter 13, "Living With Your Living Trust," Sections D, E and F.)

If you move to another country after creating a living trust, the trust remains valid. Under the 1961 Hague Convention (effective for U.S. citizens since 1981), a document notarized as a valid document in one country is recognized as valid by other countries which agreed to the treaty.

4. Out-of-State Beneficiaries or Successor Trustee

Your trust beneficiaries can live in any state, or indeed, any country. Similarly, your successor trustee does not have to live in your state.

5. Registration

A few states require "registration" of living trusts. These requirements are not a serious burden, or reason to not use a trust. (See Chapter 12, "Copying, Storing and Registering Your Trust Document," Section C.)

I. Can I Place Real Estate in a Living Trust?

Generally, it's easy—and quite common—to place valuable real estate, usually your home, in a living trust.

1. Property Tax Reassessment

In some states, some real estate transfers, such as sales to new owners who aren't family members, result in property being immediately reappraised for property tax purposes. By contrast, if the property is not transferred to new owners, it usually won't be reappraised for a set period of years, or is reappraised at a reduced rate.

In states that reappraise property when it's transferred to a new owner, placing title to property in a living trust doesn't usually trigger a property tax reappraisal. For instance, California law (Rev. & Tax. Code § 62) expressly prohibits reappraisals for transfers to a living trust where the grantor is a trustee. To be absolutely sure that this is true in your state if you're transferring real estate into a living trust, check with your local property tax collector to make sure you know exactly what reappraisal rules apply.

2. Transfer Taxes

A very few counties or cities impose hefty transfer taxes, even on transfers to a grantor's own living trust, so you do need to check this out with your County Assessor or Recorder's Office.

3. Deducting Mortgage Interest

For income tax purposes, the trust doesn't exist. You retain the right to deduct all mortgage interest from your income taxes, even though your home is technically owned by the trustee of your trust.

4. Insurance Policies

Insurance policies on your home—fire, liability, theft and other particular policies—do not have to be re-registered in the trust's name. Like the IRS, insurance companies are concerned with the real form of ownership, not legal technicalities to avoid probate (or reduce estate taxes). So there's no reason at all to contact your insurance company when you transfer your home (or other real estate) to your living trust.

5. "Rolling Over" Profits

Although your home is technically owned by the trustee of your trust, you retain your rights to defer ("roll over") profits from the sale of your home by using that gain to purchase another home within 24 months of the sale. (IRC § 1034.)

6. Tax Breaks for Sellers Over 55

If you're over 55, you have the right to sell your principal home once and exclude $125,000 of profit from income taxation. You retain that right even if you have transferred that home to a living trust. (IRC § 121.)

7. Homestead Rights

Generally, transferring your home to a living trust does not affect the protection offered by state homestead laws. These laws typically protect a homeowner's equity interest in a home, up to a designated amount, from creditors. The living trust forms in this book each contain a specific statement that the grantor(s) intend to remain eligible for the state homestead exemption they would be entitled to if they still owned the real estate outside the trust.

"HOMESTEAD" DEFINED

A homestead is a legal device, available under the laws of most states, to protect your equity in your home, up to a certain amount, from creditors. In some states that allow homesteads, you record a Declaration of Homestead with the county land records office; in others, the protection is automatic. In either case, if you qualify for a homestead, your home is protected against forced sale by creditors (other than mortgage holders) if your equity is below the dollar limit set out in the statute.

However, if you're in debt and concerned that a creditor may try to force a sale of your house, check your state's homestead rules carefully. If you are not seriously in debt, there is no need to worry about this one.

8. Selling or Refinancing Your House

If you try to sell or refinance a house that is in a living trust, you might encounter some paperwork hassles, but nothing more serious. Some banks balk at refinancing a home that technically is owned by a living trust, even if you show them the original trust document. Similarly, some title companies are reluctant to insure sales of a home from a trust while the grantor is alive. By contrast, once an owner dies and a house is transferred to the beneficiaries, title companies routinely approve the sale of that real estate, even though it was formerly owned by a trust.

If you encounter a problem trying to sell or refinance a house owned by your trust, you have two options:

- Seek a bank or title company that is reasonable and will allow the transaction in the trust's name, which is fully legal, or;

- Transfer the property out of the trust, back into your individual name(s). Then go ahead with the sale or refinancing. Once the refinancing is completed, you can prepare yet another deed, again transferring the property back to the trust. Silly, yes, but not really onerous.

9. Due-on-Sale Clauses

Federal law expressly prohibits enforcing a "due-on-sale" clause in a mortgage because of a transfer of one's home ("principal residence") to one's own revocable living trust. (The Garn-St. Germain Depository Institutions Act, 12 U.S.C. §§ 1464, 1701.) State laws that say otherwise are void.

No statute expressly prohibits a bank from enforcing a due-on-sale clause when other real estate is transferred to a trust. However, I've never heard of it happening, probably because banks know it wouldn't make sense. After all, the transfer is flatly not a sale. No money changes hands. The IRS doesn't consider the transaction a sale. If a bank did try to claim that a due-on-sale clause was activated by a transfer of, say, investment or commercial real estate to a trust, you could always rescind the transaction and transfer the property back to your individual name.

Some cautious lawyers do obtain a bank (mortgage holder's) prior consent to transfers of commercial real estate to a living trust. Sometimes banks agree to this readily, but charge a fee of $100 or $200.

10. Transfer Part Interests in Real Estate

Any portion of real estate you own, such as a time share or percentage of ownership, can be transferred to a living trust. (See Chapter 11, "Transferring Property to Your Living Trust," Section D.)

11. Rental (Income) Property

Under federal tax law, net profits received from rental property are "passive income." Losses in passive income cannot be used to offset profits or gains from "active income." However, there is a limited $25,000 exception to this rule for owners who "actively participate" in operation of the rental property. This $25,000 exception is lost if the rental property is placed in a living trust. (IRC § 469.)

Rental property. This is a new and complex tax issue. If you own rental property, want to put it in a living trust and retain the $25,000 exception, review this issue with a lawyer before completing your trust.

J. Can I Sell or Give Away Trust Property While I'm Alive?

You can readily sell, transfer or give away property in your trust.

1. Making Gifts

While you are alive, you are free to give away property held in your living trust. There are no estate tax drawbacks to making such gifts.

This wasn't always the case. Before it abruptly changed its bureaucratic mind in 1995, the IRS insisted that revocable trust property given away less than three years before the grantor's death was, for tax purposes, still part of the grantor's estate. It has now abandoned that position, which was based on esoteric legal theory, so you, as trustee, can make gifts directly from the trust.

2. Selling Trust Property

You can readily sell any property in your trust. There are two ways to go about it:

- Sell the property directly from the trust, acting in your capacities as grantor and trustee to sign the title document, bill of sale, sales contract or other document. The trust documents in this book specifically state that the trustee has the power to sell trust property, including stocks or bonds.

- In your capacity as trustee of the living trust, first transfer title of the particular item of trust property back to yourself as an individual, and then sell the property in your own name.

The only reason for using this second option, which requires more paperwork, is if some institution involved in the sale insists you sell it in your personal name. This rarely happens. For instance, stock brokerage companies are familiar with sales by a trustee from a living trust. At most you might have to point out to some overcautious bureaucrat that the specific trustee powers clause of your trust document specifically gives you authority to make the sale.

> **AMENDING YOUR TRUST AFTER SALE OR GIFT OF TRUST PROPERTY**
>
> You should amend your revocable living trust if property it leaves to a particular trust beneficiary is no longer owned by the trust because that property has been sold or given away. Obviously, the trust document cannot give away what you no longer own. (Amending living trusts is discussed in Chapter 13, "Living With Your Living Trust," Section D.)

K. Is My Bank Account in the Trust's Name Insured by the FDIC?

Yes. Any bank account in the trust's name is insured up to the $100,000 maximum if the bank is covered by the FDIC.

Banks also offer "pay-on-death" accounts, which function as de facto living trusts for the funds in the accounts, and which also are protected by the FDIC. (See Chapter 15, "A Living Trust as Part of Your Estate Plan," Section B.)

L. Will Property in My Living Trust Get a "Stepped-Up" Basis Upon My Death?

Yes. Property left through a revocable living trust does get a stepped-up tax basis. This is an important concern for many people, who rightly understand that, for inheritors of their property, a stepped-up basis is highly desirable for income tax reasons. Here's how it works.

To understand the concept of stepped-up basis, you must first understand what "basis" means. Put simply, the basis of property is the figure used to determine taxable profit when the property is sold. Usually, the basis of real estate is its purchase price, plus the cost of any capital improvements, less any depreciation. Once you know the basis, you subtract that figure from what you sell the property for. The result is your taxable profit.

Example

Phyllis buys a home for $140,000. She puts $25,000 into capital improvements (new roof and foundation). By the time she sells the house, total depreciation is $40,000. So her basis in the property is $125,000 ($140,000 plus $25,000 minus $40,000). If she sells the property for $275,000, her profit is $150,000.

Under federal law, the basis of inherited property is increased, or "stepped-up," to its market value as of the date the deceased owner died. (This is only fair, as the same property is valued, for estate tax purposes, at its market value as of the date the owner died.) At your death, the inheritors' basis of living trust property becomes the market value of that property at your death, not your original acquisition cost.

Example

Continuing the above example, Phyllis dies and, through her living trust, leaves the house (with a market value of $275,000) to her niece, Nancy. Nancy's basis in the house is $275,000. If she promptly sells it for that amount, she has no taxable profit.

In "community property" states (a total of nine, mostly in the West), both halves of property owned jointly by both spouses receive a stepped-up basis when one spouse dies. In all other states (called "common law" states), the property of a married person who dies receives a stepped-up basis. However, property already owned by the surviving spouse does not get a stepped-up basis; it retains the basis it had.

A few states require registration of a living trust. (See Chapter 12, "Copying, Storing and Registering Your Trust Document," Section C.) If you register your trust in one of these states, it is possible for others to have access to certain information about the trust. But only minimal information need be made public through registration—the name of the grantor, the date of the trust—not the key terms of the trust, such as the property in it, and who are the beneficiaries.

Whether or not to tell your beneficiaries what's in your trust and who gets what is entirely your personal decision.

Example

Alexander and Harriet, residents of New York, share ownership of a house with a basis of $200,000. When Alexander dies, the house is worth $800,000. The basis of Alexander's share is "stepped up" to its value at the time of death, or $400,000. However, Harriet's share retains its original basis, which is one-half of $200,000, or $100,000.

If Alexander and Harriet lived in Oregon, a community property state, and had the same property situation, both spouses' shares of the house would receive a stepped-up basis to $400,000 when Alexander died.

M. Who Must Know About My Living Trust?

Normally, the only person who must know about your living trust is your successor trustee. And even he or she need only know where the trust document is, not what's in it. However, most people do show the trust document to their successor trustee. After all, you should fully trust this person. And it should make his or her job easier to know in advance what property the trust owns, and who gets it after your death.

N. Could Someone Challenge My Living Trust?

Of course a trust can be challenged in court. In our legal system, any document can be challenged. But theory doesn't matter here, reality does. The important questions to ask are:

- Is there any likelihood someone will challenge my living trust?
- If there is, what can I do to protect myself?

Legal challenges to a living trust are quite rare. (Indeed, I've never encountered one, either in my own practice or that of colleagues in estate planning.) You don't need to concern yourself unless you think a close relative might have an axe to grind after your death.

Some people ask about including a "no-contest" clause as a protection against a lawsuit attacking their trust. A no-contest clause doesn't prevent anyone from contesting the validity of your trust. It simply says that if a beneficiary contests your living trust and loses, he or she gets nothing. Thus, a no-contest clause will not discourage a non-beneficiary from suing. Nor will a no-contest clause necessarily deter a disgruntled beneficiary who wants more, and is willing to risk losing what you've given them by suing.

Adding a no-contest clause. If you think you need a no-contest clause, it's an indication you have a potentially serious problem—someone who might challenge your trust. See a lawyer.

Following are the kinds of legal challenges that can theoretically be made against a living trust.

1. Challenges to the Validity of the Trust

Someone who wanted to challenge the validity of your living trust would have to bring a lawsuit and prove that:

- when you made the trust, you were mentally incompetent or unduly influenced by someone; or
- the trust document itself is flawed—for example, because the signature was forged.

Proving any of this is not easy. It's generally considered more difficult to successfully challenge a living trust than a will. That's because your continuing involvement with a living trust after its creation (transferring property in and out of the trust, or making amendments) is evidence that you were competent to manage your affairs.

2. Lawsuits by Spouses

Most married people leave much, if not all, of their property to their spouses. But if you don't leave your spouse at least half of your property, your spouse may have the right to go to court and claim some of your property after your death. Such a challenge wouldn't wipe out your whole living trust, but might take some of the property you had earmarked for other beneficiaries and give it to your spouse.

The rights of spouses vary from state to state. (See Chapter 6, "Choosing What Property to Put in Your Living Trust," Section D, and Chapter 8, "Choosing Your Beneficiaries," Section H.)

3. Lawsuits by a Child

Children usually have no right to inherit anything from their parents. There are two exceptions: laws that give minor children certain rights and laws that are designed to protect children who are unintentionally overlooked in a will.

a. Minor Children

State law may give your minor children (less than 18 years old) the right to inherit the family residence. The Florida constitution, for example, prohibits the head of a family from leaving his residence in his will (except to his spouse) if he is survived by a spouse or minor child. (Fla. Const. Art. 10, § 4.)

b. Overlooked Children

Some state laws protect offspring who appear to have been unintentionally overlooked in a parent's will. The legal term for such an overlooked offspring is a "pretermitted heir." In most states, this term means a child born after the will was signed. In a few states, the term includes any child not mentioned in the will. Though the law is unclear, it could be argued that a child omitted from a living trust was also a pretermitted heir. Fortunately, it's easy to avoid these problems. See Chapter 8, "Choosing Your Beneficiaries," Section H, and Chapter 16, "Wills," Section B.

Q. Will Congress or My State Legislature Abolish or Restrict Living Trusts?

Probate-avoidance living trusts seem clearly safe from government restrictions and limits. There would be howls of protest if Congress or a state legislature tried to abolish or restrict living trusts from being used as a probate-avoidance device. Certainly there's no legitimate reason for Congress or a legislature to do so. Probate-avoidance living trusts have been successfully used for decades, without any reports of serious problems. Literally millions of people have prepared them. Also, probate-avoidance living trusts don't cost the federal government or states serious money. (Some lost revenue from court filing fees is about it.)

Really, the only people who have an interest in curtailing probate-avoidance living trusts are some conservative probate lawyers. But their self-interest is so blatant that it's inconceivable they could persuade a legislature to restrict living trusts. Indeed, more savvy lawyers have long since moved into selling living trusts themselves.

chapter 4

WHAT TYPE OF TRUST DO YOU NEED?

No law specifies the form a living trust must take. As a result, there is no such thing as a "standard" living trust. Indeed, there are a bewildering variety of living trust forms. Some attorney-created forms contain vast piles of verbiage, which serve little real-world purpose except to generate attorney fees.

This book offers three types of fully legal living trusts, as clear and understandable as I can make them:

- a probate-avoidance trust for an individual
- a probate-avoidance trust for a couple who own property together, called a "basic shared living trust"
- a probate-avoidance and estate tax-saving AB trust for a prosperous couple.

The AB estate tax-saving trust in this book is useful for couples with a net combined estate worth between $625,000 to $750,000, on the low end, to $1,250,000 to $1,500,000 (or perhaps more, if the first spouse dies after 2001) on the high end. (See Section E, below.)

USING MORE THAN ONE LIVING TRUST

Legally, you can have more than one living trust at the same time for different types of property. Although it isn't necessary for most people, in complex property ownership situations, using more than one trust can make sense. For example, you might set up one trust for your business and another for the rest of your property, if you want one of your business associates to act as successor trustee to handle and transfer your business property, but a spouse, friend or close relative to be successor trustee to dispose of your other property.

Getting more help. If your estate is too large for you to use any of the trusts in this book, see an estate planning lawyer to discuss your tax options. A couple with an estate in excess of $1,250,000 to $1,500,000 may well benefit from this book's AB trust, but they will probably also need additional tax-saving devices, beyond what this book provides. For background information on other estate tax-saving trusts and methods, see *Plan Your Estate* (Nolo Press).

A. If You Are Single

If you are single and making a living trust by yourself, you must use the individual trust. You can use it to transfer all of your property, or any part of it, to your inheritors (beneficiaries). This includes both property you own in your name alone and your share of co-owned property. For instance, if you own a house together with your sister, you simply transfer your share of that house into your trust. Similarly, you can transfer your share of a partnership or shares in a small corporation to your trust, assuming the partnership agreement or corporate charter and by-laws permit it.

If you're a member of an unmarried couple with much of your property held in shared ownership with your significant other, the two of you can use a basic shared living trust if you want to retain shared ownership of the property while you live.

Unmarried couples who are concerned about estate taxes can create an AB trust, discussed in Section E, below.

If you're ready to begin making an individual trust, go to Chapter 6, "Choosing What Property to Put in Your Living Trust."

B. If You Are Part of a Couple

Couples—married or unmarried—often share ownership of property equally. They can legally set up a living trust that doesn't change that shared ownership. They can also include property separately owned by either spouse in their trust.

This book provides three ways for couples to create a living trust:

- Each spouse prepares an individual trust.

- Both spouses prepare one basic shared living trust.

- Both spouses prepare one AB living trust.

The next sections examine each option in detail.

C. Individual Trusts for Members of a Couple

A member of a couple can legally use a separate, individual trust for all of his or her property, or a spouse could use two living trusts, one individual trust for separately-owned property and another trust for property shared with the other spouse. But this is rarely necessary or advisable. As you'll see in Sections D and E, below, both separately owned and shared property can be conveniently handled in either of this book's shared living trusts.

Most couples prefer not to create two individual trusts because it requires dividing property they own together, which is normally the bulk of their property. Splitting ownership of co-owned assets can be a clumsy process. For example, to transfer a co-owned house into two separate trusts would require the spouses to sign and record two deeds transferring a half-interest in the house to two separate trusts. And to transfer household furnishings to separate trusts, spouses would have to allocate each item to a trust or do something as silly as each transferring a half-interest in a couch to his or her trust.

In some common law states (see list in Chapter 6, "Choosing What Property to Put in Your Living Trust," Section D), some attorneys advise couples to go this route. The claimed advantage for this is that it's then easier, upon the death of a spouse, to tell what property each spouse owns. I think this type of caution is unnecessary, and not worth the drawbacks of dividing shared property while both members of the couple are living. With a properly drafted trust—either a basic shared living trust or an AB trust—there should be no difficulty identifying what property belongs to which spouse upon the death of a spouse.

If, however, you and your spouse own most or all of your property separately, you may each want to make an individual trust. Most couples in this situation fit one of these profiles:

- You live in a community property state, and you and your spouse signed an agreement stating that each spouse's property, including earnings and other income, are separate, not community property. (See Chapter 6, "Choosing What Property to Put in Your Living Trust," for a discussion of community property.)

- You don't want to give your spouse legal authority as your successor trustee over your property when you die. (See Chapter 7, "Trustees.")

- You are recently married, have little or no shared or community property, and want to keep future property acquisitions separate. (To accomplish this, you'll both need to sign a written statement of your intentions.)

- You each own mostly separate property acquired before your marriage (or by gift or inheritance), which you conscientiously keep from being mixed with any shared property you own. Couples who marry later in life and no longer work often fit into this category. Not only is the property they owned before the marriage separate, but Social Security benefits and certain retirement plan benefits are also separate, not shared or community, property.

Example

Howard and Luisa live in Indiana, a non-community property state. Both have grown children from prior marriages. When they married, they moved into Howard's house. They both have their own bank accounts and investments, and one joint checking account that they own as joint tenants with right of survivorship.

Each makes an individual living trust. Howard, who dies first, leaves his house to Luisa, but most of his other property is left to his children. The funds in the joint checking account are not included in his living trust, but pass to Luisa, also without probate, because the account was held in joint tenancy. Howard's other accounts go to his children, under the pay-on-death arrangement he has with the bank. (Joint tenancy, pay-on-death accounts and other probate-avoidance methods are discussed in Chapter 15, "A Living Trust as Part of Your Estate Plan.")

If you and your spouse decide on separate living trusts, each of you will transfer your separately-owned property to your individual trust. If you own some property together—a house, for example—you each transfer your portion of it to your individual trust.

Preparing separate trusts. If you and your spouse decide to prepare two separate trusts and do not name each other as successor trustees, you may want to see a lawyer to be as certain as you can that there won't be any conflict between your spouse and your successor trustee.

D. A Basic Shared Living Trust

Most married couples (and many unmarried ones) own most or all of their property equally together and don't want to divide it up and transfer it into two separate trusts. They choose to make one living trust to avoid probate, and transfer all of their property—both shared and separately owned—to it. They are willing to do this because, while they live, each retains full ownership of all his or her separate property, as well as her or his share of jointly-owned property.

Example

Lorenzo and Marsha are married and own a house together. Marsha also owns, as her own property, some valuable jewels left to her by her mother. Lorenzo owns, as his separate property, some stock his uncle gave him.

Lorenzo and Marsha create one shared living trust and transfer all of their jointly-owned property to it. Marsha's jewelry is also placed in this trust, but is identified as her separate property. Similarly, Lorenzo's stock is placed in this trust, identified as his separate property. Neither loses any ownership rights to her or his separate property by placing it in the shared living trust.

If probate avoidance is your only goal, you can use a basic living trust no matter how much all of your property is worth. But if your and your spouse's combined estates exceed $625,000 to $750,000, you should at least consider estate tax-savings trust, such as the AB living trust, explained in Section E, below.

1. How a Basic Shared Trust Works

With the basic shared marital trust from this book, designed to avoid probate, you and your spouse will be co-trustees of your living trust. You'll both have control over the jointly-owned property in the trust. In theory, this means either spouse can act alone on behalf of the trust, including selling or giving away shared trust property. However, because banks, title companies and others often have their own rules requiring both signatures, as a practical matter, the consent of both spouses to sell or transfer shared property is commonly necessary.

If one spouse will not be a trustee. If for any reason—health, mistrust, whatever—you don't want your spouse to serve with you as a trustee of your basic shared trust, see a lawyer.

As I've said, each spouse retains sole control over his or her separate property, because in the trust document it's identified and listed as property owned by only that spouse. With his or her separate trust property, each spouse may:

- sell it, give it away or leave it in the trust

- in the trust document, name a beneficiary, or beneficiaries, to inherit that property

- amend the trust document to name a new beneficiary or beneficiaries for that property. Technically, trust amendments require consent of both spouses, but this is a mere formality in most all cases where a spouse wants to amend the trust to name new beneficiaries for her property. If the other spouse is recalcitrant—say the couple is getting divorced—either spouse can revoke the entire trust and prepare a new one for his or her property.

Each spouse is also free to add separately-owned property to the trust.

In the trust document, each spouse names his or her own beneficiaries for his or her share of co-owned property, as well as all of his or her separate property. Commonly, each spouse leaves all, if not the bulk, of their property to each other. But leaving all or most of your property to your spouse isn't legally required. Each spouse has complete freedom to choose whomever he or she wants to inherit his or her trust property, subject to legal restrictions in many states that entitle a spouse to a certain share of a deceased spouse's estate. (See Chapter 6, "Choosing What Property to Put in Your Living Trust," Section D.)

A spouse's separate property is kept separate in a shared trust by means of trust "schedules," which are just lists of trust property, attached to the trust document. Schedule A lists co-owned property. Property listed on Schedule B is the separate property of the wife, and all property listed on Schedule C is the separate property of the husband.

If spouses want to leave significant amounts of property to each other, a basic shared living trust provides another big advantage over individual trusts. With a basic shared trust, property left by one spouse to the survivor automatically stays in the living trust when the first spouse dies. It becomes part of the property the surviving spouse has in what is now her individual living trust. No formal transfer documents are needed. If separate, individual trusts were used, property left to the surviving spouse would need to transferred first from the deceased spouse's trust to the name of the surviving spouse; then, to avoid probate, the second spouse would have to transfer it into his or her own living trust.

Either spouse can revoke the trust at any time. If either spouse revokes the trust, the couple's property ownership situation returns to exactly what it was before the trust was formed. Shared property is returned to the ownership of both spouses, and separately-owned property to the spouse who owned it. By contrast, amendments to the trust document require the consent of both spouses. For example, both must agree to change the successor trustee or name new beneficiaries for shared property.

2. What Happens When One Spouse Dies

When one spouse dies, the shared living trust is split into two trusts, Trust 1 and Trust 2; this is automatic under the terms of the basic living trust document itself. The surviving spouse is sole trustee of both trusts. (The surviving spouse's duties are discussed in Chapter 14, "After a Grantor Dies.")

Trust 1 contains the deceased spouse's share of trust property, except any trust property left to the surviving spouse. Trust 1 is irrevocable; that is, the surviving spouse can't change its terms, which dictate what happens to the property in it.

Trust 2, the survivor's trust, contains the surviving spouse's share of the trust property, plus trust property left to him or her by the deceased spouse.

In many situations, since all property is left to the survivor, division of the property between the two trusts is all that needs to be done after a spouse dies. However, if the deceased left property in Trust 1 to others, the surviving spouse, as sole trustee of Trust 1, distributes that property to the named beneficiaries.

All gifts are distributed outright, except for gifts left to minors or young adults in a child's subtrust or through the Uniform Transfers to Minors Act (UTMA). (See Chapter 9, "Property Left to Minor Children or Young Adults.") If the property is left in a child's subtrust, the surviving spouse manages that trust for the benefit of the child until the child reaches the age specified by the deceased spouse in the trust document to receive the property outright. If the property is left to a custodian under

the UTMA, the custodian manages the property until the child is old enough to be legally entitled to the property.

When all the property in Trust 1 has been distributed to the beneficiaries (or placed in a child's subtrust), Trust 1 ceases to exist. No formal documents need be prepared or filed to officially end the trust. Once its mission is accomplished, it just evaporates.

Trust 2 (the survivor's trust) is basically a continuation of the original revocable living trust. It contains any trust property the survivor inherited from the deceased spouse, as well as the surviving spouse's share of shared trust property and any separately-owned trust property that belongs to the survivor. Since the surviving spouse is the sole trustee of Trust 2, he or she is free to change it as he or she wishes. For example, the surviving spouse might name a new successor trustee or name a new beneficiary for property that was to have gone to the deceased spouse.

Example

Harry and Maude, a married couple, set up a basic shared revocable living trust to avoid probate. In their trust document, they name themselves co-trustees and appoint Maude's brother Al as successor trustee, to take over as trustee after they have both died. They transfer much of their co-owned property—their house, money market accounts and stocks—to the living trust. Maude also puts some of her family heirlooms, which are her separate property, in the trust.

The trust document states that Maude's brother Al is to receive the heirlooms when she dies; everything else goes to Harry. Harry leaves all his trust property to Maude. Both name their son, Edward, as alternate and residuary beneficiary.

Maude dies first. The basic shared living trust splits into Trust 1, which contains Maude's heirlooms, and Trust 2, which contains everything else—Harry's half of the co-owned trust property and the trust property he inherits from Maude. Harry becomes the sole trustee of both trusts.

Following the terms of the trust document, Harry distributes Maude's heirlooms (from Trust 1) to Al, without probate. When the property is distributed, Trust 1 ceases to exist. Harry doesn't have to do anything with the trust property Maude left him; it's already in Trust 2, his revocable living trust.

EXAMPLE 1: TRUST CONTAINS ALL SHARED PROPERTY

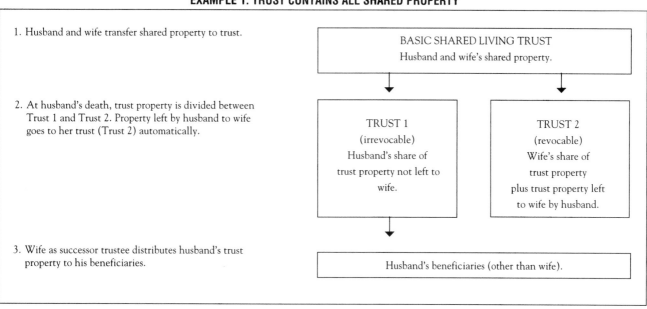

EXAMPLE 2: TRUST CONTAINS SHARED AND SEPARATE PROPERTY

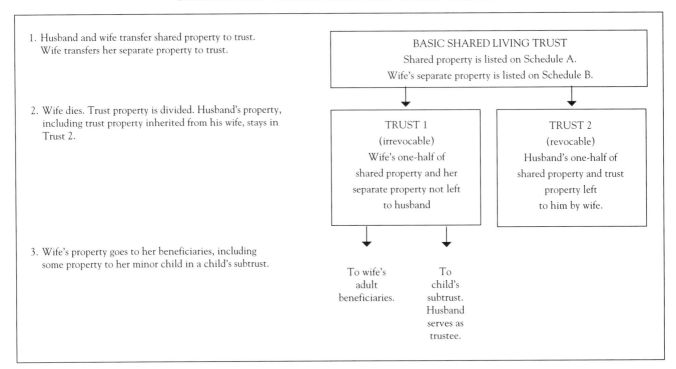

1. Husband and wife transfer shared property to trust. Wife transfers her separate property to trust.

2. Wife dies. Trust property is divided. Husband's property, including trust property inherited from his wife, stays in Trust 2.

3. Wife's property goes to her beneficiaries, including some property to her minor child in a child's subtrust.

BASIC SHARED LIVING TRUST
Shared property is listed on Schedule A.
Wife's separate property is listed on Schedule B.

TRUST 1
(irrevocable)
Wife's one-half of shared property and her separate property not left to husband

TRUST 2
(revocable)
Husband's one-half of shared property and trust property left to him by wife.

To wife's adult beneficiaries.

To child's subtrust. Husband serves as trustee.

When the second spouse dies, the person named in the original basic shared living trust document as successor trustee takes over as trustee of Trust 2. This successor trustee is responsible for distributing the surviving spouse's trust property to the surviving spouse's beneficiaries, named in the trust document, and managing any trust property left to a young beneficiary in a child's subtrust. Again, no formal documents are required to terminate Trust 2.

Example

Continuing the above example of Harry and Maude, after Maude dies, Harry needs to change and update his beneficiaries. (This is normally done when one spouse dies, if that spouse was the major beneficiary of the other spouse's trust.) Harry names his son Edward as the (new) primary beneficiary of his trust. He names Edward's three minor children as alternate beneficiaries, and creates a child's subtrust for each one. Harry also leaves some property outright to his niece, Cecelia. Finally, he names Edward as successor trustee, denoting Al as alternate successor trustee.

When Harry dies, Edward becomes trustee and distributes the trust property following Harry's instructions in the trust document. He transfers the property Harry left to Cecelia to her. The rest of the property he transfers to himself, and the trust ends.

If your combined estate isn't large enough to trigger estate taxes, and you just want to create a basic shared living trust, you can proceed to Chapter 6, "Choosing What Property to Put in Your Living Trust."

E. A Tax-Saving AB Trust

If you and your spouse have a large enough estate, you may want a trust that helps you avoid estate taxes as well as probate.

IMPORTANT TERMS

Exempt amount: The amount of property you can leave free of estate taxes at your death. This amount starts at $625,000 in 1996 and increases by $25,000 every year to the year 2001, when it reaches $750,000.

Maximum protected amount: The maximum amount of property you and your spouse can shield from federal estate tax using the AB living trust in this book, which is between $1,250,000 and $1,500,000.

UNMARRIED COUPLES

An unmarried couple can use an AB trust if it fits their needs. As with a basic shared trust, when describing an AB trust, I refer to husbands, wives and spouses, but no exclusion of unmarried couples is implied. In my experience, it's not common for an unmarried couple to want to use this type of trust, but it's certainly possible.

Suppose Anne and Frank—or Anne and Sylvia—have been an unmarried couple for a long while and have a child they both deeply love, whether both are biological parents or not. If this couple has a combined estate large enough to trigger estate taxes, they can use an AB trust and reap exactly the same benefits of probate avoidance and estate tax reduction as a married couple in a similar situation.

---

1. Why Worry About Eventual Federal Estate Taxes?

Under U.S. tax law, a spouse can leave any amount of property, no matter how much it is worth, to the surviving spouse free of estate tax (unless that spouse is not a citizen—see Chapter 15, "A Living Trust as Part of Your Estate Plan," Section C). Also, you and your spouse can each leave property worth up to the exempt amount tax-free to anyone. So what's the worry, even if your combined estate exceeds the minimum exempt amount?

In a nutshell, it's this—each spouse typically wants to leave most, or all, of his or her property to the survivor. This can pile up well over the exempt amount in the survivor's estate and lead to hefty estate taxes when the survivor dies. Suppose a couple has a combined estate worth $1,000,000. Each spouse's share is worth $500,000.

When the first spouse dies, there are no federal estate taxes, no matter who the property is left to, because that spouse's $500,000 estate is under the estate tax threshold. But if the deceased spouse leaves all that to the survivor, the survivor's estate is now worth the entire $1,000,000, well over the federal estate tax threshold, no matter what the year of death. When the second spouse dies, stiff federal estate tax rates apply—they start at 37% and increase with the size of the estate.

Estate planners call a tax due on the death of the surviving spouse the "second tax." It is this second tax that an AB trust is designed to eliminate, for combined estates that exceed the exempt amount by up to double that limit. With such an AB trust, the second spouse never becomes the legal owner of the first spouse's property. There is no tax due when that second spouse dies, since his or her own estate is below the tax threshold.

The diagram below shows what happens without a tax-saving trust, for a couple with a combined estate worth $950,000, with deaths in 1996 and 1997.

2. Who Can Use the AB Trust in This Book

If you and your spouse want to leave all, or the bulk of your property to each other, and your combined estate is likely to be subject to estate tax, consider using the AB trust in this book. With this AB trust, you can shield from taxation a combined estate worth double the tax-exempt amount. So a couple with a combined estate worth up to $1,250,000 to $1,500,000, or perhaps more, after 2001, when the first spouse dies can save on estate taxes using this trust.

If your combined estate is larger than the amount that the AB trust can shelter, you may need more tax planning than this book offers.

If your estimate of the net worth of the combined value of your estate is near the maximum protected

HOW THE SECOND ESTATE TAX CAN COST YOUR FAMILY MONEY

  Couple owns property worth $950,000

 Husband dies, leaving his $475,000 to his wife.

- less than the minimum exempt amount left by husband

- property left to citizen spouse isn't taxed

Estate Tax Due: None

 Wife dies, leaving entire $950,000 to children

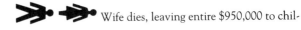

Estate Tax Will Be Payable.
(Exact amount depends on year of wife's death)

By contrast, no estate taxes would be payable on either spouse's death if the couple had used an AB trust.

amount, you need to take stock and decide whether or not you want to consult a tax attorney. If your estate is close to the limit now, isn't it likely it will be over it when a spouse dies?

If you use the AB living trust from this book, and a spouse's estate is over the tax-exempt amount at death, taxes must be paid promptly on the excess. For example, if a spouse with property worth $775,00 dies in 1998, when the exempt amount is $675,000, estate tax must be paid on $100,000. The tax rate is 39%, giving a tax of $39,000, which must be paid when the first spouse dies. This book's tax-saving trust allows no other options.

Other options are available, though, if you see an estate planner and get a more complex trust. It's possible, for example, to give the surviving spouse the option of postponing the estate tax until both spouses have died. Ask yourself: are you willing to pay some estate tax when the first spouse dies, or would the surviving spouse rather postpone payment of any tax? Many couples understandably want to preserve all their estate until both spouses die.

If your estate seems reasonably likely to be over $1,250,000 when a spouse dies, it's prudent to see an attorney to explore other estate tax-saving options. Even though the tax-saving trust in this book will work fine for a combined estate worth up to $1,500,000 or more, depending on the year of a spouse's death, if your estate is now nearing the top limit, why risk having the estate turn out to exceed the maximum protected amount? Clearly, it's better to learn now how to prepare for that possibility.

If one spouse owns property worth over the exempt amount $600,000. If either spouse has property worth over the exempt amount, because of the combination of his or her separate property and half-interest in shared property, the couple needs to see a lawyer, because that spouse's total

property will be subject to estate tax when she dies. Nolo's AB trust is designed for couples, so that neither will have to pay estate tax when one dies. A restriction here is that each spouse must own less than the exempt amount.

Example

Sam and Helen have a combined estate of $1,050,000. But their shared property totals only $500,000. Helen owns separate property worth $550,000. Her net worth is $800,000 (her $250,000 half of the community property plus her $550,000 separate property). This is over the exempt amount, no matter what the year of Helen's death. So this couple cannot use Nolo's AB trust.

3. Estimating the Value of Your Combined Estate

The first step in determining whether or not to use an AB trust is to estimate the net value of your combined property. Only if your combined estate is over the exempt amount need you be concerned about federal estate taxes in the first place. By subtracting the value of your liabilities (that is, your mortgage and other debts) from the current value of your assets, you can get a rough estimate of your current net worth.

You can use the Property Worksheet in Chapter 6, "Choosing What Property to Put in Your Living Trust," Section E, if you want to itemize your property and make written estimates of its worth. There is no need to obtain the precise dollar value of your assets. After all, this amount will surely change by the time of your death. All you need is a sensible estimate, so you can determine if it seems likely now that your estate will eventually be liable for federal death taxes. Do remember that if you own a life insurance policy, the value of the proceeds payable at death are included in your taxable estate.

Estimating your net worth for estate tax purposes raises the question of what to do about inflation or other events that could cause a substantial increase in the value of your estate before you or your spouse dies. Do you need to take these factors into account now? It depends on the current value of your estate and your prospects for savings and expenditures. Admittedly, this involves a number of speculations. If your present combined marital estate is worth nowhere near the exempt amount—say the total is $320,000—there's probably no reason to worry about estate taxes. It'll take substantial inflation and savings for a number of years to bring you to the estate tax threshold. By contrast, if you estimate your combined estate at $585,000, it's quite likely that even low inflation will push it over the exempt amount before a spouse dies—unless, of course, you are currently spending principal.

Remember that unless a spouse dies very suddenly, you can always revoke your existing shared living trust and create an AB trust later, if your combined estate nears the exempt amount. Because there are drawbacks to using an AB trust (see Section 6, below), normally it doesn't make sense to create one before you're pretty sure your family will benefit from the estate tax savings it offers.

4. How an AB Trust Can Solve the Second Estate Tax Problem

If you can't leave your spouse property without also saddling his or her estate with a large tax bill, one obvious alternative is to leave much of your property directly to your children or other beneficiaries. This makes use of the deceased spouse's estate tax exemption and doesn't combine spousal estates, which is what causes the "second tax" problem. But leaving property to others often conflicts with many couples' primary goal—to provide financial security for the surviving spouse. So here's the dilemma: How can a couple pass the maximum amount of property to their children or other beneficiaries after both spouses die (with Uncle Sam getting as little as legally possible), while at the same time being sure the surviving spouse is financially comfortable?

For couples with a combined estate over the exempt amount, the ideal result can be simply stated: you want the surviving spouse to have access to the deceased spouse's property, if he or she needs it, but you don't want the surviving spouse to become the legal owner of that property, because then hefty estate taxes will be due when the second spouse dies.

Happily, there is a way to accomplish this result. It's one of the few times in life you really can have it both ways. The neat little device that allows this to happen is called an AB trust.

Here's a summary of how it works. It's explained in more detail in Chapter 5, "The Tax-Saving AB Trust."

Both spouses create a basic shared living trust like the one just described in Section D of this chapter, with one crucial difference: As part of that living trust, each spouse creates a separate Trust A, or marital life estate trust—a trust within a trust. Instead of leaving his or her share of property outright to the survivor, each spouse leaves all, or at least the bulk, of his or her property to Trust A. And now for the key point: *When one spouse dies, the survivor gets only a "life estate" interest in all property of the deceased spouse that goes into Trust A.* In lawyer talk, the surviving spouse is the "life beneficiary" of this trust. What all this amounts to is that the *surviving spouse can use the property during the rest of his or her life, with certain restrictions, but is not given outright ownership of it.* (The surviving spouse continues to have his or her own revocable trust property, of course.)

The reason for the big tax savings is that Trust A property is subject to estate tax when the first spouse dies. And, as explained in Section 1, above, if there is less than the exempt amount in the estate of the first spouse to die, there are no federal estate taxes. The property isn't subject to estate tax when the second spouse dies, because the second spouse never legally owned it.

When setting up the "A" trusts, each spouse names final beneficiaries who will receive that trust's property when the surviving spouse dies. Spouses often name the same people—the couple's children—as final beneficiaries, but that is not mandatory. The final beneficiaries are, for estate tax purposes, the legal owners of the property in Trust A after the first spouse dies.

Example

Christine and Thierry have a combined estate of $1,100,000, all shared ownership property. If each left his or her half, $550,000, to the surviving spouse outright, that spouse would be left with an estate of $1,100,000. If the surviving spouse's estate remained at $1,100,000, it would be subject to estate tax.

By contrast, if Christine and Thierry each leave their half of their property in an AB trust, naming their five children as the trust's final beneficiaries, no estate taxes will be due, no matter which years the spouses die in. This is because when the first spouse dies, her $550,000 goes into Trust A, and is subject to estate tax at that time. But because the amount in the marital life estate trust is less than the exempt amount, no tax is due. Similarly, when the surviving spouse dies, his $550,000 is not subject to tax.

5. The Surviving Spouse's Rights Over Trust A Property

Under the law, there's no one set formula defining the rights a surviving spouse has over the property in Trust A. The spectrum runs from the maximum permitted by the IRS (any more, and the surviving spouse would become the legal owner of the trust property, exactly what you don't want) to fairly rigid restrictions and controls placed on how the surviving spouse can use the property.

The AB trust in this book gives the surviving spouse all the powers the IRS allows over a trust property. The survivor:

* receives all interest or other income from the trust property

* is entitled to use and control of the property—for example, she can live in a house that's owned by the trust, or sell it and buy another house (or do other things with the profits of the sale—from buying a retirement condo to conserving the profits in a trust account)

* is specifically authorized, as sole trustee of Trust A, to spend (invade) the trust property (principal) in any amount for his or her health, education, support and maintenance in his or her accustomed manner of living.

HOW AN AB TRUST CAN SAVE YOUR FAMILY MONEY

 Couple owns property worth $950,000. They create an AB Trust.

 Husband dies, leaving his $475,000 to the A trust, for wife to use and children to inherit at wife's death.

* less than the exempt amount left by husband.

Estate Tax Due: None

 Wife dies, leaving her $475,000 to children. Trust A also ends, so husband's $475,000 goes to children.

* less than the exempt amount left by wife.

Estate Tax Due: None

The IRS regulation specifically authorizes these powers. Even though these powers to use trust principal are fairly broad, the legal owner of the trust property, for estate tax purposes, remains the trust itself, not the surviving spouse. In other words, with an "AB" trust, the surviving spouse has the right to use Trust A principal, up to all of it, for what really concerns most couples, particularly older ones—the surviving spouse's health and other basic needs. At the same time, the property is kept out of the surviving spouse's taxable estate because it is never legally owned by the surviving spouse.

During his or her life, the surviving spouse has no power to change the final beneficiary designations for the Trust A chosen by the deceased spouse in the original trust document, since the surviving spouse is never the legal owner of the property in Trust A. After the death of the second spouse, the Trust A property is distributed to the final beneficiaries. Also, the property in the surviving spouse's Trust B is distributed to the final beneficiaries she named, either in the original trust document, or in a later amendment. Remember, although one spouse has died, the surviving spouse's trust remained revocable, and amendable, until his or her death. (The rights of the surviving spouse are discussed in more detail in Chapter 5, "The Tax-Saving AB Trust," Section D.)

6. Couples Unlikely to Want an AB Trust

Now that you know the basic workings of an AB trust, let's deal with an important question: Should all married couples who might face estate taxes use this kind of trust? No. This trust is generally not advisable for:

- Younger middle age couples—some under 60 and more if they're under 50. In this age group, you probably won't want to tie up assets in a trust, which may last for many years or decades, if one spouse dies prematurely. Commonly, younger couples create a basic shared living trust to leave each other all or most of their property. Then, once they're older—say in their late 50s or 60s—they revoke their old trust and create an AB trust. If one spouse unexpectedly dies before a younger couple gets around to making a tax-avoiding trust, the survivor will inherit everything estate-tax

free, no matter what the amount, under federal tax law. That surviving spouse will probably have years to use the money—and years to arrange for other methods of reducing the eventual estate tax. (See Chapter 15, "A Living Trust as Part of Your Estate Plan," Sections C and E.)

- Couples where one spouse is considerably younger than the other and presumably will live much longer. Again, generally there's no need to burden the surviving spouse with a trust designed to save estate taxes when he or she is likely to live for many years. (Of course, such couples may well sensibly decide to use a basic shared living trust, to avoid probate.)

- Couples who don't want to leave the bulk of their property for use of the surviving spouse, but want instead to leave substantial amounts of property directly to other beneficiaries. If you want to make many specific gifts, outside the AB trust property, that add up to a substantial amount of money—as a rough rule, over $25,000 to $50,000—you can simply use a basic shared living trust.

- Couples with estates exceeding the maximum amount the trust can shelter from tax. As noted at the beginning of this chapter, these couples need the services of an estate planning attorney. If they are older, they may well end up with some type of AB trust, but quite possibly not the specific type this book provides.

- Many couples in second or subsequent marriages. With the form in this book, each spouse can name his or her own children from prior marriages as final beneficiaries of his or her portion of the AB trust. However, the AB trust in this book gives the surviving spouse the maximum power allowed by law over the property in the "A" trust. Some couples in a second marriage want to place more controls or restrictions over the surviving spouse. For example, they may want one of their children to serve as co-trustee. Or they feel that the surviving spouse's authority, as sole trustee, to use trust principal for her "health, education, support and maintenance," is too broad. They may want to limit it to the right to receive income from and use the property, but not spend the principal. Other concerns can include: does the surviving spouse have the authority to sell trust property? What reports and accountings must be given to the children, the final beneficiaries?

In short, there are often worries about conflict of interest between the surviving spouse and the deceased spouse's children and how to allocate power over the Trust "A" property between them. If relations could become strained between your children and your current spouse, you may very well not want to set things up so that they essentially share ownership of property for many years.

When to see a lawyer. Many questions need to be resolved in setting up an AB trust for couples with estates over the maximum protected amount, or in many second marriage situations. To resolve them, see an experienced estate planning lawyer to draft a trust specifically geared to your situation and desires. (These issues are discussed further in Chapter 15, "A Living Trust as Part of Your Estate Plan," Section D.)

7. Drawbacks of an AB Trust

Before deciding to use an AB trust, both spouses should understand what they're getting into. Once one spouse dies, that spouse's Trust A becomes irrevocable. The trust imposes limits and burdens on the survivor that cannot be changed.

Possible drawbacks of an AB trust include:

a. Restrictions on the surviving spouse's use of the property. On the death of a spouse, the couple's shared property must be divided into two legally separate entities. One share is owned outright by the surviving spouse's revocable living trust and is under the surviving spouse's complete control. The other half is in Trust A, or the marital life estate trust, and the surviving spouse's use of it is subject to restrictions.

As you know, with Nolo's trust, the surviving spouse has the right to any income generated by Trust A property and fairly broad rights to use the property for health, education and support. (See Section 4, above.) But he cannot spend trust property freely on whatever he feels like, because except for legally permitted expenditures, that property is held in trust for the final beneficiaries.

b. Legal or accounting help is often necessary to divide the property. An estate lawyer or accountant may be needed on the death of the first spouse to determine how to best divide the couple's assets between the irrevocable Trust A, or marital life estate trust, and the continuing revocable living trust controlled by the surviving spouse. Each item of the couple's shared property does not have to be divided 50/50 between the two trusts. The only requirement is that the shared property in both trusts must be equal. This means there is considerable flexibility in allocating assets between the two trusts. Often it takes an expert to decide on the best division.

For example, if full ownership of a house is placed in Trust A, the house would be valued, for estate tax purposes, at its value on the death of the first spouse. By contrast, if the house were allocated to the surviving spouse, and she survives for many more years, the house would presumably be worth more (given inflation) by the date of her death. Its increased value might result in the survivor's net property being over the federal estate tax threshold.

But there can also be drawbacks to including the full value of a house in Trust A, or the marital life estate property. If an irrevocable trust owns a house, certain tax advantages are lost. For example, a person over 55 has the one-time right to sell a house and retain up to $125,000 profit (capital gain) without tax. An irrevocable trust has no such right. So if the house may be sold in the future, it can be costly, income tax-wise, to place it in Trust A.

This just scratches the surface of the complexity of dividing a couple's property between the two trusts on the death of a spouse. Of course, not every case is complex, but the surviving spouse may well have to at least check the matter out with an expert before splitting the couple's shared property between the two trusts.

c. Trust tax returns. The surviving spouse, as trustee of Trust A, must obtain a taxpayer ID number for this trust. Also, the surviving spouse must file an annual trust income tax return for that trust. This isn't a big deal, but like any tax return, it requires some work.

d. Recordkeeping. The surviving spouse must keep two sets of books and records, one for his own property (which remains in the surviving spouse's revocable living trust) and one for the property in Trust A, which (as you know by now) is legally separate from property owned by the surviving spouse.

8. Your Personal Situation

Finally—but certainly not least in importance—you need to be sure an AB trust and the particular form of that trust presented in this book (further described in Chapter 5), are right for you and your family.

From a personal, human point of view, an AB trust works best when all involved—both spouses and all final beneficiaries—understand and agree on the purposes of the trust, which is to save on estate taxes and at the same time give the surviving spouse maximum rights to use the money and property. Without this understanding, serious conflicts between the surviving spouse and the final beneficiaries may develop.

The AB trust in this book is designed for families where:

• Family members trust each other, are reasonably close and are able to work out any conflicts that might arise.

• The final beneficiaries understand that all property in Trust A, or the marital life estate trust, really belongs to the surviving spouse, or, more precisely, is available for her needs, such as health care or supporting her in her accustomed manner of living.

• The final beneficiaries understand that taking the trouble to create an AB trust is a generous act by parents, who do this not to benefit themselves, but their inheritors. After all, the estate tax savings benefit only the final beneficiaries, who receive much more of the couple's combined estate than they would if the spouses had left property outright to the other.

• The final beneficiaries can be trusted to support the surviving spouse if she (as trustee) decides she needs to spend trust principal for reasons authorized by the IRS and listed in the trust document (that is, "support, health, education and maintenance in his or her accustomed manner of living") and not to question these expenditures, in an effort to preserve the largest possible amount for themselves.

If there is any potential for conflict between the surviving spouse and the final beneficiaries of the trust (often the couple's children), an AB trust may well provoke or aggravate that conflict. After all, in theory at least, there is an inherent possibility of conflict of interest between the life estate beneficiary and the final beneficiaries. These final beneficiaries may want all the trust principal conserved, no matter what the needs or wishes of the surviving spouse.

Another possible conflict can arise if the surviving spouse becomes ill and can no longer serve as trustee. If a child who stands to eventually receive trust assets takes over as successor trustee, it's possible the child might be more concerned with preserving principal than with a parent's medical or other needs. I've heard of instances where it seemed to other family members and friends that a child, acting as trustee of Trust A, the marital life estate trust, disregarded his parent's basic needs to protect the trust principal for himself.

Conflicts can also occur if the final beneficiaries believe the surviving spouse, as trustee, is not managing the trust property sensibly—for example, he is investing in very speculative stocks or real estate. If this situation arises, there can be real trouble, possibly even a lawsuit.

Having doubts? See a lawyer. If you have any doubts about these personal matters, the AB trust in this book is not for you, and you'll need to see a lawyer to work out a more individualized trust.

Finally, to end on a note of optimism: Despite the possible drawbacks, an AB trust does work very well for many couples and families. For many older couples, the drawbacks amount to no more than relatively minor accounting and recordkeeping hassles, which they feel is well worth conserving up to tens or even hundreds of thousands of dollars worth of their property for their children or other beneficiaries. ❦

chapter 5

THE TAX-SAVING AB TRUST

$\mathcal{A}$s you know, there are three primary purposes for a couple to use an AB living trust:

1. To save on estate taxes, increasing the property that can be conserved for the couple's children or other final beneficiaries.

2. At the same time, to make the deceased spouse's property available for use by the surviving spouse, to be as sure as possible that the survivor is adequately provided during the rest of his or her life.

3. To avoid probate.

This chapter takes a deeper look at the AB trust this book offers. It shows how couples with a large combined estate can conserve for their children, or other final inheritors, substantial amounts of money by using this trust.

A couple must have a combined estate of at least $625,000 to consider using an AB trust, because that is the lowest federal estate tax threshold. Below that amount, there simply are no federal estate taxes, so obviously, there's no need to bother with a trust designed to save on federal estate taxes.

After reading this chapter, you may decide that the Nolo AB trust isn't right for your situation. Section E, below, briefly discusses different types of trusts which may be preferable. All these types of trusts, however, need to be prepared by a lawyer.

How Much the AB Trust Can Shelter From Estate Tax

If you die in	you can leave this much tax-free (the exempt amount)	and an AB trust can shelter a combined estate worth this much (maximum protected amount)
1996	$625,000	$1.25 million
1997	$650,000	$1.3 million
1998	$675,000	$1.35 million
1999	$700,000	$1.4 million
2000	$725,000	$1.45 million
2001	$750,000	$1.5 million
After 2001	$750,000 plus	$1.5 million + annual cost of living adjustment

As I cautioned in Chapter 1, "An Overview of Living Trusts," Congress and the President had not resolved their budget struggle as of the printing of this second edition of this book. The estate tax exemptions listed above are contained in the proposed Congressional budget, and it seems very likely that these exemptions will eventually become law. But until the budget conflict is resolved, the current estate tax law remains in effect. Under this current law, property worth up to $600,000 is exempt from federal tax, no matter what the year of death. If you want Nolo help to learn if the proposed Congressional changes have become law, try one of the resources listed in Chapter 1, Section D.

Limits on each spouse's estate. If you want to use the Nolo AB trust, neither spouse's estate, counting the total worth of his or her half interest in shared-ownership property, and all his or her separate property, can exceed the exempt amount. If one member has more than the exempt amount, the Nolo AB trust is not for you. See a lawyer.

A TRUST BY ANY OTHER NAME

The AB trust explained in this chapter goes by a variety of names in the world at large. You may hear the same type of trust called a "living trust with marital life estate," a "bypass" trust, an "exemption" trust, a "family" trust or a "credit shelter" trust.

A. Should You Use This Book to Do It Yourself?

Before we plunge into details of how Nolo's AB trust works, I again want to give you a serious warning. AB trusts come in a variety of forms, having different tax, legal and practical consequences. This book presents one type of AB trust, useful for many couples. As long as this trust is right for you, don't hesitate to use it. But if you conclude that your family and monetary situations are different than those discussed in Chapter 4, Section E, and summarized below, this form is not advisable for you.

Don't change the form on your own. Except where I specifically state it's permissible, please do not modify or make any changes in the AB trust form in the Appendix. If you want to make changes, see a lawyer. Beyond having a combined estate that's large enough to trigger concern about estate tax, here are the basic requirements you should meet:

- You want to leave the bulk of your property for the use of your spouse during her or his lifetime, if that spouse survives you.

- Neither spouse wants to leave more than three gifts directly to other persons or institutions.

- You and your spouse want to eventually leave your property to your children or other final inheritors in a way that avoids estate taxes as much as possible.

- Key family members understand and approve that the AB trust allows the surviving spouse broad powers over the trust property.

- If you have children from prior marriages (or children from prior marriages and children from this marriage), be sure there's enough understanding and trust among all the children and both spouses, so there won't be serious conflicts once the trust becomes functional.

The comforting truth is that Nolo's AB trust does work fine for many couples. If you're among this group, you'll find that the technical aspects of preparing your trust (covered in Chapters 10 and 11) are not onerous, and you can safely prepare this trust yourself, saving yourself at least a thousand dollars—and probably a good deal more—in attorney fees.

On the other hand, if your situation is more complex, and you can't safely use Nolo's AB trust, that means you'll have to see a lawyer. Yes, trust lawyers are expensive, but remember:

- By studying this book, you'll be far better prepared to deal with a lawyer, and can suggest ways to keep fees to a reasonable amount (such as you, yourself, transferring assets to your trust, rather than paying an attorney $200, $300 or more per hour for what is basically clerical work).

- You are seeing a lawyer to save on overall estate taxes on a combined estate that, by definition, is worth over $625,000. You can afford to spend some money on legal advice.

- AB trusts can become quite complex and technical. If you don't fully comply with IRS regulations, estate tax savings will be lost.

- Even if your trust qualifies under IRS rules, if it isn't properly geared to your situation, you may not achieve your goals and desires. If you and your spouse both have children from prior marriages, for example, you may need a carefully prepared trust to minimize possibilities of family conflict. This can be doubly true if one spouse has far more money than the other, and if the spouse married late in life. An AB trust that is technically and legally okay can nevertheless lead to disastrous conflicts if the personal concerns of all involved haven't been addressed and resolved as best they can be.

B. Federal Estate Tax Rules

At the beginning, let's go over some basic federal estate tax rules. All U.S. citizens (and anyone owning property in the U.S.) may be subject to federal estate taxes, which can take a large bite of a good-sized estate. The tax rate is determined by the size of the taxable estate; the general rule is that the more you own, the higher the rate.

Federal estate tax rates are stiff: They start at 37% for amounts between $625,000 and $750,000. The tax rate is graduated, reaching a maximum of 55% for estates worth over $3 million. (Federal estate and gift taxes are discussed further in Chapter 15, "A Living Trust as Part of Your Estate Plan," Section C.)

More information on estate taxes. A more comprehensive explanation of federal estate taxes, including a chart of the tax rates, is contained in *Plan Your Estate* (Nolo Press).

Fortunately, several exemptions allow you to transfer substantial amounts of property free of federal estate taxes. The major exemptions are:

- **The personal exemption.** Under this exemption, in 1996, $625,000 worth of property in an estate is free of tax, no matter who the property is left to. This amount is scheduled to increase each year. (See chart above.) This assumes you haven't made any taxable gifts during your lifetimes. See Chapter 15, "A Living Trust as Part of Your Estate Plan," Section C.

- **The marriage exemption.** All property, no matter how large the dollar value, left by a deceased spouse to a surviving spouse who is a United States citizen is free of federal estate tax. (This is called the "marital deduction," in tax lingo.) If the surviving spouse is not a citizen of the U.S., the marital deduction does not apply. (See Chapter 15, Section C.)

- **The charity exemption.** All property left to tax-exempt charities is tax-free.

- **The state tax exemption.** Amounts used to pay any state death taxes are tax-free.

NO ESTATE TAX EXEMPTION FOR UNMARRIED COUPLES

There is no exemption similar to the marital deduction for lovers or "significant others" or whatever other name unmarried couples, whether gay or heterosexual, use for their mates. Quite simply, the estate tax laws are written to encourage and reward traditional relationships. (Don't blame me; I didn't write the laws.) However, the marital deduction is available for couples who entered into a legal common law marriage. Such marriages may legally be created in Alabama, Colorado, District of Columbia, Georgia, Idaho, Iowa, Kansas, Montana, New Hampshire (for inheritance only), Ohio, Oklahoma, Pennsylvania, Rhode Island, South Carolina, Texas and Utah.

State death taxes. Some states impose death taxes on estates that aren't big enough to reach the federal tax threshold. Many other states impose no death taxes at all. Unless you can move from a high death tax state to one with no or low death taxes, it's rarely worth the trouble to plan to reduce or avoid state death taxes, which are relatively small compared to federal estate taxes. If this matter concerns you, see a lawyer.

C. Estate Tax Savings With an AB Trust

To summarize it again, the key to the usefulness of an AB trust is this: While the deceased spouse's property is left for the use of the surviving spouse, as long as that spouse remains alive, the survivor never becomes the legal owner of that property. The legal owners, in effect, are the trust's final beneficiaries—the people who ultimately inherit the property. These final beneficiaries were named by the deceased spouse in the original living trust document. The surviving spouse has no right to change these final beneficiaries.

An AB trust is sometimes called a "bypass" trust, because legal ownership of property in the trust bypasses the surviving spouse. Because she never legally owns it, the property does not become part of her taxable estate (the property she owns when she dies). Instead, the property in Trust A is subject to estate tax when the first spouse dies. Having it taxed at this point is desirable because the first spouse to die has an estate tax exemption of at least $625,000, depending on the year of death, so no tax is due if the property in his total estate (including what's in Trust A) is worth less than that amount. The second spouse has a separate estate tax exemption, which can be used at her death exclusively to shelter her property (up to the exempt amount) from estate tax.

To sum up the tax advantages, an AB trust saves on estate taxes because it allows each member of the couple to use a separate estate tax exemption. It prevents the surviving spouse from ending up as legal owner of all the property that originally belonged to both spouses and, assuming this is more than the exempt amount, having a hefty estate liability upon her death.

Example

Jacob and Annette, a married couple in their 60s, have a total estate of $950,000—$800,000 of shared property and $150,000 of Annette's separate property. They have three children, and understandably would like their entire estate to pass equally to the kids, with none being used on taxes. ("Spend it on yourselves," a daughter urged. "Bah," Annette replied, "We have all we need. What do I want with a deluxe trip to Las Vegas?") Because their combined estate is under the maximum amount that can be protected by Nolo's AB trust, and neither spouse's estate exceeds the exempt amount (Jacob's estate is $400,000; Annette's is $550,000), they decide to create an AB trust from this book.

Each leaves all his or her living trust property in Trust A (the life estate trust), and each names the children as the final beneficiaries of his or her life estate trust.

Annette dies in 1997, and all of her living trust property goes into the "A" portion of her AB trust. This means that Jacob receives a life estate interest in this trust property as well as the right to use it if needed for his health or support.

When Jacob dies in 1999, Annette's Trust A property is divided equally among their three children. (Because Jacob has no spouse to leave property for in a life estate, the final beneficiaries he named in the original trust document inherit his own living trust property outright.) No federal estate tax has been paid.

Here's a more detailed example, complete with math.

Example

Mabel and Anthony, who together own property worth $1,100,000, create an AB trust. Here are the estate tax consequences:

At Mabel's death, 1996

Value of Mabel's net estate	=	$550,000

(Net estate means the net worth of the estate after all liabilities, including any last debts or taxes, have been paid.)

Exempt amount	=	$625,000
Amount subject to federal estate tax	=	0

Mabel's estate goes into a marital life estate trust

At Anthony's death, 1998

Value of Anthony's net estate	=	$550,000

(Obviously, this assumes his net estate has remained the same over a year—perhaps not often exactly true in reality.)

Exempt amount	=	$675,000
Amount subject to federal estate tax	=	0

By contrast, here are the estate tax consequences if all property had been left outright by the deceased spouse to the surviving spouse:

At Mabel's death, 1996

Value of Mabel's net estate	=	$550,000

Exempt amount is unlimited
(because of marital deduction)

Amount subject to federal estate tax	=	0

At Anthony's death, 1998

Value of Anthony's net estate		$1,100,000
Exempt amount	-	675,000
Amount subject to tax	=	425,000
Federal estate tax due	=	$ 166,250

If your estate grows. Whatever you earlier estimated your estate would be worth, if the estate of either spouse actually exceeds the exempt amount at death and you use this book's AB trust, a federal estate tax return must be filed and any taxes due paid within nine months of the first spouse's death.

D. How Nolo's AB Trust Works

This section focuses on precisely how Nolo's AB trust works.

1. Creating the Trust

To create an AB trust using this book, use Form 3 in the Appendix. (Specific, step-by-step instructions for completing this form are in Chapter 10, "Preparing Your Living Trust Document.") In general, the process is:

- Both spouses create an overall shared living trust by naming themselves trustees and listing all property they plan to transfer to the trust on trust schedules.

- Within this overall living trust, each spouse creates an AB trust. The "A" portion leaves property of the first spouse to die in an irrevocable trust, with the surviving spouse as the life beneficiary. The "B" portion is that part of the shared property that will be owned outright by the surviving spouse. Each spouse names the other as the life beneficiary and trustee of his or her A (marital life estate) trust.

- Each spouse names his or her final beneficiaries (and alternates) to receive his or her trust property after the surviving spouse has died. Spouses can name different final beneficiaries, but since this can create serious risks of conflict, be sure all final beneficiaries of the trust will get along among themselves and with both spouses.

- The spouses name a successor trustee, to take over and distribute trust property after both spouses have died.

That's basically all there is to it. (That's enough, no?) All the terms and phases necessary to create a legal AB trust, following the IRS rules to ensure estate tax savings, are printed in Form 3.

When a couple creates an AB trust, they cannot absolutely know (although some couples may be pretty sure) which spouse will be the first to die. So each spouse must create a separate Trust A, and fate will decide which one becomes fully operational.

Example

Meredith and Gary have a total estate (all shared property owned equally) of $900,000. They use Nolo's Form 3 to create an AB trust in which:

- Both transfer all property into the living trust.

- Meredith leaves her share of the property in her Trust A with Gary as the life beneficiary and their children, equally, as the final beneficiaries.

- Gary leaves his share of the property in his Trust A with Meredith as the life beneficiary and to their children, equally, as the final beneficiaries.

- Gary and Meredith name their daughter Alice to serve as successor trustee after both spouses die.

    In practical, day-to-day terms, so long as Meredith and Gary live, nothing really changes after they've created their AB trust. The living trust is revocable, and all trust transactions (such as any sale of trust property, or other income from trust property) are reported on the couple's regular income tax return. But when one spouse dies, the trust really becomes operational.

2. How an AB Trust Becomes Operational

Only one of the "A" trusts will ever become operational. When one spouse dies (called, for our purpose, the "deceased spouse"), that spouse's Trust A becomes irrevocable and fully effective. The surviving spouse no longer has any need for his or her Trust A, because he or she cannot, by definition, have a spouse survive him or her. (However, if he or she remarries, the surviving spouse and new mate can create a new, separate living trust with

a new AB trust.) So the surviving spouse's Trust A will always remain inoperative. At the second spouse's death, his or her Trust B property goes directly to the final beneficiaries he or she named originally.

When the deceased spouse's Trust A becomes operational, this means it exists as a distinct taxable entity. The surviving spouse has all the rights in that trust property specified in Section D6, below. The final beneficiaries of this trust receive whatever trust property remains when the surviving spouse dies.

3. Property Left to Specific Beneficiaries

Nolo's AB trust allows each spouse to make three specific gifts, in addition to the property left in Trust A. These gifts will go to the named beneficiaries at the deceased spouse's death. Legally, you can make as many specific gifts as you want. However, from my experience, it's rare for someone to want to both leave a number of specific gifts while simultaneously leaving the bulk of property for use of the surviving spouse.

Making these gifts is, of course, not mandatory; many couples simply leave all their property in Trust A. You can make separate gifts from either your separate property (if you have any), or from your half of shared property or some combination of both. If you choose to make specific gifts, they should be relatively minor, totaling no more than $25,000 to $50,000. After all, a central purpose of an AB trust is to leave the bulk, or all, of one spouse's property for the use of the other spouse during his or her lifetime.

Example

Shauna is married and has an estate worth $516,000. She decides to leave some of her separate property heirlooms to her sister and nieces: an old music box to her sister Bernice, an antique clock to her niece Danielle and several lace dresses to her niece Moira. The total monetary value of these gifts is approximately $7,000. Shauna leaves all the rest of her property, both separate and her half of shared property, in an AB trust, where her spouse will be able to use it during his lifetime.

4. Division of AB Trust Property When One Spouse Dies

Eventually, one spouse dies. At this point, the property in the AB trust must be divided between the deceased spouse's property in Trust A and the property owned by the surviving spouse in Trust B. From Trust A property, any gifts the deceased spouse left to specific beneficiaries are distributed; then all the rest of his or her property is retained in Trust A, the marital life estate trust.

The deceased spouse's trust is now irrevocable. None of its terms—who is the life beneficiary, final beneficiaries or successor trustee—can be changed by the surviving spouse, or anyone else.

Example

Bill and Rachel make an AB trust. Bill dies first. The property in the living trust (worth $980,000, all shared property) is divided into two equal shares. Bill made no specific gifts of trust property, so his entire share of the living trust property ($490,000) is placed in Trust A, with Rachel as the life beneficiary. This trust is now irrevocable. It will last until Rachel dies, and then the remaining trust property will be distributed to the final beneficiaries Bill named in the original trust document, who are Bill's and Rachel's children, in equal shares.

The surviving spouse's property in the original living trust goes into what is called Trust B, or "the surviving spouse's trust," which is really a continuation of her portion of the original living trust. The trust is given a distinct name to help make clearer that it's a separate entity from Trust A. The surviving spouse can amend or revoke her Trust B if she wishes. The property in Trust B includes:

- The surviving spouse's 50% share of co-owned trust property. (Each item does not have to be divided 50-50, but the total value of the deceased spouse's share of co-owned property must be the same as the value of the surviving spouse's share.)
- All separate trust property of the surviving spouse.

Dividing the trust property is the responsibility of the surviving spouse, as trustee of both trusts. She must decide which of the couple's living trust property she wants placed in the (irrevocable) Trust A, and which she wants retained in her (revocable) Trust B. All that is legally required is that the total dollar amount of shared ownership property in each trust be equal. Ownership of each individual item of property does not have to be split in half.

If your goals include maximum future income tax savings and estate tax savings (beyond what's automatically saved by using an AB trust), deciding which property goes where isn't always clear or simple.

Suppose a couple shares ownership of a house worth $400,000 and money market accounts of $550,000, and the husband has separate property worth $100,000. What's the wisest way to divide up this property when the first spouse dies? It depends on the couple's needs and circumstances, and requires a bit of trying to see into the future.

First, let's just look at the house. If all the $400,000 value of the house is put in Trust A, it will not be subject to estate tax (even if the husband's $100,000 of separate property is added in as well), because the total in the A trust is less than the exempt amount. So if over the years, the value of the house rises to $750,000 before the surviving spouse dies, the final beneficiaries will receive all this increase in value without paying any estate tax at all on it. (Remember, this property was subject to estate tax only once, when the deceased spouse died and Trust A became operational and irrevocable.) If the house weren't in Trust A, it would be assessed at $750,000 for estate tax purposes when the second spouse died.

But, as some folks have recently learned, it's not a law of nature that house prices always rise. House prices are set by a free market, and the only thing we really know about a free market is that (as Bernard Baruch said of the stock market) "prices will fluctuate." If real estate prices go down or even remain flat, maybe the couple (and the children, as the final inheritors) would be better off if the money market funds were all put in Trust A. Maybe they'll increase in value more, even much more, than that house. Or maybe splitting both the house and the money market funds between Trust A and the Trust B will prove wisest.

A spouse faced with dividing up property between the two trusts may well decide to hire a good accountant or estate tax lawyer to determine the most advantageous division. Since this should cost a few hundred dollars—but not thousands—it often makes sense to spend the money. An expert can discuss your situation with you and explain what's likely to be most desirable, say, if you think you'll sell the house soon, and how IRS rules regarding sale of your home could affect you.

But experts are not fortune tellers. They can't guarantee which property will appreciate most in the future. Some surviving spouses simply split all shared property equally between the two trusts—that is, half the house to Trust A, half to Trust B, half the money market funds to one trust, half to the other. These spouses decide it's not worth the bother and expense to try to guess which property will appreciate more.

Some paperwork is required to officially allocate property between the two trusts. All property with documents of title that is placed in Trust A must have new title documents prepared (and recorded, if need be, as with real estate deeds), listing Trust A as owner. Property without title must be listed on a schedule attached to the

Trust A document. (Instructions are in Chapter 14, "After a Grantor Dies.")

No new paperwork is required to create Trust B, or the surviving spouse's trust. It happens automatically under the terms of Nolo's Form 3. Property in Trust B does not have to be formally retitled or renamed. The name "Trust B, surviving spouse's trust," is used (technically, added onto the name of the original living trust) to make it clearer that there now are two trusts—one, Trust A, which is now irrevocable, and two, the ongoing trust of the surviving spouse, or Trust B, which is revocable. Using this terminology can also be helpful to the IRS. They're familiar with it, and they'll surely want to know what property is in Trust A when the annual trust tax return is filed. (Since the surviving spouse's Trust B remains revocable, all transactions of that trust can continue to be reported to the IRS on the surviving spouse's personal income tax return.)

5. Managing the Property in Trust A

The surviving spouse, as trustee, must manage Trust A as a separate legal entity. The minimum required here is to:

- obtain a federal taxpayer ID for the trust
- keep separate, clear tax records of all trust transactions (a checkbook will usually suffice), and
- file a separate trust tax return for Trust A each year.

While all of this requires energy and involves some paperwork hassles, few spouses find it truly onerous, given the tax savings they're achieving for their children.

If the gross value of the property in Trust A turns out to exceed the exempt amount, the surviving spouse, as trustee, is responsible for filing a federal estate tax return and paying any taxes due within nine months of death. However, as you know by now, you shouldn't have to worry about this, because the value of the property in Trust A should be under the exempt amount (so no federal tax return is required or taxes assessed). But it's possible that the value of your combined estate could grow to exceed the maximum protected amount (and each spouse's share would exceed the exempt amount). If you

HE DECIDED TO TAKE IT WITH HIM.

don't see a lawyer to revise your trust before a spouse dies, an estate tax return will be required and taxes will have to be paid from some property in Trust A.

Once Trust A is legally established, the surviving spouse, as trustee, must manage the trust property responsibly. For example, any property taxes due on real estate in Trust A should be paid from funds or property of that trust. (If there are no liquid assets—cash, or property that can be turned into cash—in Trust A, the surviving spouse is stuck and must pay them from some other source. But remember, she could always refinance the house, assuming there was some equity in it, to obtain cash.)

Legally, as trustee, the surviving spouse has what is called in legalese a "fiduciary duty" to the final beneficiaries. That means she must manage the trust property reasonably, and protect the final beneficiaries' interest in the trust property (principal), except as otherwise authorized in Trust A document. With Nolo's Trust A, the surviving spouse has the authority to hire financial advisers or consultants, paid for from trust funds (including principal), if need be.

With Nolo's AB trust, the surviving spouse has no obligation to provide reports about the property in Trust A to any of the final beneficiaries, except to provide them with copies of the annual trust income tax return. This is a compromise between allowing the final beneficiaries no rights at all to know what is going on in the trust and allowing them far more extensive rights or controls. Since the surviving spouse must prepare and file an annual trust income tax return for Trust A, it does not seem unduly burdensome or intrusive that she give copies of that tax report to the trust's final beneficiaries.

6. The Surviving Spouse's Rights to Use Property in a Nolo Trust A

Because this subject is a matter of such vital concern to many couples, I want to stress here, even at the risk of some repetition, what the rights of the surviving spouse are. Nolo's Trust A is designed to allow the surviving

spouse to have substantial control over that trust's property, while, of course, still achieving estate tax savings. To accomplish this, the trust uses the specific language required by the IRS so that Trust A property is never legally owned by the surviving spouse. At the same time, the surviving spouse has all of the following rights to Trust A property:

- The right to all income from the trust property

- The right to use trust property (for example, to live in a house owned, or partially owned, by the trust)

- The right to sell trust property, reinvest trust funds or buy new property in the name of the trust, as long as principal is not used up. For example, the surviving spouse, as trustee, can sell a house owned or co-owned by the trust and buy a condo in Florida or North Carolina, but cannot use the proceeds to gamble at Las Vegas.

- The right to use the trust principal for any amount necessary for the surviving spouse's "health, education, support and maintenance in his or her accustomed manner of living." (IRS Reg. 20.2041-1(c)(2).)

The only practical effect of the IRS limitations is that the surviving spouse cannot spend the money any way she wants, say for a painting by Elmer Bischoff or a six-month vacation in Europe.

How would the IRS find out if the surviving spouse were improperly spending money from Trust A? First, you must realize that this is mostly a lawyer's theoretical question. Surely the overwhelming majority of couples who create and use an AB trust do so in good faith and want to conserve the trust principal for their children.

Improper spending of Trust A principle might be detected by an IRS audit of the annual trust tax return, or perhaps one of the final beneficiaries would learn of these improper expenses and oppose them. (It might take a lawsuit, though, to actually prevent the spouse from continuing to abuse her position.) But even if the children had no objection to the parent spending the money, if the IRS decided it had been spent for an improper purpose, it could conclude that there was never any intention of creating a bona fide AB trust. In that case, the trust is disallowed, for tax purposes, and all Trust A property treated as owned by the surviving spouse—exactly what you don't want.

Don't change a word. The language permitting the surviving spouse to spend "A" trust principal for "health, education, support and maintenance in accord with his or her accustomed manner of living" (printed in Form 3) is crucial. If you add a word like "well-being" or "comfort" to the list, the IRS would claim that the standard for spending principal was "subjective"—a fatal mistake. If a "subjective" standard is used, IRS rules state that Trust A property is legally owned by the surviving spouse. This means this property is included in the survivor's estate for estate tax purposes. As you know, the whole point of setting up an AB trust in the first place is to keep the husband's and wife's estates from being lumped together for estate tax purposes.

The right of the surviving spouse to invade the trust principal for any amount needed for "support, health, education and maintenance in his or her accustomed manner of living" can be of great importance. It means that if the surviving spouse faces any serious financial need—a costly medical emergency, housing crisis or other necessity of life—and doesn't have enough other funds or assets to pay them, she's legally authorized, as trustee, to spend any amount needed of trust principal to pay for these needs. If a spouse couldn't use the A trust principal for these needs, this type of trust would be far less popular.

The surviving spouse is not required to use up all her assets before using trust principal to pay for, or help pay for, such costs. For example, a survivor doesn't have to sell her house and spend all the proceeds on medical care before using Trust A property for medical needs. The IRS regulations specifically provide that she's entitled to continue to live in "her accustomed manner of living."

What's required here is simply that the surviving spouse's use of trust principal be reasonable, under the circumstances, and for one of the IRS-authorized purposes.

Example

A couple, Kumar and Hari, has assets of $1 million—a house worth $400,000 (equity) and stocks and money market funds worth $600,000. They establish an AB trust, with each spouse having the maximum legal rights over the trust's property.

Kumar dies. Hari continues to own outright her half of the property. Kumar's half goes into Trust A. Hari is both the life beneficiary and trustee of this trust, and the couple's kids are the final beneficiaries.

The real world effect is that Hari remains in the house. She also receives all the income from the $600,000 in stocks and money market funds—half because she owns half the stocks and money market funds directly, half as trust income.

Hari has some serious health problems over the next couple of years. The costs of the illness are mostly covered by her insurance and Medicare. But one medical bill is not covered, and Hari's income is not sufficient to pay it. Hari, as trustee, can spend some of the trust principal to pay this bill.

7. Amending Trust B

Trust B, or the surviving spouse's trust, which contains the survivor's portion of the living trust property, remains revocable while the survivor lives. The survivor can amend the terms of Trust B, or revoke it entirely, as long as he or she is mentally competent.

A surviving spouse often doesn't name new beneficiaries for some or all of her Trust B property, because the most common situation is where both spouses want to leave their property to their children, and this desire doesn't change after one spouse dies.

Normally, it's inadvisable for the surviving spouse to change the successor trustee of her trust, unless there are compelling reasons. That's because when the surviving spouse dies, there would be two trustees involved in transferring the property of the two trusts—Trust A, the marital life estate trust, and Trust B, the surviving spouse's trust—to the same final beneficiaries (assuming the final beneficiaries are the same for both trusts). It seems self-evident that there are risks of conflict and tension between two different trustees for different trusts for what is all, basically, "family" money.

However, if the surviving spouse amends her trust to name new final beneficiaries, it may well make sense to also name a new successor trustee for this trust. When she dies, this new successor trustee will distribute her trust property to her new beneficiaries. And the successor trustee for Trust A will distribute that trust's property to the final beneficiaries named by the deceased spouse in the original living trust document. (See Section E8, below.)

8. After the Surviving Spouse Dies

After the death of the surviving spouse (the life beneficiary of Trust A), the successor trustee named in the original living trust document (often one of the couple's children) distributes Trust A property to that trust's final beneficiaries. In addition, the surviving spouse's own living trust, Trust B, becomes irrevocable on his or her death, and the successor trustee distributes that trust's property as the trust document directs.

This usually involves some paperwork and dealing with financial institutions such as stock brokerage companies and title companies. (See Chapter 14, "After a Grantor Dies," for a full discussion of this process.) In ad-

dition, the successor trustee manages any children's subtrusts created by either spouse's trust. Finally, the successor trustee is responsible for handling any other trust-related matters. For example, if the gross value of the surviving spouse's estate exceeded the tax-exempt amount, the successor trustee would have to file a federal estate tax return and pay any tax due from the estate. As I've discussed, the estate of the surviving spouse may grow to exceed the tax-exempt amount. This is true particularly if she lives a number of years after the first spouse dies, and even more particularly if she owns property—say real estate or stocks—that substantially appreciates between her husband's death and her own.

Example

Lamont and Iola create an AB trust, with their three children as the final beneficiaries to share equally. Lamont leaves some of his separate-property art works to his sister, Coreen. They name their daughter Thelma as the successor trustee.

When Lamont dies, Iola, serving as trustee of the living trust, divides the trust property in half. From Lamont's half, she makes the specific gift Lamont left to his sister. All Lamont's remaining property becomes the property of Trust A. Iola, the surviving spouse, is the trustee and life estate beneficiary of this trust. She receives all income from that trust property and has the right to use it and manage it (as trustee) for the rest of her life.

When Iola dies, Thelma, the successor trustee, divides property in Trust A equally among the three children. Since one child, Willie, is only 20 years old, his property stays in a child's subtrust, managed by Thelma, until Willie becomes 35. (See Chapter 9, "Property Left to Minor Children or Young Adults," Section C.) Thelma also divides Iola's trust B property equally among the three children. Again, Willie's share (of Iola's trust property) is placed in the child's subtrust, with Thelma as the trustee.

E. Other Options

Many options can be used for couples' estate planning needs. Some of these options are other forms of an AB trust. Other options are different types of trusts. I briefly mention some of these options here, and discuss them and others further in Chapter 15, "A Living Trust as Part of Your Estate Plan," Section F. Because each of these options can be complicated, and none fits the needs of large numbers of people without modification, no forms for them are included in this book. If you wish to pursue any of them, see a lawyer. I discuss them here so it will be clear exactly what you cannot do with Nolo's AB trust, and so that if you do decide to see a lawyer, you'll understand some of the terms and concepts she's likely to throw at you.

All these options require a lawyer. They are for people with large estates, over $625,000 for an individual, or $1,250,000 for a couple.

1. The "5 and 5" Power Trust

Under present IRS rules, the surviving spouse of an AB trust can be given the right to obtain annually, for any reason whatsoever, up to a maximum of 5% of the A trust principal or $5,000, whichever is greater. Estate planners call this the "5 and 5" power. There can be drawbacks to including this in an AB trust, including adverse tax con-

DIVISION AND DISTRIBUTION OF TRUST PROPERTY WHEN A SPOUSE DIES

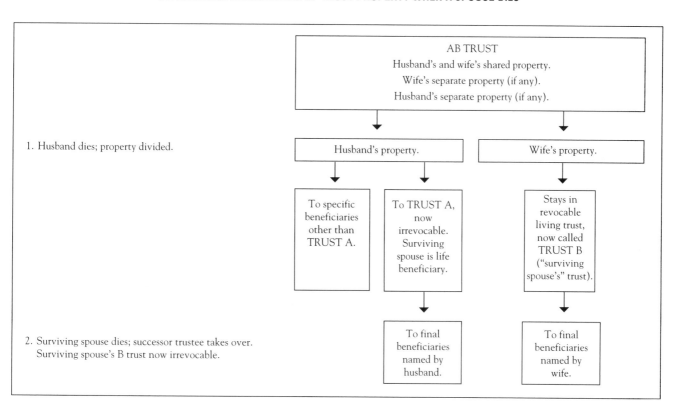

sequences if the money isn't actually taken annually by the surviving spouse. Still, some estate planners like to include the "5 and 5" power because it allows, to a limited extent, the surviving spouse to use the Trust A principal for any reason.

This "5 and 5" power is not included in this book's AB trust because the surviving spouse already has authority to obtain trust principal in any amount for "health, education, support and maintenance." In my view, an additional general power for the spouse to use the principal for any reason seems unnecessary and possibly unwise. In addition, Congress or the IRS might change this "5 and 5" power. You shouldn't have to keep up with federal estate tax laws and regulations and then amend your trust if need be to get rid of a power you never really needed in the first place.

2. Limiting the Rights of the Surviving Spouse

As I've mentioned, an AB trust does not have to grant the surviving spouse the broadest powers allowed by law. It's possible to limit, or prohibit altogether, the surviving spouse's right to spend (invade) the Trust A principal. Some AB trusts impose lesser restrictions on the surviving spouse, such as requiring regular trust reports to trust beneficiaries, or requiring the consent of a specific final beneficiary before spending principal.

Imposing these types of restrictions is somewhat atypical. They tend to occur in second or subsequent marriages, where each spouse wants to ensure that his or her children from a prior marriage are protected and will actually receive the principal of Trust A. Because these trusts raise many concerns related to the couple's personal needs and financial circumstances, people who want them should consult a lawyer.

The goal of imposing limits and controls on the property left to the surviving spouse can be combined with estate tax savings, or it can be independent. Thus, even if a couple has no estate tax problems—their combined estate is less than the exempt amount—they may want to create an AB trust to control property left to a surviving spouse. For example, a spouse in a second mar-

riage wants to leave his property for the use of his wife during her lifetime, but also to ensure that the property goes to their children from first or prior marriages. (Limiting the rights of a surviving spouse is discussed further in Chapter 15, Section F.)

3. A Formula Trust

A "formula" trust defines the value of the property placed in Trust A when the first spouse dies. It does this by way of a clause or, more accurately, a series of clauses, in the trust document, which in essence say "put in the maximum amount federal law exempts from estate taxes, but no more." All property in excess of the exempt amount is transferred by other methods—frequently by what's called a "QTIP" trust. QTIP is IRS jargon for "Qualified Terminal Interest Property." (That clears it all up, right?) This type of trust allows a surviving spouse to postpone estate taxes that would otherwise be due on the death of the first spouse.

Example

Damian and Victoria have a combined estate worth $1,800,000. They create a "formula" AB trust and a QTIP trust. When Damian dies in 1998, his estate is worth $900,000. The estate tax exemption for that year is $650,000, so that amount goes by the formula into Trust A. The balance of Damian's estate, $250,000, goes into the QTIP trust. No estate taxes are paid on Damian's death.

A formula AB trust makes sense only when another trust is created to handle any property worth more than the formula covers. This book does not offer a do-it-yourself QTIP or other advanced estate tax-saving trust. Creating these trusts requires a lawyer. They are too complex to risk preparing yourself. Because this book does not offer any additional trusts to handle property worth over the exempt amount, no purpose would be served by having a "formula" define what amount of property goes into Trust A. This book's AB trust simply provides that all of a deceased spouse's property, less any left in specific gifts, goes into the deceased spouse's Trust A. As I've urged before, if you think that sum may be over the tax-exempt amount, see a lawyer to explore more complex estate planning.

4. Other Estate Tax-Saving Trusts

Other types of estate tax-saving trusts and devices are discussed in Chapter 15. To very briefly summarize here, they include:

- **Disclaimers.** Basically, a disclaimer permits someone who's been given a gift to decline to accept it. The gift then goes to an alternate beneficiary originally named by the gift giver. The person who disclaims the gift does so to lower overall estate taxes.

- **Charitable remainder trusts and generation-skipping trusts.** These trusts can be used to save taxes by couples with estates over the amount that can be protected by the Nolo AB trust, or a single person with an estate over the exempt amount. ❧

chapter 6

Choosing What Property to Put in Your Living Trust

*O*kay, it's time to begin hands-on work. Here in this chapter you'll make your initial decisions regarding what property to put in your trust.

You can place all your property in your living trust, or leave some or even most of it by other means. This chapter alerts you to when a living trust may not be the best method for transferring your property. Other methods are discussed further in Chapter 15, "A Living Trust as Part of Your Estate Plan."

For many people, deciding what property to transfer to their living trust is not a difficult matter. They have one, or a few, "big ticket" items—for example, their house, some stocks and a money market account—and they know they want to avoid probate of this property. But for many other people, matters aren't quite so simple. Some have questions about different types of property— say, about personal checking accounts, retirement accounts or more unusual items such as copyrights or patents. And if you're married, you may need to determine which property is shared in equal amounts and which is the separate property of one spouse.

This chapter:

- Discusses types of property you'll probably want to put into your trust

- Reviews state marital property laws that can require you to leave property to your spouse

- Provides a Property Worksheet you can use to make a thorough inventory of what you own and estimate the net value of your property. You can use this estimate of your net worth to see if your individual, or combined (if you are a couple), estate exceeds $625,000, the federal estate tax threshold.

Even if you believe you are already sure what property you want to put in your trust, read these materials carefully to be sure your decisions pose no potential problems. Of course, you can always revise your decisions before preparing your actual trust document. The point isn't to lock you in now, but to get you started.

A. Listing the Property to Be Put in Your Trust

You must list, in the trust document, each item of property the trust owns. Any property you don't list will not go into your living trust and will not pass under the terms of the trust. It may instead have to go through probate.

A list of trust property is called a "schedule" and is attached to the trust document. (This is explained in detail in Chapter 10, "Preparing Your Living Trust Document," Section C.) A trust for one person has only one schedule. A trust for a married couple (either a basic shared trust or an AB trust) has three schedules: one for shared-ownership property, one for any separate property of the wife, and another for any separate property of the husband. If a spouse doesn't have any separate property, you can simply eliminate the appropriate schedule.

Transferring title to the trustee. You must also prepare separate documents formally transferring legal title to the trust. Technically, you do that by placing title in the trustee's or trustees' name(s), "as trustee(s) for the ___[name]___ Trust." Property with a document of title—like a deed to a house, or a stock account—must be transferred by preparing and signing a new document of title. Property without a document of title—such as household goods, jewelry and clothes—can be transferred simply by listing them on a trust schedule. Preparing these documents is vital, and is explained in detail in Chapter 11, "Transferring Property to Your Trust." But for right now, your concern is simply to make basic decisions regarding the property you want in the trusts and to write down how you'll list that property.

Many people instinctively think of their trust beneficiaries and property together: The antique dresser goes to Mary; the house will be divided between the kids, and so on. But to be thorough and sure you do the job right, I suggest that you separate these two key elements. Here, list your trust property. Then, in the next chapter, you'll learn about trust beneficiaries and name yours.

ADDING PROPERTY TO THE LIVING TRUST LATER

If you acquire valuable property in your name after you create your living trust, you will be able to amend your trust and easily add that property to it. Also, once you've set up the trust, if you're buying property you intend to keep for a while, you can simply acquire it in the name of the trustee(s) of your trust. Finally, if you mistakenly leave something out of your trust, you can add it later by amending your trust. (See Chapter 13, "Living With Your Living Trust.")

B. Property That Should Not Be Put in Your Living Trust

You don't automatically need to put everything you own into a living trust to save money on probate. Property that is of relatively low value (the amount depends on state law) may be exempt from probate or qualify for a streamlined probate procedure that's relatively fast and cheap. And in some states, at least some of the property left to a surviving spouse can probably be transferred without a full-blown probate court proceeding.

Generally, it's better not to include the following types of property in your trust:

- **Your personal checking account**, unless you want to pay your bills in the name of the trust. A checking account in the name of a trust can cause raised eyebrows—even refusal to accept the check—by people or institutions who wonder, "Why can't she write the check in her own name? What's this trust business?"

- **Property you buy or sell frequently.** If you don't expect to own the property at your death, there's no compelling reason to transfer it to your living trust. (Remember, the probate process you want to avoid doesn't happen until after your death.)

- **Automobiles**. Some insurance companies won't insure a vehicle owned by a trust. They worry that an un-

known number of people could be entitled, under the terms of the trust, to drive the vehicle. Anyway, the value of most people's car or cars isn't so high that they need to worry about transferring them by living trust. Also, most state Departments of Motor Vehicles have special forms that conveniently allow cars to be registered in joint tenancy, a handy way to avoid probate for an auto. And California, Minnesota, Missouri, North Dakota and Oregon allow "transfer-on-death" vehicle registration, where you name, on your vehicle registration, who receives the vehicle upon your death. No probate is necessary.

But if you own a very valuable vehicle, or several, it can be worth your while to seek out an insurance company that will allow you to own and transfer them by living trust. Some insurance companies will insure a vehicle owned by a trust.

- **IRAs, Profit-Sharing Plans, Annuities and other retirement plans.** Legally, a trust cannot be an owner of an IRA (Individual Retirement Account) Profit-Sharing Plans, 401(k) plan or most annuities. But the funds in any retirement plan can still avoid probate; you can directly name a beneficiary (on a form provided by the custodian of the account) to receive any funds left in the account when you die. The funds go directly to the beneficiary without going through probate.

> **NAMING YOUR LIVING TRUST AS A BENEFICIARY OF YOUR IRA**
>
> This is a bad idea. If you designate your living trust as the primary beneficiary of your individual retirement account, certain limitations will apply at the time distributions from that account are made. First, mandatory distributions must begin at age 70½, if a trust is the beneficiary. Distributions will be based on your life expectancy alone and not the joint life expectancy of you and another beneficiary (as is possible if you'd named a living person as beneficiary of your IRA). Second, at your death, any account balance must be fully distributed within five years instead of longer periods that might be available if the trust weren't the beneficiary. To avoid these limitations, you should make the primary beneficiary of your IRA your spouse or another individual of your choice.

- **Life insurance.** When you buy an insurance policy, you name beneficiaries to receive the proceeds of the policy outside of probate. However, if you have named a minor or young adult as the beneficiary of an insurance policy, you may want to change the beneficiary to your living trust or, more precisely, the trustee, as trustee of the child's subtrust of the living trust. Then, in the trust document, you name the child as beneficiary of any insurance proceeds paid to the trust. The trustee manages the policy proceeds, as part of the child's subtrust, if the beneficiary is still young when you die. If you don't arrange for this type of management of the insurance money, and the beneficiary is still a minor (under 18) when you die, a court will have to appoint a financial guardian after your death. (See Chapter 9, "Property Left to Minor Children or Young Adults.")

  Technically, passing the proceeds of a life insurance policy through your living trust is a bit more complicated than leaving other property this way. You must take two steps:

  1. Name the trustee, as trustee of the child's subtrust of the living trust, as the beneficiary of your life insurance policy. Your insurance agent will have a form that lets you change the beneficiary of the policy. Tell the agent what you want to do and make sure you've got forms that are acceptable to the insurance company.

  2. When you list property items in the living trust document (that is, property owned by the trust), list the proceeds of the policy, not the policy itself. The trust should not be the actual owner of the policy. You, personally, remain the owner. (Chapter 10, "Preparing Your Living Trust Document," Section D, contains an example of how to list beneficiaries for insurance proceeds left to your trust.)

- **Income or principal from a trust.** If you are the beneficiary of an established trust and have the right to leave any of your interest in this trust to someone else, you cannot do that in your own living trust. The reason is that you cannot transfer title of the trust that benefits you into your own living trust, because you are not the owner of the trust. And as I've emphasized, your trust cannot give away what it doesn't technically own. You can leave your rights to this type of trust income property by your will. (See Chapter 16, "Wills.")

  Other probate-avoidance methods, such as joint tenancy or pay-on-death bank accounts, are explained in Chapter 15, "A Living Trust as Part of Your Estate Plan."

C. Property to Put in Your Living Trust

Whatever type of trust you create with this book, one primary goal is avoiding probate fees. As a general rule, the more an item is worth, the more it will cost to probate it. That means you should transfer at least your most valuable property items to your living trust (or use some other probate-avoidance device to leave them at your death). Think about including:

- houses and other real estate
- small business interests, including stock in closely-held corporations
- money market accounts
- other financial accounts
- stocks, bonds and other security accounts held by brokers
- royalties, patents and copyrights
- valuable jewelry, antiques, furs and furniture
- precious metals
- valuable works of art
- valuable collections of stamps, coins or other objects.

Property you owe money on. Some items of property are commonly not owned free and clear. The most common example is a house with a mortgage. When you use your living trust to leave that house to a beneficiary, he or she will receive it subject to the mortgage. Similarly, if you give someone a car subject to a loan and lien, those debts go with the car.

If you have sufficient assets, it's legally possible to use your trust to provide that these debts are paid off. That way, the beneficiary receives a house, car or other previously debt-encumbered property free and clear. See a lawyer to arrange this.

1. Real Estate

The most valuable thing most people own is their real estate: their house, condominium or land. Other types of real estate include property such as a boat marina dock space or a time-share interest in a piece of property, like a vacation house used twice a year. You can save your family substantial probate costs by transferring your real estate through a living trust.

If you own real estate in joint tenancy or tenancy by the entirety, however, you've already arranged to avoid

probate for that property, so there's much less reason to transfer it to a living trust. (See Chapter 15, "A Living Trust as Part of Your Estate Plan," Section B.) One advantage of owning real estate in a living trust over joint tenancy is that, in a living trust, you can provide for who will receive the real estate in the event of simultaneous death—both owners die at the same time. You cannot provide for this with real estate owned in joint tenancy. Another reason for transferring joint tenancy real estate into a living trust is if you use an AB living trust and want the real estate to be part of the Trust A property.

IF YOU'RE NOT SURE HOW YOU HOLD TITLE

If you own real estate with someone else but aren't sure how the title is held, look at the deed. It should say how title is held:

- in joint tenancy (sometimes abbreviated JT or JTWROS, for "joint tenancy with right of survivorship")
- tenancy in common
- community property (in community property states). In a community property state, if the deed says the property is owned "as husband and wife," that means community property
- tenancy by the entirety.

If you own real estate with someone else, you can transfer just your interest in it to your living trust.

Co-op apartments. If you own shares in a co-op corporation that owns your apartment, you'll have to transfer your shares to your living trust. You may run into difficulties with the corporation; some are reluctant to let a trust, even a revocable living trust completely controlled by the grantor, own shares. Check the co-op corporation's laws and rules, then do some good lobbying, if necessary.

Mobile homes. The rules on when an attached mobile home becomes "real estate" vary in different states. If this matters to you, see a lawyer or look up your state's law in the law library. (Legal research is discussed in Chapter 17, "If You Need Expert Help," Section D.)

Leases on real estate. If you're the owner of a lease on real estate (you've leased a store for five years, say, and the lease has two years to run), that lease is generally considered an interest in real estate. You can transfer it to your living trust if you wish.

2. Small Business Interests

The delay, expense and court intrusion of probate can be especially detrimental to an ongoing small business. Using your living trust to transfer business interests to beneficiaries quickly and after your death is almost essential if you want the beneficiaries to be able to keep the business running, or even to be able to sell it for a fair price.

Controlling management of a business. If you want to impose controls on the long-term management of your business, a revocable living trust is not the right device. See an estate planning lawyer to draft a different kind of trust, with provisions tailored to your situation.

Different kinds of business organizations present different issues when you want to transfer your interest to your living trust.

Sole proprietorships. If you operate your business as a sole proprietorship, with all business assets held in your own name, you can simply transfer your business property to your living trust like you would any other property. You should also list the business's name itself on a trust schedule; that transfers the customer goodwill associated with the name.

Partnership interests. If you operate your business as a partnership with other people, you can probably transfer your partnership share to your living trust. If there is a partnership certificate, it must be changed to show the trust as owner of your share.

Some partnership agreements require the people who inherit a deceased partner's share of the business to sell that share to the other partners if they want it. But that happens after death, so it shouldn't affect your ability to transfer the property through a living trust.

It's not common, but a partnership agreement may limit or forbid transfers to a living trust. If yours does, you and your partners may want to see a lawyer before you make any changes. If the other partners won't agree to revise your partnership agreement to allow this transfer, you're stuck.

Solely-owned corporations. If you own all the stock of a corporation, you should have no difficulty transferring it to your living trust. All you need do is prepare the appropriate corporate papers—for example: Notice of Meeting of Shareholders, and Resolution of Shareholders (there's only one, remember)—authorizing the transfer of the shares of stock to the living trust. The precise corporate paperwork needed depends on what's required by your Articles of Incorporation and the bylaws of your corporation.

Closely-held corporations. A closely-held corporation is a corporation that doesn't sell shares to the public. All its shares are owned by a few people who are usually actively involved in running the business. Normally, you can use a living trust to transfer shares in a closely-held corporation by listing the stock in the trust document and then having the stock certificates reissued in the trust's name.

You'll want to check the corporation's bylaws and Articles of Incorporation to be sure that if you transfer the shares to a living trust, you will still have voting rights in your capacity as trustee of the living trust; usually, this is not a problem. If it is, you and the other shareholders should be able to amend the corporation's bylaws to allow it.

There may, however, be legal restrictions on your freedom to transfer your shares to a living trust. Check the corporation's bylaws and articles of incorporation, as well as any separate shareholders' agreements.

One fairly common rule is that surviving shareholders (or the corporation itself) have the right to buy the shares of a deceased shareholder. In that case, you can still use a living trust to transfer the shares, but the people who inherit them may have to sell them to the other shareholders.

Subchapter S or professional corporations. Special IRS rules apply if you want to transfer shares in a Subchapter S corporation to a living trust. The trust must contain special provisions that make it a "Qualified Subchapter S Trust" under the IRS regulations. You must see a lawyer to draft the appropriate provisions for your trust. Also see a lawyer if your business is a professional corporation, such as one for lawyers, doctors or architects.

3. Money Market and Bank Accounts

Money market funds can be readily transferred into your trust. Often, these money market funds contain substantial amounts of cash, so it's wise to place them in your living trust.

It's not difficult to hold bank accounts (aside from your personal checking account) in your living trust. But you may well decide that you don't need to, because there's another easy way to avoid probate of the funds. In what's called a "pay-on-death" account (or Totten Trust, or sometimes a revocable trust account), you can designate a beneficiary for the funds in a bank account. The beneficiary receives whatever is in your account at your death, without probate.

A living trust, however, offers one advantage that most pay-on-death arrangements do not: If you transfer an account to a living trust, you can always name an alternate beneficiary to receive the account if your first choice as beneficiary isn't alive at your death. The lack of an alternate may not be a problem if you use a pay-on-death account and name more than one beneficiary to inherit the funds, however; if one of the beneficiaries isn't alive, the other(s) will inherit the money.

Pay-on-death accounts are discussed in Chapter 15, "A Living Trust as Part of Your Estate Plan," Section B.

4. Stocks and Securities

If you buy and sell stocks regularly, you may not want to go to the trouble of acquiring them in the living trust's name and selling them using your authority as trustee of the trust.

Fortunately, there's an easier way to do it: hold your stocks in a brokerage account that is owned in the living trust's name. All securities in the account are then owned by your living trust, which means that you can use your living trust to leave all the contents of the account to a specific beneficiary. If you want to leave stock to different beneficiaries, you can either establish more than one brokerage account or leave one account to more than one beneficiary to own together.

AN ALTERNATIVE: PAY-ON-DEATH REGISTRATION

A number of states allow ownership of securities to be registered in a "transfer-on-death" form. In those states, you can designate someone to receive the securities, including mutual funds and brokerage accounts, after your death. No probate will be necessary. The Uniform Transfers-on-Death Security Registration Act has been adopted in the following states:

Arizona	Missouri	Oregon
Arkansas	Montana	South Dakota
Colorado	Nebraska	Tennessee
Florida	New Jersey	Utah
Illinois	New Mexico	Washington
Kansas	North Dakota	West Virginia
Maryland	Ohio	Wisconsin
Minnesota	Oklahoma	Wyoming

---

5. Cash

It's common for people to want to leave cash to beneficiaries—for example, to leave $5,000 to a relative, friend or charity. However, there's no way to transfer cash to a living trust—you can't put a stack of dollar bills into a document. Nor does listing $5,000 on a trust schedule work by itself. Where is this $5,000?, the successor trustee would ask.

You can, however, easily transfer ownership of a cash account—a savings account, money market account or certificate of deposit, for example—to your living trust. (Don't transfer a pay-on-death account, since the beneficiary for it is already named.) You can then name a beneficiary to receive the contents of the account or any specified sum from it. So if you want to leave $5,000 to cousin Fred, you can put this amount in a bank or money market account, transfer it to your living trust and name Fred, in the trust document, as the beneficiary. Or you could put an account with a larger amount in your trust, leave $5,000 from it to Fred and the balance to another beneficiary.

Example

Michael would like to leave some modest cash gifts to his two grown nephews, Warren and Brian, whom he's always been fond of. He puts $25,000 into a money market account and then transfers the account into his living trust. In his trust document, he names Warren and Brian as beneficiaries of $5,000 each from that, with whatever is left to go to Michael's wife. After Michael's death, the two nephews will each receive $5,000 from the trust.

If you don't want to set up an account to leave a modest amount of cash to a beneficiary, think about buying a savings bond and leaving it to the beneficiary.

6. Royalties, Copyrights and Patents

You can transfer your right to future royalties, or copyrights and patents you own, to your living trust. Simply list the royalty, copyright or patent in your trust property schedule and then transfer your interest in a copyright, patent or royalty, to the trust, using the proper legal form. (Instructions are in Chapter 11, "Transferring Property to Your Trust," Sections K, L and M.)

7. Other Valuable Property

Many other types of valuable property can be placed in your trust, including valuable jewelry, antiques, furs, furniture, precious metals, works of art and collectibles—from Depression china to antique soldiers to old dolls to stamps to whatever objects people will pay money for.

The common denominator of all these types of property is that none of them has any formal ownership papers, like a deed for real estate. Some may have papers authenticating them, but these are not documents of title, and don't need to be changed. So you can transfer any of these valuables to your trust simply by listing it on the trust schedule.

D. Marital Property Laws

If you are married, you need to know what property is owned by each spouse separately, and what property is held in shared ownership, to properly complete your trust. Whether you make separate trusts (because most or all of each spouse's property is owned separately) or a shared trust (either the basic shared trust or a living trust with marital life estate), you need to clarify which spouse owns what to know which schedule—basically "ours," "his" and "hers"—to list the property on. Each spouse controls, in the trust document, who will inherit his or her own trust property.

To figure out who owns what, you need to know a little about the law of the state where you live (and of any other state in which you own property) regarding marital property. Marital property laws can be divided into two basic groups: community property states and common law states.

SEPARATE PROPERTY

1. Community Property States

Arizona	Louisiana	Texas
California	Nevada	Washington
Idaho	New Mexico	Wisconsin

In these states, the general rule is that spouses own everything acquired during the marriage 50-50, unless the spouses agree otherwise. It doesn't matter whose name is on the title slip.

There are a few important exceptions to the general rule. Property acquired before marriage is not community property; it is the separate property of that spouse. Likewise, property given to one spouse, by gift or inheritance, is separate property.

COMMUNITY PROPERTY BASICS

Community Property includes:
- money either spouse earns during marriage

- things bought with that money
- separate property that has become so mixed (commingled) with community property that it can't be identified

Separate Property includes:
- property owned by one spouse before marriage
- property given to just one spouse
- property inherited by just one spouse

Married couples don't have to accept these rules. They can sign a written agreement that makes some or all community property the separate property of one spouse, or vice versa.

Typically, most property owned by spouses is community property, especially if they have been married for a number of years. For example, if while married you bought real estate with money you earned during marriage, your spouse legally owns a half interest in it, unless you both signed an agreement keeping it separate.

Sometimes it's not obvious who owns what. For example, are life insurance proceeds shared property or the separate property of the deceased spouse? The answer depends on the source of the funds used to pay for the insurance and the intention of the couple. If the insurance was paid for with shared marital property, the proceeds are co-owned. Similarly, if the couple agreed (in writing) that the proceeds were shared property, no matter who paid for them, that agreement controls. But if the policy was paid for from the separate property of the deceased, with no agreement that it was a shared ownership policy, the proceeds are the separate property of the deceased.

If you move from a common law state to California, Idaho or Washington, some of your property may be reclassified as community property. In these three states, the rule is that property acquired by a couple during marriage, no matter who owned it in a common law state, is treated as community property, owned equally by each spouse, if it would have been community property had the couple acquired it in one of these states. The legal term for such property is "quasi-community property." This means each spouse owns half of this property and can leave only that share at death.

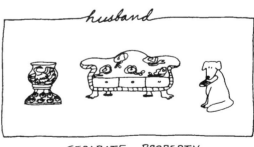

SEPARATE PROPERTY

Example

Cora and Eric Gustafson live in Florida, a common law state. Cora buys some stocks with money she earned while married. She owns the stocks in her own name and is free to leave them by will or trust to whomever she pleases, subject to state law on the inheritance rights of spouses.

Later, Cora and Eric move to California. Because the stocks, had they been bought in California, would have been Cora and Eric's community property, they are now "quasi-community property." At death or divorce, the stocks will be treated as community property, owned 50-50 by each spouse. Cora now owns only half and can leave only half in her trust or will.

If you move from a community property state to a common law state, your ownership rights in the property already acquired stay the same. The new state's law applies only to property acquired in the new state.

Separate property may, however, turn into community property if it is mixed ("commingled") with community property. For example, if you deposit separate property funds into a joint bank account and then make more deposits and withdrawals, making it impossible to tell what part of the account is separate money, it's all considered community property.

Example

Roberto and Celia live in Nevada, a community property state. They have been married for 20 years. Except for some bonds that Celia inherited from her parents, virtually all their valuable property—house, stocks, car—is owned together. The money they brought to the marriage in separate bank accounts has long since been mixed with community property, making it community property too.

In community property states, there are restrictions on one spouse's freedom to transfer community property. Especially in the case of real estate, the consent of both spouses is necessary for either to sell or give away his or her half-interest in the property. Each spouse can, however, leave his or her half-interest in the property through a will or living trust.

If you live in a community property state, and you and your spouse create a living trust together, property you transfer to the trust will stay community property, even though it is technically owned by the living trust. Separately owned property (property of only one spouse) will also remain separate property. That means that community property transferred to a living trust is still eligible for the favorable tax treatment given community property at one spouse's death. (Both halves of community property left to the surviving spouse get a "stepped-up basis" for income tax purposes; see Chapter 15, "A Living Trust as Part of Your Estate Plan.")

It also means that if either spouse revokes the living trust, ownership of the property will go back to the spouses as it was before the property was transferred to the living trust. Community property goes back to both spouses equally, and separate property goes to the spouse who owned it before ownership was transferred to the trust.

2. Common Law Property States

Alabama	Kentucky	North Dakota
Alaska	Maine	Ohio
Arkansas	Maryland	Oklahoma
Colorado	Massachusetts	Oregon
Connecticut	Michigan	Pennsylvania
Delaware	Minnesota	Rhode Island
District of Columbia	Mississippi	South Carolina
Florida	Missouri	South Dakota
Georgia	Montana	Tennessee
Hawaii	Nebraska	Utah
Illinois	New Hampshire	Vermont
Indiana	New Jersey	Virginia
Iowa	New York	West Virginia
Kansas	North Carolina	Wyoming

In a non-community property state, it's usually fairly easy for spouses to keep track of who owns what. The spouse whose name is on the title document (deed, brokerage account paper or title slip, for example) owns it. In these states, if the property doesn't have a title document, it belongs to the spouse who paid for it or received it as a gift. It's possible, though, that if there were a dispute about ownership, a judge could determine, based on the circumstances, that a spouse whose name is not on the title document might own an interest in the property.

It's increasingly common for couples, especially if they are older and have children from a prior marriage, to sign an agreement (before or during the marriage) to own property separately. Or they may not make a formal agreement, but carefully avoid mixing their property together.

If you want to co-own property equally, you can do that simply by taking title to property in both names, for new property, or preparing a new ownership deed for previously-owned property, listing the new owners as both of you. You should also state you own the property "equally, as tenants in common," if you intend to place the property in your living trusts. (For married couples, no state taxes will be assessed because of any transfer of title, because any transfer of property between spouses is free of tax.)

In common law states, see a lawyer if you don't want to leave at least half of your living trust property to your spouse. This matter is discussed further in Chapter 8, "Choosing Your Beneficiaries," Section H.

IF YOU'RE UNSURE OF YOUR MARITAL STATUS

Most people are quite certain of their marital status. If you're not, here's what you need to know.

The divorce decree. You're not divorced until you have a final decree of divorce (or dissolution, as it's called in some states) issued by a state court in the United States.

If you think you're divorced but never saw the final decree, contact the court clerk in the county where you think the divorce was granted. Give the clerk your name, your ex-spouse's name and the date, as close as you know it, of the divorce.

Legal separation. Even if a court has declared you and your spouse legally separated, and you plan to divorce, you are still married until you get the divorce decree.

Foreign divorces. Divorces issued to U.S. citizens by courts in Mexico, the Dominican Republic or another country may not be valid if challenged, especially if all the paperwork was handled by mail. In other words, if you or your spouse got a quickie foreign divorce, you may well be still married under the laws of your state. If you think that someone might make a claim to some of your property after your death based on the invalidity of a foreign divorce, see a lawyer.

Common law marriages. In some states, a couple can become legally married by living together, intending to be married and presenting themselves to the world as a married couple. Even in states that allow such common law marriages, most couples who live together don't have common law marriages. If you really do have a valid common law marriage, you must go to court and get a divorce to end it—there's no such thing as a common law divorce.

Common law marriages can be created in Alabama, Colorado, District of Columbia, Georgia, Idaho, Iowa, Kansas, Montana, New Hampshire (for inheritance purposes only), Ohio, Oklahoma, Pennsylvania, Rhode Island, South Carolina and Texas. If a common law marriage is created in one of these states, and the couple moves to another state, they are still legally married.

Gay or lesbian couples. No state allows marriage between two people of the same sex, even if a religious ceremony is performed.

E. Completing the Property Worksheet

On the worksheet below, you can list your property. This groundwork should make preparing your actual trust document easier. But completing it is not mandatory; use it if you think it will help you.

Even if you plan to leave everything to your spouse or children, you need to describe your property sufficiently on a trust schedule so that it is readily identifiable. In other words, every item (or group of items, in some circumstances) must be specifically described and listed as part of the trust document. (Examples are given in Chapter 10, "Preparing Your Living Trust Document.") Also, you can use the worksheet to estimate your net worth to see if you are near the $600,000 federal estate tax threshold.

Remember, this worksheet is purely for your convenience. It can be as messy or as neat as you care to make it. Pencil is recommended (unless you're the type who does the *New York Times* crossword puzzle in ink).

ORGANIZING IMPORTANT INFORMATION

While you're taking stock of all your valuable property, it might be a good time to go a step further and gather the information your family will need at your death. You can use your computer to get organized by using *Nolo's Personal RecordKeeper* database program. It can keep track of all the important information in your family's life, including securities data, investments, real estate records, medical information, insurance records, credit card information and more. (Ordering information is in the back of this book.)

---

1. Section I, Assets

Column 1, Property Description

Here you write out what you own. How specific you should be depends in part on how you plan to leave your property (who your beneficiaries are), which you'll pin down in Chapter 8, "Choosing Your Beneficiaries." For example, if you're going to leave all your books to your daughter, there's no need to list them individually. But if you own several rare first editions, which you'll leave to separate beneficiaries, list each book.

Column 2, Net Value of Your Ownership

In Column 2, estimate the net value of each item listed. Net value means your equity in your share of the property—the market value of your share, less your share of any debts on that share, such as a mortgage on a house or the loan amount due on a car.

If you're a couple, "your share" means the value of both of your interests. For estate tax purposes, it's the value of what you both own that really counts.

Obviously, listing net values for your property means making estimates. That's fine; there's no need to burden yourself with seeking precise figures. After all, your death taxes, if any, will be based on the net value of your property when you die, not its current worth. For example, if you think the net worth of your house, after you subtract the mortgage, is about $200,000, your car $5,000, and your stamp collection would fetch $2,000 if you put an ad in a philatelist's journal, use those numbers.

If you own property with someone other than a spouse or mate, simply estimate the worth of your share of that property.

Example

Paul owns a house with a market value of $250,000 as a tenant in common with his sister Ava; each owns half. Paul computes the net value of his share by first subtracting the amount of mortgages, liens and past due taxes from the market value to arrive at the total equity in the property. There's a $100,000 mortgage and a $10,000 lien against the property. The total equity, then, is $250,000 minus $110,000, or $140,000. The net worth of Paul's half of the property is $70,000.

With some common sense, you can probably safely make sensible estimates yourself. Only with more complex types of property, such as business interests, might you want expert help.

Example

Stacey is sole owner of the Maltese Falcon Restaurant, a successful business she has run for 20 years. She has only a vague notion of its market value since she has never been interested in selling it. Making a reasonable estimate of the worth of the business is difficult, since the market value of her restaurant includes the intangible of "good will." Stacey talks to an accountant to help her arrive at a sensible estimate of the worth of the restaurant.

Column 3, Who Owns It

Because you need to identify which property is shared and which is separate, indicate that here. Use whatever symbols you want to identify the ownership—for example, O (ours); H (Husband); W (Wife) or S (shared); M (Mary); N (Neil).

Column 4, Transfer to Trust

In Column 4, indicate whether or not you want to transfer this item of property to the trust. For each item you'll put in the trust, put a "T."

2. Section II, Liabilities

Here, list any liabilities (debts) you haven't already taken into account in Section I. For example, list any significant personal debts—the $10,000 loan from a friend or $5,000 unsecured advance on a line of credit. Also list all other liabilities, such as tax liens or court judgments and add up all these liabilities.

Property Worksheet

I. ASSETS

Description of Your Property	Net Value of Your Ownership	Who Owns It	Transfer to Trust?

A. Liquid Assets

1. cash (dividends, etc.)

_____	_____	_____	_____
_____	_____	_____	_____
_____	_____	_____	_____
_____	_____	_____	_____
_____	_____	_____	_____

2. savings accounts

_____	_____	_____	_____
_____	_____	_____	_____
_____	_____	_____	_____
_____	_____	_____	_____
_____	_____	_____	_____

3. checking accounts

_____	_____	_____	_____
_____	_____	_____	_____
_____	_____	_____	_____
_____	_____	_____	_____
_____	_____	_____	_____

4. money market accounts

_____	_____	_____	_____
_____	_____	_____	_____
_____	_____	_____	_____
_____	_____	_____	_____
_____	_____	_____	_____

5. certificates of deposit

_____	_____	_____	_____
_____	_____	_____	_____
_____	_____	_____	_____
_____	_____	_____	_____
_____	_____	_____	_____

Description of Your Property	Net Value of Your Ownership	Who Owns It	Transfer to Trust?

B. Other Personal Property

(all your property except liquid assets, business interests and real estate, houses, buildings, apartments, etc.)

1. listed (private corporation) stocks and bonds

_____ _____ _____ _____
_____ _____ _____ _____
_____ _____ _____ _____
_____ _____ _____ _____

2. unlisted stocks and bonds

_____ _____ _____ _____
_____ _____ _____ _____
_____ _____ _____ _____
_____ _____ _____ _____

3. government bonds

_____ _____ _____ _____
_____ _____ _____ _____
_____ _____ _____ _____
_____ _____ _____ _____

4. automobiles and other vehicles, including
   planes, boats and recreational vehicles

_____ _____ _____ _____
_____ _____ _____ _____
_____ _____ _____ _____
_____ _____ _____ _____

5. precious metals

_____ _____ _____ _____
_____ _____ _____ _____
_____ _____ _____ _____

6. household goods

_____ _____ _____ _____
_____ _____ _____ _____
_____ _____ _____ _____
_____ _____ _____ _____

Description of Your Property	Net Value of Your Ownership	Who Owns It	Transfer to Trust?
7. clothing			
8. jewelry and furs			
9. art works, collectibles and antiques			
10. tools and equipment			
11. valuable livestock/animals			
12. money owed you (personal loans, etc.)			
13. vested interest in profit sharing plan, stock options, etc.			

Description of Your Property	Net Value of Your Ownership	Who Owns It	Transfer to Trust?

C. Miscellaneous Receivables

(mortgages, deeds of trust or promissory notes held by you; any rents due from income property owned by you; and payments due for professional or personal services or property sold by you that are not fully paid by the purchaser)

_____   _____   _____   _____

_____   _____   _____   _____

_____   _____   _____   _____

_____   _____   _____   _____

D. Real Estate

1. address

_____   _____   _____   _____

_____   _____   _____   _____

_____   _____   _____   _____

_____   _____   _____   _____

2. address

_____   _____   _____   _____

_____   _____   _____   _____

_____   _____   _____   _____

_____   _____   _____   _____

3. address

_____   _____   _____   _____

_____   _____   _____   _____

_____   _____   _____   _____

_____   _____   _____   _____

4. address

_____   _____   _____   _____

_____   _____   _____   _____

_____   _____   _____   _____

_____   _____   _____   _____

5. address

_____   _____   _____   _____

_____   _____   _____   _____

_____   _____   _____   _____

_____   _____   _____   _____

E. Total Net Value of Your Assets $_____

II. LIABILITIES

To Whom Debt Is Owed	Amount

A. Personal Property Debts

    1. personal loans (banks, major credit cards, etc.)

    2. other personal debts

B. Taxes (include only taxes past and currently due. Do not include taxes due in the future or estimated estate taxes)

C. Any Other Liabilities (legal judgments, accrued child support, etc.)

D. Total Liabilities (excluding those liabilities already deducted in Section I) $_____

III. NET WORTH (Total Net Value of Your Assets, from Section I.E above, minus Total Liabilities, from Section II.D above) $_____

chapter 7

TRUSTEES

$\mathcal{T}$o be legally valid, your living trust must have a trustee—someone to manage the property owned by the trust. Indeed, as I've said, the trust property is technically held in the trustee's name. When you create a trust from this book, you are the initial trustee. If you create a basic shared living trust or AB trust, you and your spouse are co-trustees.

When the initial trustee, or both trustees, have died, the "successor trustee" takes over. This person is responsible for transferring trust property to the beneficiaries and handling any other matters required by the trust—such as managing a child's subtrust or filing federal or state estate tax returns. Technically, the executor of your will is responsible for filing tax returns, but normally, the executor and successor trustee are the same person. In any case, the executor and successor trustee will have to work together.

For many people, the decision of who to name as successor trustee is clear, but for others, complexities and uncertainties can arise.

A. The Initial Trustee

A key to how a living trust works is that you, or you and your spouse, are the initial trustees. Grasping this point is essential to understanding what a living trust is—a device that allows you to absolutely control your own property while you are alive, and at the same time avoid probate of the property after you die.

Naming someone else as initial trustee. If you want to name someone besides yourself to be your initial trustee because you don't want to, or cannot, continue to manage your own assets, see a lawyer; don't use the trust forms in this book. When you make somebody else your initial trustee, you create a more complicated trust, often necessitating much more detailed controls on the trustee's powers to act. In addition, under IRS rules, if you aren't the trustee of your own living trust, separate trust records must be

maintained, and a fiduciary trust tax return (Form 1041) filed each year.

1. Your Responsibilities as Trustee

You won't have any special duties as trustee of your trust. As a day-to-day, practical matter, it makes no difference that you now manage your property as trustee, rather than in your own name. You do not need to file a separate income tax return for the living trust. As long as you are trustee, any income the trust property generates must be reported on your personal income tax return, as if the trust did not exist. (IRS Reg. § 1.671-4.) Likewise, you don't have to obtain a trust taxpayer ID number or keep separate trust records.

As explained in Chapter 3, you have the same freedom to sell, mortgage or give away trust property as you did before you put that property into the living trust. Normally, the only difference is that you must now sign documents in your capacity as trustee. It's that easy.

$\mathcal{E}xample$

Celeste and Angelo want to sell a piece of land that is owned in the name of their living trust. They prepare a deed transferring ownership of the land from the trustees of the trust to the new owner. They sign the deed as "Celeste Tornetti and Angelo Tornetti, trustees of the Celeste Tornetti and Angelo Tornetti Living Trust dated February 4, 1992."

If you make a shared living trust (either a basic shared trust or an AB trust), it's important to realize that once the property belongs to the trust, either trustee (spouse) has authority over it. Either spouse can sell or give away any of the trust property—including the property that was co-owned or was the separate property of the other spouse before it was transferred to the trust. In practice, however, both spouses will probably have to consent (in writing) to transfer real estate out of the living trust. Especially in community property states, buyers and title insurance companies usually insist on both spouses' signatures on transfer documents.

If you don't want to give your spouse legal authority over your separately owned property, it's best to make a separate living trust for that property.

Naming only one spouse as trustee. If you want only one spouse to be the original trustee of a basic shared living trust or an AB trust, there's an unusual—and unequal—distribution of authority over shared property, and you should see a lawyer.

2. Naming a Co-Trustee

If you think you'll want or need someone else to manage your trust property for you, but don't want the hassles of having a separate trustee, you can consider naming yourself and another person to both be the initial trustees of your trust. Both of you would have authority to act on the trust's behalf. No fiduciary trust tax return is required, since *one* of the trustees is the original grantor.

Example

Beatrice is in her 80s. She doesn't want to abandon control over her property but has difficulty managing things—keeping track of bills and payments, for example. So she creates a living trust, naming herself and her daughter Polly as initial co-trustees. Either trustee can act for the trust. Because Beatrice is one of the initial trustees, she does not have to keep separate records or file a trust tax return. And as a practical matter, Polly can handle most trust transactions on her own.

Get help if you want initial co-trustees. If you want to have a co-trustee to serve with you, it's best to see a lawyer, so the authority of the trustees is clearly defined and specifically geared to your situation. Don't rely on the forms in this book.

B. The Trustee After One Spouse's Death or Incapacity

If you create a basic shared living trust or an AB trust, when one spouse dies or becomes incapacitated and unable to manage his or her affairs, the other becomes sole trustee.

Using the trust forms in this book, a spouse's physical or mental incapacity must be certified in writing by a physician. If that occurs, the other spouse, as sole trustee, takes over management of both spouses' trust property. That's the extent of his or her authority; he or she has no power over property of the incapacitated spouse not owned by the living trust, and no authority to make health care decisions for the incapacitated spouse. For this reason, it's also wise for each spouse to create documents called Durable Powers of Attorney and Living Wills, giving the other spouse authority to manage property not owned in the name of the trust and to make health care decisions for an incapacitated spouse. (See Chapter 15, "A Living Trust as Part of Your Estate Plan," Section E.)

The duties of a surviving spouse as trustee are summarized below. They are discussed in more detail in Chapter 4, "What Type of Trust Do You Need?" and Chapter 5, "The Tax-Saving AB Trust."

C. The Successor Trustee

Your trust document must name a successor trustee. The successor trustee takes over after you have died, or, for a basic shared trust or an AB trust, after both members of the couple have died. The successor trustee also takes over if you, or both you and your spouse, become incapacitated and are unable to manage the trust property.

Incapacity means the inability to manage your affairs. The trust forms in this book require that incapacity be documented in writing by a physician before the successor trustee can take over management of the trust property. For a basic shared trust or AB trust, the successor trustee has no authority to act if one spouse is alive and capable of managing trust property.

Picking your successor trustee is an important decision. Not only must you pick someone you trust who can do the job and is willing to do it, you also probably don't want to ruffle any family feathers when making your choice. You can name successor co-trustees, if this fits your needs.

When you decide on your successor trustee, your job isn't done. You should also name an alternate successor trustee, in case the successor trustee dies before you do or for any other reason can't serve. If you named two or more successor trustees, the alternate won't become trustee unless none of your original choices can serve.

1. The Job of the Successor Trustee

Obviously, when you choose your successor trustee, it helps for you both to understand what he or she will need to do. The primary job of the successor trustee is to turn trust property over to the beneficiaries you named in the trust document. This is normally not difficult if the property and beneficiaries are clearly identified. Still, some effort is required.

Usually, the successor trustee obtains several certified copies of the death certificate of the grantor. Then she presents a copy of the death certificate and a copy of the living trust document, along with proof of her own identity, to financial institutions, brokers and other organizations that have possession of the trust assets. They will then release the property to the beneficiary. If any documents of title (ownership) must be prepared to transfer trust property to the beneficiaries, the successor trustee prepares them. For example, to transfer real estate owned by a living trust to the beneficiaries after the death of the grantor, the successor trustee prepares, signs and records (in the local land records office) a deed from herself, as trustee of the living trust, to the specified beneficiaries. No court or agency approval is required.

What happens if an institution won't cooperate with the successor trustee? Happily, such problems are unlikely. Institutions that deal with financial assets—from title companies to county land records offices to stock brokers—are familiar with living trusts and how they work.

NO GOVERNMENT FILING REQUIRED

A successor trustee who takes over because the original grantor(s) have died doesn't need to file any documents to establish his or her authority with any court or governmental agency. Of course, if a trust is ongoing, such as an AB trust or child's subtrust, the successor trustee must contact the IRS and maintain proper tax records.

It's even easier for the trustee to distribute trust assets that don't have documents of title—household furnishings, jewelry, heirlooms, collectibles—to the appropriate beneficiaries. The trustee just turns the property over to the beneficiaries.

When all beneficiaries have received the trust property left to them in the trust document, the successor trustee's job is over, and the trust ends.

In some situations, additional tasks may be required of the successor trustee before the trust can end:

- **Managing AB trust property if one trust grantor remains alive but is incapacitated.** If you create an AB trust, the successor trustee could wind up managing two separate trusts—the "A" trust of the deceased spouse and the surviving spouse's "B" trust for the spouse who is alive but incapacitated.

- **Preparing and filing death tax returns.** If a death tax return (state, federal or both) must be filed, and death taxes paid, the successor trustee is responsible for these tasks. Also, a final income tax return must be filed for the deceased grantor. The executor you name in your back-up will (see Chapter 16, "Wills") shares legal responsibility for filing these tax returns. Usually, the same person is appointed as the successor trustee and executor.

- **Managing children's subtrusts.** The trust forms in this book allow you to leave trust property to young beneficiaries, who are under 35 when you die, in simple children's trusts, called "subtrusts." (See Chapter 9, "Property Left to Minor Children or Young Adults," Section C.) If you die before any child reaches the age you've specified, your successor trustee will manage subtrust property left for the benefit of that child until she reaches that age. Thus, the successor trustee can have ongoing management responsibilities for a child's subtrust. Annual trust income tax returns are required for each operational child's subtrust, and are the responsibility of the successor trustee.

2. The Successor Trustee's Authority

The trust forms in this book spell out the specific powers granted the successor trustee.

a. The Successor Trustee's Powers

The living trust forms in this book grant the successor trustee all power permitted under state law. The forms also spell out certain specific powers—for example, that the trustee has authority to buy and sell real estate and stocks. Some banks, title companies, stock brokerage companies or other financial institutions demand this level of detail before approving a trust transaction, even though such authority is clearly included in a general grant of power under state law.

The living trust forms also give the successor trustee broad authority to manage any child's subtrust, including the power to spend any amount of each child's subtrust income or principal for that child's "health, support, maintenance or education." As long as you trust your successor trustee, defining the power to manage young beneficiaries' trust property in this broad way is the best approach.

Once in a while, a financial institution gets quirky and demands that a trust specifically authorize some relatively unusual transaction the trustee wants to engage in. For example, a brokerage company may claim that some sophisticated maneuver isn't authorized by the Trustee's Power clause in your trust. The simple solution here is to learn exactly what wording the institution wants in your trust, and then add it to the Trustee's Power clause of your trust. See Chapter 13, "Living With Your Living Trust," Section F.

b. The Successor Trustee's Duty to Act Responsibly

The successor trustee must manage any trust property, including any property in a child's subtrust, in a "prudent manner." Practically, this means the trustee must always act honestly and in the best interests of the beneficiary. For example, the trustee must not make risky investments with subtrust property.

Legally, the trustee cannot personally profit or benefit from a transaction (this is called "self-dealing"). Basically, this means personally profiting or benefiting from a transaction involving trust property, such as buying a house from the trust. But remember, legal restrictions can only be enforced by a lawsuit. As successor trustee, be sure you have someone you trust, to minimize the possibility of litigation.

The successor trustee has authority to get professional assistance if necessary and pay for it with trust money. For example, the successor trustee might want to pay a tax preparer for help with the child's subtrust income tax return, or consult a financial planner for investment advice.

c. Payment of the Successor Trustee

Typically, the successor trustee of a basic probate-avoidance living trust isn't paid. This is because the successor trustee's duty is simply to distribute the deceased grantor's trust property, which is not normally an arduous job. Also, the successor trustee is usually a major beneficiary of the trust. For these reasons, the trust forms in this book provide that no compensation be paid to the successor trustee, with two exceptions:

- for managing an ongoing child's subtrust, and
- for managing an "A" (marital life estate) trust if the surviving spouse is incapacitated.

The trust forms provide that, in these situations, a successor trustee is entitled, without court approval, to "reasonable" compensation for services. The successor trustee decides what is reasonable and takes it from the appropriate trust property, in either the child's subtrust or the "A" trust.

In these situations, the successor trustee might have to actively manage the trust property for some time, so some pay for that work seems fair. The duties and burdens of a successor trustee who manages a child's subtrust can be substantial. The trust can last for decades and entail extensive financial responsibilities. If you have more than one subtrust, the job can become even more demanding.

Similarly, a successor trustee who takes over an A (marital life estate) trust for an incapacitated spouse will be required to do all the paperwork and other chores needed to keep the trust valid in the eyes of the IRS. Again, it seems fair to provide for reasonable compensation for this work.

Restricting the trustee's authority. Consult a lawyer if you are uneasy about:

- the broad grant of powers to the successor trustee
- the successor trustee's authority to manage trust property if you become incapacitated
- the lack of specific restrictions on the successor trustee
- the successor trustee's authority to manage and invest trust funds, or
- allowing open-ended compensation for managing a child's subtrust or "A" trust.

Such a concern may well indicate potential serious problems, which require careful professional attention.

Also, if you decide that you want your successor trustee to be compensated for tasks entailed in transferring trust property to adult beneficiaries, see a lawyer. Compensation might be appropriate if your estate is a large one, and federal estate tax returns will have to be filed.

3. Choosing Your Successor Trustee

Clearly, your successor trustee will play a vital role in carrying out the aims of your living trust.

In most situations, the successor trustee does not need extensive experience in financial management; common sense, dependability and complete honesty are usually enough. A successor trustee who may have long-term responsibility over a young beneficiary's subtrust property probably needs more management and financial skills than a successor trustee whose only job is to distribute trust property. But as I've said, the successor trustee does have authority, under the terms of the trust document, to get any reasonably necessary professional help—from an accountant, lawyer or tax preparer, perhaps—and pay for it out of trust assets.

Your successor trustee should be whomever you feel is most trustworthy to do the job, who's willing to do it and can actually do it. Often a major beneficiary, such as a spouse or adult child, is named as successor trustee.

However, you aren't compelled to name a beneficiary as trustee. If you believe the beneficiary (much as you love him or her) will be troubled by having to handle the practical details and paperwork, it is preferable to name someone else, often another family member. Or as a last resort, consider naming an institution as trustee. (See Section C7, below.)

If you are married and create a basic shared trust, keep in mind that the successor trustee does not take over until both spouses have died (or become incapacitated). That means that after one spouse's death, the surviving spouse may well have time to amend the trust document and name a different successor trustee if he or she wishes.

The situation is different with an AB trust. The A trust becomes irrevocable upon the death of the first spouse. Therefore, the successor trustee for the A trust cannot be changed by the surviving spouse, so your choice here is particularly important. The surviving spouse remains free, of course, to amend or revoke her own B surviving spouse's trust and name a new successor trustee for it.

AVOIDING CONFLICTS BETWEEN YOUR TRUST, YOUR WILL AND OTHER DOCUMENTS

Your living trust, will (see Chapter 16, "Wills") and Durable Power of Attorney for Finances (see Chapter 15, "A Living Trust as Part of Your Estate Plan," Section E) all give someone the authority to make decisions about your property if you can't. If you choose different people to act for you in these different documents, each will become involved in case of your incapacity, and when you die. Clearly, you don't need three heads here. Pick the same person for all three tasks.

 If for some reason you want to name different people to be your successor trustee, executor in your will and to act for you in your Durable Power of Attorney for Finances, see a lawyer.

Obviously, you should confer with the person you've chosen to be your successor trustee to be sure your choice is willing to serve. If you don't, you risk creating problems down the line. No one can be drafted to serve as a successor trustee. The person you've chosen may not want to serve, for a variety of reasons. And even if the person would be willing, if he or she doesn't know of his or her responsibilities, transfer of trust property after your death could be delayed.

4. Naming More Than One Successor Trustee

Legally, you can name as many successor co-trustees as you want, to serve together with power divided among them as you specify. However, as a general rule, because of coordination problems and possible conflicts among multiple trustees, it's generally best to name just one successor trustee. This isn't invariably true, however. For example, a parent may not want to be seen to favor one child over others, and to avoid this could name two or more children as successor co-trustees. This can be especially appropriate if the children are equal beneficiaries of the trust. If the children all get along, it rarely causes a problem.

When appointing successor co-trustees, you must decide how authority is shared among them—whether each can act separately for the trust, or all must agree in writing to act for the trust. Consider giving each the power to act for the trust without the formal written consent of the others. Especially if they live far away from one another or travel often, this could speed up the eventual property transfer process, avoiding delays that might otherwise be caused if one co-trustee were temporarily unavailable.

But what is most important is that you have complete confidence that all your successor trustees will get along. Do be cautious here. Power and property can lead to unexpected results (ask King Lear). If the co-trustees are prone to conflict, you may well create serious problems (and are doing none of them a favor) by having them share power as trustees.

If the co-trustees can't agree, it could hold up the distribution of trust property to your beneficiaries. In extreme situations, the other trustees might even have to go to court to get a recalcitrant trustee removed, so that your instructions can be carried out. The result might be much worse, and generate much more bad feeling, than if you had just picked one person to be trustee in the first place and let the chips fall as they will.

Having more than one successor trustee is especially risky if the successor trustees may be in charge of property you have left to a young beneficiary in a child's subtrust. The trustees may have to manage a young beneficiary's property for many years, and will have many decisions to make about how to spend the money—greatly increasing the potential for conflict. (Children's subtrusts are discussed in Chapter 9, "Property Left to Minor Children or Young Adults," Section C.)

If you name more than one successor trustee, and one of them can't serve, the others will serve. Only if none of them can serve will the alternate successor trustee you name take over.

Handling conflicts between successor co-trustees. If you're naming successor co-trustees and fear potential conflicts, see a lawyer. Such situations are too touchy to resolve without careful individual analysis. For this reason, the trust forms in this book don't contain clauses for resolving conflicts between successor co-trustees. A lawyer may recommend requiring the trustees to submit disputes to arbitration or mediation, or providing that if there is a dispute, one identified trustee gets to make the call.

5. Naming a Sole Beneficiary as Successor Trustee

It's perfectly legal to name a beneficiary of the trust as successor trustee. In fact, it's common.

Example

Santiago names his only child, Jaime, to be his sole trust beneficiary. Santiago also names Jaime as successor trustee. So when Santiago dies, Jaime's only task is to turn the trust property over to himself.

6. Naming an Out-of-State Trustee

Your successor trustee does not have to live in the same state as you do. But if you are choosing between someone local and someone far away, think about how convenient it will be for the person you choose to distribute the living trust property after your death. Someone close by will probably have an easier job, especially with real estate transfers. But for transfers of property such as securities and bank accounts, it usually won't make much difference where the successor trustee lives.

7. Naming a Bank or Trust Company as Successor Trustee

In my experience, it is almost always a bad idea to name a bank as successor trustee. I've heard some horror stories involving the indifference or downright rapaciousness of banks acting as trustees of family living trusts. Institutional trustees also charge hefty fees, which come out of the trust property and leave less for your family and friends. And banks probably won't even be interested in "small" living trusts—ones that contain less than several hundred thousand dollars worth of property.

Your successor trustee is your link with the ongoing lives of your loved ones. You want that link to be a human being you trust, not a corporation dedicated to the enhancement of its bottom line. However, if there is no person you believe will act honestly and competently as your successor trustee, you'll need to select some financial institution to do the job. Probably the best choice here is a private trust company. These companies generally offer more humane and personal attention to a trust than a bank or other large financial institution. Also, they can be more reasonable about fees charged to wind up a living trust.

For a very large living trust, another possibility is to name a person and an institution as successor co-trustees. The bank or trust company can do most of the paperwork, and the person can keep an eye on things and approve all transactions. ❧

chapter 8

CHOOSING YOUR BENEFICIARIES

*a*fter deciding what property you'll put in your trust and who will be your successor trustee, your next step is to decide who will be your trust's beneficiaries. Who gets what? Obviously, this is the heart of preparing your living trust.

This chapter raises some important concerns about choosing beneficiaries and provides a worksheet where you can list each beneficiary and what property you want to leave him or her.

Even if you believe your beneficiary decisions are cut-and-dried and you are tempted to skip this chapter, please read at least Sections A through G. They contain important information you should take into account even if you have already decided who will inherit your property. For instance, you may initially think you don't want to bother naming alternate beneficiaries, to cover the contingency that a primary beneficiary will die before you do. But to make that decision sensibly, you should understand how alternate beneficiaries are used in living trusts, and why often it's wise to name them.

A. Kinds of Trust Beneficiaries

Several different classes of trust beneficiaries are used in trusts in this book.

1.   Individual or Basic Shared Trusts

When you make a simple probate-avoidance living trust, you can name three kinds of beneficiaries:

- *Primary beneficiaries*, who you name to receive specific property. Primary beneficiaries include individuals, institutions, groups who receive property together.

- *Alternate beneficiaries*, who you name to receive property left to a primary beneficiary if that primary beneficiary predeceases you.

- *Residuary beneficiaries (and alternate residuary beneficiaries)*, who receive all trust property not left to primary or alternate beneficiaries (including where both have predeceased you). You can, if you choose, leave all trust property to your residuary beneficiary, and not name any primary or alternate beneficiaries.

KEEP IT SIMPLE

Some living trust books argue:

- You cannot be trusted to choose who your beneficiaries should be without professional help.
- You need to create all sorts of complex gift provisions, to cover all sorts of contingencies, such as providing for what happens if a child's needs change long after you die, or a spouse remarries.

It's not hard to dream up future contingencies, often rather remote, about beneficiaries. While this certainly makes work for lawyers, it isn't what most people want. They are wise enough to understand it's rarely sensible to try to impose controls over property given to beneficiaries after their death.

This book assumes you'll leave property outright, with no strings attached (except for gifts to minors or young adults, discussed in Chapter 9, "Property Left to Minor Children or Young Adults," or property in an AB trust, discussed in Chapter 5).

If you do want to impose conditions on gifts—for instance, distributing money quarterly over a six-year period or varying the amount left a beneficiary, depending on future needs—see a lawyer.

2. AB Living Trusts

If you and your spouse create an AB trust to save on estate taxes, you each will name:

- Up to three *primary beneficiaries* who will inherit specific gifts left by the deceased spouse.
- The *life beneficiary*, who is always the surviving spouse.
- *Final beneficiaries*. Each spouse names these. They are the person or persons: (1) named by the deceased spouse to receive the property in the "A" trust when the surviving spouse dies; (2) named by the surviving spouse to receive the property in the surviving spouse's "B" trust.

B. Naming Your Primary Beneficiaries

For single people, or couples using a basic shared living trust, choosing your primary beneficiaries is often the heart of your trust. Deciding on your primary beneficiaries is, of course, entirely up to you. Your beneficiaries can include a spouse, mate, friends, young adults, children or institutions, often charitable institutions.

Disinheriting a spouse or child. If you are married and live in a common law state and you don't plan to leave at least half of what you own to your spouse, consult a lawyer experienced in estate planning. Whatever your wishes, state law entitles your spouse to some of your estate, including the property in your living trust. (See Section H, below.) In most circumstances, you don't have to leave anything to your children. But if you want to disinherit a child, you should state that expressly in your will. (See Section H, below.)

PROPERTY RECEIVED BY BENEFICIARIES IS NOT SUBJECT TO INCOME TAX

Beneficiaries who inherit property are not liable for any federal income tax on that property. Of course, large estates may have had to pay estate taxes, but once they've been paid, the recipient of a gift is not subject to income tax on the worth of it. If that gift generates income, the beneficiary is responsible for paying income tax on any future income derived from the property.

a. Individual Trust

Naming beneficiaries here is simple. Just list on the worksheet, and later on Form 1, whomever you want to receive your trust property. That's it!

b.   Basic Shared Living Trust

Each spouse names beneficiaries separately, because each spouse's share of trust property is distributed when that spouse dies. When the first spouse dies, his or her trust property is distributed to the beneficiaries he or she named in the trust document. If property is left to the other spouse, it stays in the ongoing revocable trust of that spouse. When the second spouse dies, all the property in his or her trust is distributed to his or her beneficiaries.

Example 1

Roger and Marilyn Foster create a basic shared living trust. Each puts shared, equally-owned property and separately owned property in the trust. When Roger dies, Marilyn takes over as sole trustee. The property Roger left to Marilyn stays in the trust. Marilyn distributes the trust property Roger left to other beneficiaries named in the trust document to those persons. When Marilyn dies, her trust property will be distributed by her successor trustee to her beneficiaries.

Example 2

Marcia and Perry transfer all the property they own together into their basic shared living trust. Marcia names Perry as the beneficiary of all her interest in the trust property. Perry names Marcia to inherit all of his half except his half-interest in their vacation cabin, which he leaves to his son from a previous marriage, Eric. If Perry dies first, Perry's half-interest in the cabin will go to Eric, who will co-own it with Marcia.

c.   AB Trust

If you use an AB trust, you have much less concern with primary beneficiaries. The bulk of your property is left in the "A" trust, with the surviving spouse as life beneficiary. While with this book's AB trust form each spouse can name up to three primary beneficiaries to receive gifts outside of the trust property, these individual gifts are relatively minor. (See Chapter 5, "The Tax-Saving AB Trust.") Each spouse can also name alternate beneficiaries for any primary beneficiaries.

As discussed in Chapter 5, the property in the "A" trust is left for the surviving spouse to use during his or her lifetime. Each spouse names final beneficiaries—the people who will eventually inherit the life estate trust property when the second spouse dies. It's best for each spouse to name the same final beneficiaries. This is commonly done when the couple are in their first marriage and both want their property eventually to go to their children. When each member of a couple wants to name different final beneficiaries, that's usually because each has children from prior marriages.

Each spouse can name different final beneficiaries using Nolo's AB trust, but as I've urged, be cautious. As a general rule, there's likely to be less tension and conflict if a surviving spouse and final beneficiaries have a parent-child relationship than if they do not. But if you feel secure that all people involved trust each other and will cooperate and get along, you can name different final beneficiaries.

You can also name alternate final beneficiaries, in case a final beneficiary predeceases you.

Both spouses create an "A" trust, on paper, since you can't know which spouse will die first. However, the surviving spouse's "A" trust never goes into effect (by definition, since there's no spouse for the surviving spouse to leave property to). Still, both spouses need to name final beneficiaries for their trust property to insure their property ends up going to those whom they want to get it. (See Chapter 10, "Preparing Your Living Trust Document," Section D.)

SOME THOUGHTS ABOUT GIFTS

Before plunging into technical concerns about how to name beneficiaries or shared gifts, let's pull back for a moment and consider what gifts are. In our predominantly commercial culture, gifts are special, whether they are made during life or at death. Gifts are free, voluntary transfers of property, made without any requirement or expectation of receiving anything in return. The essence of gift-giving is generosity, an open spirit. To say one makes gifts "with strings attached" is not a compliment.

Much of the real pleasure of estate planning comes from contemplating the positive effects your gifts will have on those you love. Sometimes, these pleasures are focused—you know how much Judith has always liked your mahogany table, and now she'll get to enjoy it. Others are more general—your son will be able to buy a house with the money you leave him, which will relieve some of the financial pressure that has been weighing on him.

I mention the spirit of giving here because it's easy to get entrapped by the mechanics of preparing a living trust and lose sight of your real purpose. So, if technicalities and legalities start to get to you, take a break and remember who you're giving your property to, and why. And if you wish to explore in profound depth what gift-giving is, or can mean, read Lewis Hyde's *The Gift* (Vintage/Random House), a brilliant exploration of how gifts work in many cultures.

C. Simultaneous Death of Spouses

I address this problem early on in this chapter because it's a real concern to many couples. The statistical probability of simultaneous death is very low, but still it's one of the first concerns many couples have about a shared living trust or living trust with marital life estate. "What happens if we're both killed in a plane crash?"

If you leave all your trust property directly to your spouse or in an AB trust, and your trust document doesn't have a clause to cover simultaneous death, and you and your spouse die in circumstances that make it difficult to tell who died first, your property could pass to your spouse or mate, and then immediately to your spouse's inheritors. That might not be the result either of you want.

The forms in this book (for a basic shared living trust or AB trust, and will for a member of a couple) all contain a simultaneous death clause to prevent this. These clauses are worded slightly differently, because the trust is one joint form used by both spouses and the will is a separate form for each spouse. But each clause provides that when it's difficult to tell who died first, the property of each spouse is disposed of as if he or she had survived the other.

Example

In their shared living trust, Edith and Archie leave much of their property to each other. However, Archie wants his property to go to his daughter from his first marriage if Edith dies before he does. Edith wants her property to go to her sister if Archie dies before she does. Edith and Archie are killed in a car crash. Under the simultaneous death clause, Archie's property would go to his daughter, and Edith's to her sister.

You may ask, "How, logically, can simultaneous death clauses work? How can I be presumed to have outlived my spouse when she's also presumed to have outlived me?" Yes, it is a paradox, but it does work. Under the law, each person's trust property is handled independently of the other. This allows both spouses to achieve the results each wants in the event of simultaneous death. (As Oliver Wendell Holmes put it, "The life of the law has not been logic, it has been experience.")

D. Co-Beneficiaries

You can name more than one beneficiary (primary, alternate, residuary or final) to inherit any item of trust property. People frequently want to make shared gifts to their children, for example.

When making a gift to be shared by two or more beneficiaries, always use the beneficiaries' actual names; don't use collective terms such as "my children." It's not always clear who is included in such descriptions. And there can be serious confusion if one of the people originally included as a beneficiary dies before you do; the law may give the beneficiary's children the right to inherit their parent's share, which may not be the result you intend.

Obviously, if you name co-beneficiaries for a piece of property that can't be physically divided—a house, for example—give some thought to whether or not the beneficiaries are likely to get along. If they are incompatible, disagreements could arise over taking care of property or deciding whether or not to sell it.

You need to resolve these important questions before naming co-beneficiaries:

1. What percentage of ownership will each beneficiary receive?

2. What happens down the line if the co-beneficiaries can't agree on how to use the property?

3. What happens if one co-beneficiary dies before you do?

The rest of this section discusses these concerns.

1. Percentage of Ownership

The key here is to say in your living trust document how ownership is to be shared between the beneficiaries. If you don't specify shares of ownership, it's generally presumed that you intended equal shares, but this rule isn't ironclad, and there's no good reason to be silent on this matter. If you want a gift shared equally, say so.

Here is what the language in your trust document might look like:

"The Grantor's three children, Anne Pasquez, Rob Pasquez and Tony Pasquez, shall be given the house at 1123 Elm St., Centerville, in equal shares."

or

"The Grantor's daughters, Maxine Jones and Simone Jones, shall be given all stock accounts, in equal shares."

The beneficiaries can share ownership any way you want. For example:

"The Grantor's spouse and children shall be given all the Grantor's interest in the Grantor's house and real estate known as 111 57th St., Muncy, Iowa, in the following shares:
        50% to the Grantor's spouse, Mary
        25% to the Grantor's son, Jon
        25% to the Grantor's daughter, Mildred."

2. Conflict

Conflict between beneficiaries is the basic risk with shared ownership. Suppose the people to whom you've left property disagree about how to use it. In most states, any co-owner can go to court and force a partition and sale, with the net proceeds divided by percentage of ownership. Let's say, for example, you leave your house to your three children. Suppose two want to sell it, and one doesn't. The house would be sold even if one child wanted to live in it.

If you are apprehensive, discuss it with the proposed beneficiaries. If there's genuine agreement among them, potential problems are less likely to become real ones. If you conclude there's no risk of conflict, you can simply make the shared gift without any conditions or directions, leaving it up to the beneficiaries to resolve any problems.

It's possible to put provisions governing the issue of what the shared owners can do in your trust document, but I don't recommend it. For instance, you could state, "The house cannot be sold unless all three of my children agree on it." But often other problems follow. If two want to sell the house, but one doesn't, who manages the house? Does it have to be rented at market value? Can the child who wants to keep the house live in it? If so, must that child pay the others rent? And what happens if one child dies? The difficulties of dealing with these types of complications are why it's usually more sensible not to specify details of long-term control of property you leave beneficiaries. Let them work it out. If you don't think the beneficiaries can work out any such problems, a shared gift probably isn't appropriate.

Imposing controls on co-beneficiaries. If you fear conflict between co-beneficiaries and want to impose controls on the use of the property they inherit, see a lawyer.

3. What Happens If One Co-Beneficiary Dies Before You Do

You can name alternate beneficiaries for each co-beneficiary. See Section F, below.

E. Some Common Concerns About Beneficiaries

Here are some common concerns and choices you may face when choosing your beneficiaries.

1. One Primary Beneficiary

Unless you make an AB trust, you can name one person (or one institution) as your only primary beneficiary. For instance, many people want their spouse or mate to receive all their trust property. You can name one person as your primary beneficiary either by listing that person as a sole primary beneficiary or by leaving everything in your residuary clause to your residuary beneficiary.

With an AB trust, to repeat again, most or all of each spouse's property must be left to the "A" trust itself.

2. Married Beneficiaries

When you leave property to someone who's married, the gift is that person's individual or separate property if you make the gift only in his or her name. For example, suppose your trust document says: "Mary Kestor shall be given the antique clock," or "Mary Kestor shall be given the grantor's interest in the house at 279 18th St., San Francisco." Mary would be entitled to keep the entire gift if she divorces (assuming the gift had been kept separate, not commingled (mixed) with shared marital property so that the gift could no longer be separately identified).

If you want to emphasize your wishes, you could say: "Mary Kestor shall be given the grantor's antique clock as her separate property." But if Mary later commingles the gift with shared property, it may lose its separate property status. Proof once again that you have only limited control over what happens to your property after you die.

If you want to make a gift to a member of a couple and have it be his or her separate property, note that on the beneficiary worksheet, to remind you that when you prepare your living trust in Chapter 10, you should expressly state that.

By contrast, if you wish to make a gift to a married couple, simply make it in both their names. For example: "Edna and Fred Whitman shall be given the grantor's silver bowl." Again, you can provide clarity by expressly stating your intent: "Edna and Fred Whitman shall be given the grantor's silver bowl as co-owners."

3. Children from Prior Marriages

If you or your spouse have children from a prior marriage and you're using a basic shared living trust, you may well each want to leave your own children trust property. A common way to do this is to leave the children specific items—real estate, life insurance policy proceeds, bank accounts or whatever—and leave everything else to your spouse. One way to do this is by making the specific gifts to your children and then naming your spouse as residuary beneficiary. (See Section G, below.)

A more complicated way of ensuring that both your spouse and children from an earlier marriage are taken care of is to create a certain type of AB trust. As previously discussed, the form in this book is advisable only if all children and spouses get along and really trust each other. (See Chapters 5, "The Tax-Saving AB Trust," and 15, "A Living Trust as Part of Your Estate Plan.")

Conflict between a surviving spouse and children. If there is a risk of conflict between your surviving spouse and your children after your death, see a lawyer.

4. Minors or Young Adults

If a beneficiary you name is a minor (under 18) or a young adult who can't yet manage property without adult help, you can arrange for an adult to manage the trust property for the beneficiary. The management will take effect only if the beneficiary is still too young to sensibly manage property when she inherits it. (See Chapter 9, "Property Left to Minor Children or Young Adults.")

5. Your Successor Trustee

It's very common and perfectly legal to leave trust property to the person you named to be successor trustee—the person who will distribute trust property after you (or if you are making a trust with your spouse, you and your spouse) die.

Example

Nora and Sean name their son Liam as successor trustee of their basic shared living trust. Each spouse names the other as sole beneficiary of his or her trust property, and both name Liam as alternate beneficiary. When Nora dies, her trust property goes to Sean and stays in the trust. Unless Sean amends the trust document to name someone else as successor trustee, after Sean's death, Liam, acting as trustee, will transfer ownership of the trust property from the trust to himself.

6. Pets

As a part of their estate planning, many pet owners arrange informally for a friend or relative to care for a pet. But you can make more formal arrangements. Here are a few things to keep in mind:

- You can use your living trust (or will) to leave your pets, and perhaps some money for expenses, to someone you trust to look out for them. Don't make the gift of an animal a surprise—make sure the people you've chosen are really willing and able to care for your pets.

- You can't leave money or property to a pet, either through a will or a trust. The law says animals are property, and one piece of property simply can't own another piece. In most states, if you do name a pet as a beneficiary in your will or living trust, whatever property you tried to leave it will probably go, instead, to the residuary beneficiary (the person who gets everything not left to the beneficiaries named in the will or trust). If there's no residuary beneficiary, the property will be distributed according to state law.

- Consider making arrangements for emergency care for your animals in case you suddenly can't care for them.

These issues are discussed in detail in *Dog Law*, by Mary Randolph (Nolo Press).

7. People Who Cannot Legally Inherit

Some felons, and anyone who unlawfully caused the death of the grantor of the living trust, cannot legally inherit property.

F. Naming Alternate Beneficiaries

You can name an alternate beneficiary, or beneficiaries, for each gift made to a primary beneficiary. The alternate beneficiary receives the gift if the primary beneficiary predeceases you (and you haven't amended your trust to name a new primary beneficiary for that gift).

Naming alternate beneficiaries can be sensible, for a number of reasons. Perhaps you've left property to older people, or ones in poor health. Or you're just a cautious person. Or you don't want the bother of redoing your trust document if the unlikely occurs and a beneficiary does die before you. Or you're concerned that you might not have time, before your own death, to revise your estate plan after a beneficiary dies.

On the other hand, some people decide they don't want the morbid bother of worrying about their beneficiaries dying before they do. They leave their property—as many people do—to those considerably younger than they are. If the unlikely occurs and a beneficiary dies before the grantors, normally they'll be able to modify the trust to name a new beneficiary.

Here are some examples of how alternate beneficiaries are named in a trust document:

"Mike McGowan shall be given the Grantor's outboard motor and boat. If he doesn't survive the Grantor, they shall be given to his son, Pat McGowan."

or

"The Grantor's children, Bert Wemby and Cherrie Wemby, shall be given the Grantor's interest in the house at 221 Maple Avenue, Winton, New York. If one beneficiary doesn't survive the Grantor, the house shall be given to the other. If neither survives the Grantor, the house shall be given to Kamal Abram."

You don't have to name an alternate for a charity or other institution you name as a beneficiary. If the institution is well established, it seems safe to assume that it will still exist at your death.

1. Basic Shared Trust

With a basic shared living trust, each spouse makes his or her own separate gifts, and each spouse has the right to name his or her own alternate beneficiaries. They do not need to be the same as the other spouse's.

Example

Larry and Louisa create a basic shared trust. Each leaves a one-half interest in their house to the other. Larry names his two children from a previous marriage as alternate beneficiaries for his half-interest in the house. Louisa names her sister as her alternate beneficiary for her gift.

2. AB Trust

Alternate beneficiaries play a different role with an AB trust. If you do make gifts to primary beneficiaries, outside the ongoing "A" trust, you can name alternates for those beneficiaries.

As you know, the surviving spouse is always the life beneficiary of the property that remains in the "A" trust when the first spouse dies. You do not name an alternate beneficiary for the surviving spouse.

When both spouses die, the AB trust property goes to the final beneficiaries. Each spouse can name alternate final beneficiaries for the final beneficiaries of his or her portion of the AB trust. Often, with couples in a first marriage, both spouses name the same alternate final beneficiaries, commonly grandchildren.

Example

Vittorio and Sophia create an AB trust. Each names their two children, Luigi and Anna, as final beneficiaries. Vittorio and Sophia also each name the same alternate final beneficiaries: for Vittorio, his child Alfonso; for Sophia, her children Gina, Carmela and Marcello, in equal shares.

As you know, the surviving spouse's "B" trust remains revocable during his or her life. The surviving spouse named final beneficiaries, and alternate beneficiaries, for this trust in the original trust document. Of course, as long as he or she is competent, the surviving spouse can amend this trust to name new (final) beneficiaries, and alternates, disposing of the trust property anyway she chooses.

3. Naming Alternate Co-Beneficiaries

You can name more than one person or institution as alternate beneficiaries. If you do, you must define how these co-alternate beneficiaries will share the property.

Example 1

Rosa names her husband Ramon as beneficiary of her interest in their house, which they have transferred to their basic shared living trust. As alternate beneficiaries, she names their three children, Miguel, Constanza and Guillermo, to share equally.

Ramon dies just before she does, leaving his half of the house to Rosa. Under the terms of the trust document, it stays in the living trust. At Rosa's death, the house goes to the three children, because Ramon is not living. All three own equal shares in all of it. If they sell the property, each will be entitled to a third of the proceeds.

Example 2

Benjamin names Bela, his wife, as his primary beneficiary of his interest in their house. He names their children, Susan and Zelda, as alternate beneficiaries. However, Benjamin and Bela have paid many thousands of dollars to help Zelda through medical school. Susan has been self-supporting since she left college. So Benjamin and Bela decide to leave Susan 75% of the house and Zelda 25%, and state this in the trust document when naming them as alternate beneficiaries.

4. Naming Alternate Beneficiaries for Co-Beneficiaries

Things can become complicated if you decide to move on to the next level of contingencies—naming alternate beneficiaries for a shared gift. Say you want to leave your house to your three children. What are your options if you want to name alternate beneficiaries?

- You can specify that a deceased child's share is to be shared by the remaining beneficiaries.

- You can provide that a deceased child's share is to be shared equally by that beneficiary's own children, and, if there are none, then between the remaining beneficiaries.

- You can name an "outside" alternate beneficiary (a friend or other relative) to receive the interest of any child who dies before you do.

- You can name three separate alternate beneficiaries, one for each child—for example, each of their spouses.

Often the wisest solution is to provide that the other beneficiaries of a shared gift share the interest of a deceased beneficiary. Here's how the clause would look in your trust document:

"Mollie Rainey, Allen Rainey and Barbara Rainey Smithson shall be given the Grantor's house at 1701 Clay St., Peoria, IL. If any of them fails to survive the Grantor, his or her interest in the Grantor's house shall be shared equally by the survivors."

Before plunging into complexities about alternate beneficiary provisions for a shared gift, consider whether or not you really want to worry about this contingency. Some people don't like to consider the possibility of one of their children dying before them (and you can always revise your trust if that remote possibility occurs). And once you get started worrying about these kinds of possibilities, where do you stop? You could also worry about what happens if all your alternate beneficiaries, as well as the beneficiaries themselves, die before you. There's no total security, no matter how many alternate beneficiaries you name.

5. Imposing a Survivorship Period

Some people want to impose what is called a "survivorship period" on gifts made to primary and/or alternate beneficiaries. This means that the beneficiary must outlive the grantor by a set period of time, defined in the living trust, to receive the gift. If the beneficiary doesn't live this long, the gift goes to the alternate beneficiary.

The trust forms in this book do not impose a survivorship period. Many people (including me) think they are unnecessarily cautious. And people who do want them differ widely as to how long the period should be.

If you decide you do want to impose a survivorship period on your primary beneficiaries, you can add one to the trust document. (See Chapter 10, "Preparing Your Living Trust Document," Section C.) I recommend a relatively short period, between 15 and 45 days. Imposing a longer period normally just unnecessarily delays distribution of gifts to the primary beneficiaries.

Example

In Laura's basic shared living trust, she imposes a 15-day survivorship requirement on all her beneficiaries.

Laura leaves all her trust property to her husband Juan-Carlos, and names her daughter from a previous marriage as alternate beneficiary. Laura and Juan-Carlos are seriously injured in a car accident; Juan-Carlos dies four days after Laura does. Because Juan-Carlos did not survive Laura by at least fifteen days, the trust property he would have inherited from Laura goes to Laura's daughter instead.

If there had been no survivorship requirement, Laura's trust property would have gone to Juan-Carlos.

When he died four days later, it would have gone to beneficiaries he had named in the trust document.

G. Residuary Beneficiaries

Residuary beneficiaries are the person, persons or institutions you name to receive trust property that isn't given, for whatever reason, to a primary beneficiary or an alternate. For example, if a primary beneficiary predeceases you or can't be located, and you didn't name an alternate, the property would go to the residuary beneficiary.

1. Individual or Basic Shared Living Trusts

With these trusts, you must name a residuary beneficiary. With a living trust for one person, you should always name a residuary beneficiary and an alternate residuary beneficiary, who will inherit if the residuary beneficiary dies before you.

With a basic shared living trust, each spouse names his or her own residuary beneficiary and alternate residuary beneficiary. They may name different people.

Example

Peter leaves a house to his wife Jane, or if Jane dies before him, to Jane's sister Carolyn. He names his sister Julie as residuary beneficiary. Jane and Carolyn are killed in a car crash three days before Peter dies. Because the primary and alternate beneficiaries are dead, the house goes to Julie. (Pretty cheerful example of how living trusts can work, huh?)

You can name co-residuary beneficiaries, and co-alternate residuary beneficiaries as well. But if you do, you must handle all the potential problems of naming co-beneficiaries (discussed in Section D, above).

For instance, a person could split the bulk of her estate among her children by leaving it all to the children as residuary beneficiaries. For example, she could name as her residuary beneficiaries: "Henry McCormick, Aaron McCormick and Joanne Guiliam, in equal shares."

Another approach is to make a few relatively minor gifts and leave the bulk of your property to your residuary beneficiary.

Example 1

Jennifer wants to leave her two Tiffany lamps to her friend Linda, $5,000 in a money market account to her niece Martha and her car to her sister Joan. She wants to leave all the rest of her extensive estate—houses, stocks, limited partnerships—to her long-time living-together partner, Paul. She can simply name Paul as her residuary beneficiary, after listing the three specific gifts. She names Joan as her alternate residuary beneficiary.

Example 2

Claudia and John are in their second marriage. They have no children together. Each has children from their first marriage—Claudia's are Wendy and Linus, John's are Krystin, Phil and Gary. Claudia and John each name the other as residuary beneficiary. But as alternate residuary beneficiaries, Claudia names Wendy and Linus. John names Krystin, Phil and Gary.

The residuary beneficiary of a living trust for a single person, or of one person's portion of a basic shared living trust, will receive:

- any trust property for which both the primary and alternate beneficiaries you named die before you do

- any trust property that you didn't leave to a named beneficiary (This could include property you transferred to the trust later but didn't name a beneficiary for, and trust property that was owned by your spouse, which he or she left you.)

- any property you leave to your living trust through a "pour-over" will (Because property left through a pour-over will doesn't avoid probate, there's usually no reason to use one. See Chapter 15, "A Living Trust as Part of Your Estate Plan.")

- any property that you actually transferred to your living trust but didn't list in the trust document.

2. AB Trusts

With this type of living trust, residuary beneficiaries have no role. Aside from any specific gifts given to primary beneficiaries or alternates, all property of a deceased spouse goes into the "A" trust. After the death of the surviving spouse, this trust property is distributed to the final beneficiaries. If both a primary beneficiary and alternate for a specific gift predecease a grantor, and the trust is not amended to name a new beneficiary for the gift, that gift becomes part of the "A" trust property, or part of the property in the surviving spouse's trust left to his or her final beneficiaries.

H. Disinheritance

You can disinherit most people simply by not leaving them anything in your living trust or will. If you don't leave someone any of your property, he has no rights to it, period. However, when it comes to your spouse, no disinheritance is possible except in the eight community property states. And, when it comes to your children, you should either leave them something, or expressly disinherit them in your will.

1. Disinheriting a Spouse

Whether or not you can legally disinherit a spouse (not that many people want to) depends on whether you live in a community property state or common law state.

a. Community Property States

In community property states (listed below), the general rule is that spouses together own all property that either acquires during the marriage, except property one spouse acquires by gift or inheritance. Each spouse owns a half-interest in this "community property."

Arizona	Louisiana	Texas
California	Nevada	Washington
Idaho	New Mexico	Wisconsin

You are free to leave your separate property and your half of the community property to anyone you choose. Your spouse—who already owns half of all the community property—has no right to inherit any of your half.

UNMARRIED COUPLES

Unmarried couples living together have no right to inherit any of each other's property. In short, each person can leave his or her property to anyone he or she wants to. However, if the couple has created a valid contract that gives each one the specific right to inherit specific property, that contract will normally be enforced if the person who feels cheated goes to court.

---

b. Common Law States

If you live in one of these 41 common law states or the District of Columbia, you cannot exclude your spouse from receiving some of your property after your death.

Alabama	Kentucky	North Dakota
Alaska	Maine	Ohio
Arkansas	Maryland	Oklahoma
Colorado	Massachusetts	Oregon
Connecticut	Michigan	Pennsylvania
Delaware	Minnesota	Rhode Island
District of Columbia	Mississippi	South Carolina
Florida	Missouri	South Dakota
Georgia	Montana	Tennessee
Hawaii	Nebraska	Utah
Illinois	New Hampshire	Vermont
Indiana	New Jersey	Virginia
Iowa	New York	West Virginia
Kansas	North Carolina	Wyoming

In a common law state, a surviving spouse who doesn't receive one-third to one-half of the deceased spouse's property (through a will, living trust or other method) is entitled to insist upon a set share of the property. The exact share depends on state law. So, a spouse who doesn't receive the minimum he or she is entitled to under state law (the "statutory share") may be able to claim some of the property in your living trust. To be safe, give your spouse at least half your property in your trust (except, of course, in an AB trust, where he or she receives only a life interest in the "A" trust's property).

Even property given away before death may legally belong to the surviving spouse under these laws. For example, take the case of a man who set up joint bank accounts with his children from a previous marriage. After his death, his widow sued to recover her interest in the accounts. She won; the Kentucky Supreme Court ruled that under Kentucky law, a spouse is entitled to a half-interest in the other spouse's personal property (everything but real estate). Her husband had not had the legal right to give away her interest in the money in the accounts. (*Harris v. Rock*, 799 S.W.2d 10 (Ky. 1990).) Most non-community property states have similar laws, called "dower" or "curtesy" laws.

State law may also give your spouse the right to inherit the family residence, or at least use it for his or her life. The Florida constitution, for example, gives a surviving spouse the deceased spouse's residence, no matter what the deceased spouse's will says. (Fla. Const. Art. 10, § 4.)

Plan Your Estate, by Denis Clifford and Cora Jordan, (Nolo Press), contains a state-by-state list of surviving spouses' rights, including which states allow a spouse to waive, in writing, that spouse's marital property rights.

Disinheriting your spouse. If you live in a common law state and you want to leave your spouse less than half of your property from a basic shared trust, see a lawyer.

2. Disinheriting a Child

With rare exceptions, it is legal to disinherit a child. (The Florida constitution prohibits the head of a family from leaving his residence to anyone else in his will except to his spouse or child if he is survived by a spouse or minor child. (Fla. Const. Art. 10, § 4.)

You do not have to leave your child anything in your living trust. But to completely disinherit a child (or the children of a deceased child), your state laws require you to do so in your will, even if you transfer all your property by a living trust.

There are two ways to disinherit a child in a will. One is to expressly disinherit the child in the will, by stating that you aren't leaving him anything. The other is to leave the child a minimal amount, which ensures the child cannot successfully claim to have been overlooked or accidentally omitted. If you don't mention a child in your will, state law may consider that child a "pretermitted heir" (accidentally overlooked) and give him or her the right to a certain share of your property.

The will forms in this book require you to list all your children. The forms then state that if you haven't left any property to a listed child, that failure to do so is intentional. So, if you leave a child nothing (by will or otherwise), this functions as a disinheritance clause.

3. Children Born After a Will or Trust Is Prepared

Some state laws protect offspring who were born after a parent's will was prepared. Although these laws mention only wills, not living trusts, it's possible that a court could apply them to a living trust, reasoning that the living trust is serving the function of a will. And as living trusts become more widespread, state legislatures may expand their laws to include children not mentioned in living trusts.

These laws presume that the parent didn't mean to disinherit a child who is born after the parent's will has been signed, and thus is not mentioned in a parent's will. They presume, instead, that the parent simply hadn't yet gotten around to writing a new will. Such a child is legally entitled to a share (the size is determined by state law) of the deceased parent's estate, which may include property in a living trust.

The simple answer to this problem is to amend your living trust after a child is born. Most parents want to provide for a new child, so it's simply a matter of getting the work done. Amending your trust to provide for a new beneficiary is not difficult. (See Chapter 13, "Living With Your Living Trust," Sections D and F.)

4. Grandchildren

Grandchildren have no right to inherit from their grandparents unless their parent has died. In that case, the grandchildren essentially take the place of the deceased child and are entitled to whatever he or she would have been legally entitled to.

5. General Disinheritance Clauses

You may have heard that some lawyers recommend leaving $1 to close relatives in your trust or will. This is not legally necessary. There's generally no need to mention anyone but your spouse in your trust. No one else has a legal right to any of your property.

Lawsuits contesting a living trust are very rare. A relative could conceivably try to contest your trust by claiming that you, the grantor, were mentally incompetent when you prepared your trust, and were duped by someone to leaving most or all of your property to them, while you really wanted to leave it to this relative.

Heading off contests by relatives. If you think a relative might try to contest your trust, you might leave that relative $1, to make it absolutely clear you did consider that person and wanted to give no more. But before you settle on that option, see a lawyer and review what your wisest course of action is.

6. No-Contest Clauses

A "no-contest clause" in a living trust (or a will) is a device used to discourage beneficiaries of your trust or will from suing to void the trust or will and claiming they are entitled to more than you left them. Under a no-contest clause, a beneficiary who challenges a living trust or will and loses forfeits all his inheritance under that document. Without a no-contest clause, someone left property from a living trust can sue, lose and still collect the amount given him in the trust.

Example

Pip leaves his daughter Estelle $10,000 in his living trust, and includes a no-contest clause in that document. If Estelle challenges the trust and loses, she does not receive the $10,000.

No-contest clauses can be sensible if there's a risk a beneficiary might challenge your estate plan. On the other hand, many people do not like to include a no-contest clause in their estate planning documents, because it seems to imply a suspicion of their beneficiaries that they don't actually feel. The trust and will forms in this book do not contain no-contest clauses.

Adding a no-contest clause. If you think you may need a no-contest clause, that's an indication of a potential serious problem. In this situation, it's not wise to rely solely on a no-contest clause. You need to see a lawyer to discuss how you can best arrange to handle the risk of a court fight; often, a no-contest clause is just one part of a larger strategy.

I. Putting Conditions on Beneficiaries

Occasionally a person wants to make a gift with restrictions or conditions on it. If done thoughtfully, this is usually a complex task. The trust forms in this book do not allow you to make conditional gifts. (You can, however, appoint someone to manage trust property inherited by a minor child or young adult. See Section E, above.)

Example

Ravi wants to leave money to a nephew, Monir, if he goes to veterinary school, but, if he doesn't, to his niece Sheela. This sounds simple, but here are just a few problems inherent in this approach: How soon must Monir go to veterinary school? What happens if he applies in good faith but fails to get in? Who decides if he's really studying? What happens to the money before Monir goes to veterinary school? What happens if Monir goes to veterinary school but drops out after a year and says he'll go back eventually? What happens if he graduates but doesn't become a vet?

Imposing restrictions and controls on beneficiaries is sometimes called "dead-hand control." The obvious risk of dead-hand control is that circumstances can change, so you must try to anticipate what is likely—or even possible—to occur in the future, and provide for it. This, at best, is complex work, and helps to enrich estate planning lawyers.

1. Long-Term Trusts

Except for an AB trust or child's subtrust, you cannot create long-term trusts using this book. Some major types of long-term trusts are discussed in Chapter 15, "A Living Trust as Part of Your Estate Plan."

The issues that must be resolved and the forms necessary to establish these specialized types of trusts are too complex to explain in this self-help book, so you'll have to see a lawyer if you decide you want one.

J. Property You Leave in Your Trust That You No Longer Own at Your Death

If you make a gift of specific property in your trust, but then remove that property from your trust before you die—that is, you sell it or give it to someone—the beneficiary for that gift is simply out of luck, and is likely to be quite upset (if he knew he was supposed to get it). So if you do transfer property from your trust, be sure to amend your trust document and formally delete the provision that left it to a beneficiary. (Chapter 13, "Living With Your Living Trust," Section F, shows how to amend your trust document.)

K. Beneficiary Worksheets

On one of the following worksheets, you'll list your beneficiaries and the property you want to leave to each.

- Use Worksheet 1 for an individual living trust.
- Use Worksheet 2 for a basic shared living trust. Each spouse names beneficiaries separately.
- Use Worksheet 3 for an AB trust. Each spouse can name at most three beneficiaries of specific gifts, aside from the surviving spouse and final beneficiaries.

To get started, go back to the Property Worksheet in Chapter 6, where you listed what items you will transfer to your trust. On these worksheets, you will name a beneficiary for each item. If you're making a gift to co-beneficiaries and naming alternate co-beneficiaries, you need to decide what share each co-beneficiary receives.

If you need more space than the worksheet provides, attach additional sheets (or scribble in the margins, for that matter). Also, if you think you may do a substantial amount of revising, photocopy the blank worksheet before you begin filling it out.

Beneficiary Worksheet 1: For an individual trust

1. Specific Gifts

_____
Primary Beneficiary

_____
Item of Property

_____
Alternate Beneficiary

_____
Primary Beneficiary

_____
Item of Property

_____
Alternate Beneficiary

_____
Primary Beneficiary

_____
Item of Property

_____
Alternate Beneficiary

_____
Primary Beneficiary

_____
Item of Property

_____
Alternate Beneficiary

_____
Primary Beneficiary

_____
Item of Property

_____
Alternate Beneficiary

_____
Primary Beneficiary

_____
Item of Property

_____
Alternate Beneficiary

_____
Primary Beneficiary

_____
Item of Property

_____
Alternate Beneficiary

_____
Primary Beneficiary

_____
Item of Property

_____
Alternate Beneficiary

_____
Primary Beneficiary

_____
Item of Property

_____
Alternate Beneficiary

_____
Primary Beneficiary

_____
Item of Property

_____
Alternate Beneficiary

2. Residuary Beneficiary or Beneficiaries

_____
Residuary Beneficiary(ies)

_____
Alternate Residuary Beneficiary(ies)

Beneficiary Worksheet 2: A basic shared living trust

WIFE'S BENEFICIARIES

1. Specific Gifts

Primary Beneficiary

Item of Property

Alternate Beneficiary

Primary Beneficiary

Item of Property

Alternate Beneficiary

Primary Beneficiary

Item of Property

Alternate Beneficiary

Primary Beneficiary

Item of Property

Alternate Beneficiary

Primary Beneficiary

Item of Property

Alternate Beneficiary

Primary Beneficiary

Item of Property

Alternate Beneficiary

Primary Beneficiary

Item of Property

Alternate Beneficiary

Primary Beneficiary

Item of Property

Alternate Beneficiary

Primary Beneficiary

Item of Property

Alternate Beneficiary

2. Residuary Beneficiary or Beneficiaries

Residuary Beneficiary(ies)

Alternate Residuary Beneficiary(ies)

Beneficiary Worksheet 2 (continued)

HUSBAND'S BENEFICIARIES

1. Specific Gifts

Primary Beneficiary

Item of Property

Alternate Beneficiary

Primary Beneficiary

Item of Property

Alternate Beneficiary

Primary Beneficiary

Item of Property

Alternate Beneficiary

Primary Beneficiary

Item of Property

Alternate Beneficiary

Primary Beneficiary

Item of Property

Alternate Beneficiary

Primary Beneficiary

Item of Property

Alternate Beneficiary

Primary Beneficiary

Item of Property

Alternate Beneficiary

Primary Beneficiary

Item of Property

Alternate Beneficiary

Primary Beneficiary

Item of Property

Alternate Beneficiary

2. Residuary Beneficiary or Beneficiaries

Residuary Beneficiary(ies)

Alternate Residuary Beneficiary(ies)

Beneficiary Worksheet 3: AB Trust

1. Wife's Specific Beneficiaries

_____
Specific Beneficiary

_____
Item of Property

_____
Alternate Beneficiary

_____
Specific Beneficiary

_____
Item of Property

_____
Alternate Beneficiary

_____
Specific Beneficiary

_____
Item of Property

_____
Alternate Beneficiary

4. Husband's Specific Beneficiaries

_____
Specific Beneficiary

_____
Item of Property

_____
Alternate Beneficiary

_____
Specific Beneficiary

_____
Item of Property

_____
Alternate Beneficiary

_____
Specific Beneficiary

_____
Item of Property

_____
Alternate Beneficiary

2. Wife's Final Beneficiaries

_____

_____

_____

_____

5. Husband's Final Beneficiaries

_____

_____

_____

_____

3. Wife's Alternate Final Beneficiaries

_____

_____

_____

_____

6. Husband's Alternate Final Beneficiaries

_____

_____

_____

_____

chapter 9

Property Left to Minor Children or Young Adults

*I*f any of the beneficiaries (including alternate, residuary or final beneficiaries) you've named might inherit trust property before they are ready to manage it responsibly, you'll want to arrange for an adult to manage that beneficiary's property.

If your young beneficiaries won't inherit anything of great value—if you're leaving them objects that have more sentimental than monetary value—you don't need to arrange for an adult to manage the property.

Here are the beneficiaries you should arrange management for:

• **Any beneficiary now under 18.**

Children under 18 cannot, by law, directly manage substantial amounts of money—roughly, anything over $2,500 to $5,000, depending on state law.

If a minor inherits valuable trust property, and you have not arranged for the property to be managed by an adult, a court-appointed guardian will have to manage the property. Contrary to what you might expect, a child's parent does not automatically have legal authority to manage any property the child inherits. So even if one or both of the beneficiary's parents are alive, they will not automatically have authority to manage the property. They will have to ask the court to grant them that authority, and will be subject to the court's supervision. If neither of the beneficiary's parents are alive, there may be no obvious person for the court to appoint as property guardian. In that case, it may be even more important for you to name someone in your living trust.

Reminder. If you have a child under age 18, you must nominate a personal guardian—the adult responsible for raising the child—in your will. You can't do this in your living trust.

• **Any beneficiary over 18 you believe is not mature enough to responsibly handle your gift.**

If a beneficiary is over 18 when he or she inherits trust property, you do not need, legally, to have anyone manage the property on the beneficiary's behalf. If you don't make any arrangements, the beneficiary will get the property with no strings attached. But with the forms in this book, you can arrange for property management to last until a young adult beneficiary turns any age up to 35—that is, you can choose any age between 19 and 35 when the young adult receives the property outright.

WHY 35?

We've created a rule that any beneficiary must receive a gift made from a Nolo living trust outright by age 35 at the latest. We've chosen 35 for the cut-off age because it seems reasonable to conclude that an adult who can't manage financial matters responsibly by that age may never be able to do so. If you want someone else to manage the trust property of a beneficiary who's over 35, you'll probably want to create a special type of trust, usually called a "spendthrift trust," and resolve specific problems, such as who will be the trustee many years down the line if the beneficiary survives to old age. Ending a trust when a beneficiary turns 35 means long-term problems shouldn't be as complex.

Obviously, whether or not you want to provide for management of property inherited by a young adult beneficiary is a personal decision. Some young adults are fully capable of managing money at age 21, while others at the same age might indulge recklessly, even disastrously, if they received a large inheritance outright.

A. Property Management Options

If you want to provide for property management for a gift to a minor or young adult beneficiary, you have several options.

• Leave the property directly to an adult to use for the child. Many people don't leave property directly to a child. Instead, they leave it to the child's parent or to the person they expect to have care and custody of the child if neither parent is available. There's no formal legal arrangement, but they trust the adult to use the property for the child's benefit.

- **Create children's subtrusts.** You can establish "children's subtrusts" in your living trust. If you do, your successor trustee will manage the subtrust property you left each child or young adult and spend it for that child's education, health and other needs. If you create a shared living trust or an AB trust, the surviving spouse would manage property left to minors by the deceased spouse; the successor trustee would act only after both spouses die. Each child's subtrust ends at whatever age you designate for that child (between 18 and 35), and any remaining property is then turned over to the beneficiary outright.

- **Name a custodian under the Uniform Transfers to Minors Act (UTMA).** This is a model law written by a national panel of experts. A majority of states have adopted this law, sometimes with minor modifications. In states with the UTMA, you can use this law to name a "custodian" to manage property you leave a child until the child reaches 18 or 21, depending on state law (up to 25 in Alaska, California and Nevada). If you don't need management to last beyond the age your state law allows, a custodianship is often preferable to a child's subtrust.

Children with special needs. These property management options are not designed to provide long-term property management for a child or young adult with serious disabilities. You'll need to see a lawyer and make arrangements geared to your particular situation.

A good book on estate planning for a child with a disability is *Planning for the Future: Providing a Meaningful Life for a Child With a Disability After Your Death,* by Russell, Grant, Joseph and Fee (American Publishing Co.).

B. Which Method Is Best for You: Subtrust or Custodianship?

Both a child's subtrust and a custodianship are safe, efficient ways of managing trust property that a young person inherits. Under either system, the person in charge of the young beneficiary's property has the same responsibility to use the property for the beneficiary's support, education and health. For example, you can leave a gift of life insurance to a child's subtrust, or to a custodian under UTMA, and in either case, the proceeds will be held in trust by an adult for benefit of the child you name to be the beneficiary. So use whichever method works best for you, but don't get hung up worrying about technicalities or puzzling over possible legal intricacies.

The most significant difference between a child's subtrust and an UTMA gift is that a child's subtrust can last longer than a custodianship, which must end at age 18 to 21 in most states (up to 25 in Alaska, California and Nevada). For that reason, a child's subtrust is a good choice when it's conceivable that a young person could inherit a large amount of property, and you want the money handled by a more mature person, at least through the child's middle 20s.

STATES THAT HAVE ADOPTED THE UTMA	
State	**Age at which minor gets property**
Alabama	21
Alaska	18-25
Arizona	21
Arkansas	18-21
California	18-25
Colorado	21
Connecticut	21
District of Columbia	18
Florida	21
Georgia	21
Hawaii	21
Idaho	21
Illinois	21
Indiana	21
Iowa	21
Kansas	21
Kentucky	18
Maine	18-21
Maryland	21
Massachusetts	21
Minnesota	21
Mississippi	21
Missouri	21
Montana	21
Nebraska	21
Nevada	18-25
New Hampshire	21
New Jersey	18-21
New Mexico	21
North Carolina	18-21
North Dakota	21
Ohio	21
Oklahoma	18
Oregon	21
Pennsylvania	21
Rhode Island	18
South Dakota	18
Tennessee	21
Texas	21
Utah	21
Virginia	18-21
Washington	21
West Virginia	21
Wisconsin	21
Wyoming	21

A few other states still have the earlier version of this act—The Uniform Gifts to Minors Act—which you cannot use for property left in a living trust.

An UTMA custodianship is usually preferable to a child's subtrust if the beneficiary will inherit roughly $50,000 worth of property (or perhaps up to $100,000 or so if the child is quite young). That amount is likely to be used up for living expenses by the time the child reaches age 18, let alone 21. And if your state allows the UTMA gift to be kept in custodianship until the child is 21 or older, amounts up to $100,000 can surely be consumed by four years of college costs. In these situations, there's probably no need to create a subtrust to last beyond the UTMA cutoff age.

A custodianship can have other advantages as well:

• Handling a beneficiary's property can be easier with a custodianship than with a trust. A custodian's powers are written into state law, and most institutions, such as banks and insurance companies, are familiar with the rules. Trusts, on the other hand, vary in their terms. So before a bank lets a trustee act on behalf of a beneficiary, it may demand to see and analyze a copy of the trust document.

• You can name whomever you wish to be a custodian, and you can name different custodians for different beneficiaries. So if you want to arrange custodianships for grandchildren, for example, you could name each child's parent as custodian. A child's subtrust is not so flexible: The surviving spouse, or the successor trustee, will be the trustee of all child's subtrusts created for your young beneficiaries.

• It may offer better income tax rates than a trust. A trust is taxed at 28% on retained income over $1,500 annually, with the top rate reaching 39.6% on income over $7,500. By contrast, property managed by an UTMA custodian is taxed as income paid directly to the child, often a lower rate than paid by a trust. (This can get complicated, because income paid to a child under 14 is taxed at the child's parent's, or parents', tax rate.)

C. Children's Subtrusts

As I've said, if you have left any trust property to minors or to young adults who cannot responsibly manage property, you can create, within your living trust, a separate child's subtrust for each such beneficiary. These trusts are called subtrusts because each is a component of your overall living trust. Your surviving spouse or successor trustee manages all child's subtrusts.

1. How a Child's Subtrust Is Created

The first step is to make your gifts in your living trust document, including gifts left to any children or young adults. Then you complete another clause in your trust document, the children's subtrust clause, where you list each child's name and the age (from 18 to 35) at which this beneficiary is to receive his or her subtrust property outright. If at your death the beneficiary is younger than the age you specified, a subtrust will be created for that beneficiary. If the beneficiary is older, he or she gets the trust property with no strings attached, and no subtrust is created.

Example

In their basic shared living trust, Roger and Victoria each leave their trust property to the other. They name their daughters, who are 22 and 25, as alternate beneficiaries, and arrange for any trust property they may inherit to stay in children's subtrusts until each daughter reaches 30. They name Victoria's sister, Antoinette, as successor trustee.

Roger and Victoria die in a car accident when one daughter is 28 and the other is 31. The 28-year-old's half of the trust property stays in a subtrust, managed by Antoinette, until she turns 30. The 31-year-old gets her half outright; no subtrust is created for her.

If a child's subtrust becomes operational, your successor trustee (or surviving spouse, if you made a trust together) must obtain a separate trust taxpayer ID number for each child's subtrust, file separate tax returns and keep separate accountings and records for each subtrust. The successor trustee must manage each subtrust individually.

So an operational child's subtrust is both a component of the overall living trust and a distinct entity. If light can be both a wave and a particle, surely this kind of duality is acceptable. And indeed it is, in the real world of the IRS, banks and trust beneficiaries.

HOW A CHILD'S SUBTRUST WORKS

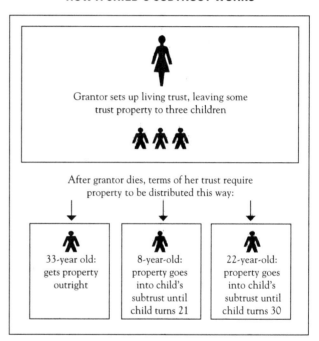

Grantor sets up living trust, leaving some trust property to three children

After grantor dies, terms of her trust require property to be distributed this way:

33-year old: gets property outright

8-year-old: property goes into child's subtrust until child turns 21

22-year-old: property goes into child's subtrust until child turns 30

Example

In his individual living trust, Stanley names his 14-year-old son Michael as beneficiary of $75,000 worth of stock. He specifies that any stock Michael becomes entitled to when Stanley dies should be kept in a subtrust until Michael is 28, subject to the trustee's right to spend it on Michael's behalf.

Stanley dies when Michael is 19. The stock goes into a subtrust for him, managed by the successor trustee of Stanley's living trust. The trustee is free to use the stock (and the income it produces) to pay for Michael's education and support. Michael will receive what's left of the stock when he turns 28.

A separate subtrust is created for each beneficiary you list. If these subtrusts ever become operational, Nolo's living trust forms provide that each one is given the name of its particular beneficiary. This allows the subtrust to be readily identified and managed in the real world.

Example

Leo Goldstein's living trust creates children's subtrusts for his grandchildren, Janet and John Ronninger, which are to last until each is 30. Leo dies while Janet and John are minors. Leo's successor trustee manages the subtrusts, one of which is called "The Leo Goldstein Living Trust, The Jane Ronninger Subtrust" and the other of which is called "The Leo Goldstein Living Trust, The John Ronninger Subtrust." Thus these trusts are identified as independent entities, while technically they are part of the original living trust as well.

With an AB trust, children's subtrusts are also possible. With an AB trust, you can make up to three independent gifts. If any of these gifts is made to a minor or young adult, you can create a child's subtrust for these beneficiaries.

All the other property of the deceased spouse must go into the "A" trust. Clearly, there will be no need to create a child's subtrust for the surviving spouse and, in most cases, even the final beneficiaries of these trusts are over 35. But if a final beneficiary or, more likely, an alternate final beneficiary, is not over 35 (such as grandchildren of the grantors), you can create a child's subtrust for any of them.

2. The Trustee of Children's Subtrusts

The trustee for each child's subtrust is your successor trustee or, if you made a trust with your spouse, then your spouse. After both spouses are deceased, the successor trustee takes over any operational children's trusts. The trust forms in this book do not allow you to name another person to be a trustee for a child's subtrust.

The reason is that naming separate trustees creates serious paperwork and practical problems. Which trustee gets the original of your living trust document? Do you create several originals? Besides, it's usually hard enough to find one competent person who'll serve as trustee for all children's subtrusts. If you really want to name someone other than your successor trustee to be custodian for a gift to a minor, in most states you can use the UTMA. (See Section D, below.)

Choosing someone else to be trustee of a child's trust. If you want to have children's subtrusts managed by someone other than your surviving spouse or your successor trustee, see a lawyer.

3. The Subtrust Trustee's Duties

The trustee's powers and responsibilities are spelled out in the trust document. The subtrust trustee must:

- Manage each subtrust's property until that subtrust's beneficiary reaches the age set out in the trust document—which can take years.

- Use each subtrust's property or income to pay for that subtrust beneficiary's expenses, such as support, education and health care.

- Keep separate records of subtrust transactions and file income tax returns for each subtrust.

- A very few states require periodic reports to the beneficiary of a child's trust. However, in most cases, it doesn't matter whether or not it's done, since everything is within the family.

If the subtrust trustee needs to hire an accountant, tax lawyer or other expert to help manage a subtrust, he or she can use that subtrust's assets to pay a reasonable amount for the help.

The trust document also provides that the trustee of a subtrust is entitled to reasonable compensation for his or her work as trustee. The trustee decides what is a reasonable amount, without court approval; the compensation is paid from the assets of the particular subtrust involved.

When the beneficiary reaches the age designated by the trust document, up to 35, the trustee must give the beneficiary what remains of the subtrust property.

D. Custodianships

Creating a custodianship for a gift under your state's Uniform Transfers to Minors Act (UTMA) may be a preferable alternative to a child's subtrust, at least for some of your younger beneficiaries.

1. How a Custodianship Is Created

After you make all your gifts in your living trust, in a separate section of the trust form you can create as many custodianships as you want for minor or young adult beneficiaries. You do this by identifying the property and the beneficiary it is left to and appointing a custodian to be responsible for supervising that property. The form provides that the custodian is to act "under the [your state] Uniform Transfers to Minors Act." You can also name an alternate custodian in case your first choice can't do the job. Finally, you list the age at which the minor is to receive the property outright, using the list in Section B as your guide. In most states, you have no choice and must list the age that state's UTMA decrees. In a few states, you can choose an age in a set range.

The custodian manages any trust property the young beneficiary inherits until the beneficiary reaches the age at which state law says the custodianship must end. (See Section B, above.)

OTHER TYPES OF TRUSTS FOR MINORS OR YOUNG ADULT BENEFICIARIES

In some situations, you may want a different type of child's subtrust than the separate one-for-each-beneficiary provided in this book's living trust forms. Consult a lawyer if you want to:

- Place extensive controls over the use of property in the trust (for example, if you place real estate in the trust that you want managed in a specific way).
- Provide for special care for a disadvantaged child.
- Create a trust for any beneficiary who is already over age 35.
- Combine property for different children into a single trust (often called a "family pot" trust). In this type of trust, the trustee doles out money to different children as he sees fit, according to their needs. Establishing this sort of trust is often not a good idea, for several reasons. It's harder (and therefore more expensive) to prepare tax returns, the trust doesn't end until the youngest child reaches the designated age (the older ones can't get their share outright before this) and the trustee may prefer one child's needs over another's, setting up the possibility of conflict or at least resentment. On the other hand, precisely because the trustee is empowered to spend any amount of the pot for any beneficiary, this sort of trust may be a good idea if one child turns out to need a lot more financial help than others.

HOW A CUSTODIANSHIP WORKS

```
┌─────────────────────────────────────────────────┐
│         LIVING TRUST PROPERTY                     │
│                                                   │
│         Grantor dies.                             │
│                                                   │
│    To           Custodianship    Custodianship    │
│   adult           created.         created.       │
│ beneficiaries.                                    │
│                                                   │
│ Beneficiary reaches                               │
│ age set out in trust   Beneficiary #1.  Beneficiary #2. │
│ document; custodian                               │
│ turns property over                               │
│ to beneficiary.                                   │
└─────────────────────────────────────────────────┘
```

Example

Sandra and Don make a basic shared living trust. Sandra leaves 100 shares of Nike stock to her niece Jennifer Frankel. She names Hazel Frankel, Jennifer's mother, as custodian under the Illinois Uniform Transfers to Minors Act.

At Sandra's death, Jennifer is 13. So Don, as trustee of the living trust, turns the stock over to the custodian, Hazel. She will manage it for Jennifer until Jennifer turns 21, the age Illinois law says she must be given the property outright.

As discussed, in some states, you can specify—within limits—at what age the custodianship will end. If your state allows this, you must state the age at which you want the custodianship to end.

Example

Alexis and Jonathan, who live in New Jersey, make a basic shared living trust. They leave most of their trust property to each other and leave some property to their young children, Ian and Noel. They both specify, in the trust document, that any trust property the children inherit should be managed by the other spouse as custodian, under the New Jersey Uniform Transfers to Minors Act, until the boys turn 21. Under New Jersey law, they could have specified any age from 18 to 21. As alternate custodian, both name Jonathan's mother.

Alexis and Jonathan die simultaneously in an accident. Jonathan's mother, as custodian, takes over management of the trust property left to her grandchildren. When each boy turns 21, he will receive whatever of his property hasn't been used for his support or education.

2. Changes in State Law

States are free to change their rules about the age at which custodianships terminate. If your state does this after you make your living trust, it could affect any custodianships you have set up.

- If your state raises the age at which custodianships terminate, the new age will determine when your beneficiary's custodianship ends.

- If your state adopts a flexible scheme allowing you to choose the age at which the custodianship ends, you can amend your living trust document to designate an age. If you don't amend it, the custodianship will end when the beneficiary reaches the youngest age allowed under the law—in most cases, 18.

3. If You Move

If you move to a state that hasn't adopted the UTMA, it's usually necessary to revise your living trust by creating children's subtrusts for any gifts previously made using a custodian. However, if the beneficiary of the gift, or the custodian for it, remains in a state that has an UTMA, you can still use that law for your gift. Finally, if you move from one UTMA state to another, you can keep your UTMA clause as it is, unless you've moved to a state that has a lower age for turning over the gift to the minor than the age allowed in your old state. If this is the case, you'll have to amend your trust to establish a new age for the gift to be turned over to the child.

4. The Custodian's Responsibilities

A custodian has roughly the same responsibility as the trustee of a child's subtrust: to manage the beneficiary's property wisely and honestly. The custodian's authority and duties are clearly set out by the Uniform Transfers to Minors Act, as enacted by your state. No court directly supervises the custodian.

The custodian must:

- Manage the property until the beneficiary reaches the age at which, by law, he or she gets the property outright. If the child is quite young at your death, this can be a number of years.

- Use the property or income to pay for the young beneficiary's support, education and health care.

- Keep the property separate from his or her own property.

- Keep separate records of trust transactions. The custodian does not have to file a separate income tax return; income from the property can be reported on the young beneficiary's return. (By comparison, the trustee of a child's subtrust must file a separate tax return for the subtrust.)

A custodian who needs to hire an accountant, tax lawyer or other expert can use the property to pay a reasonable amount for the help.

If state law allows it, the custodian is entitled to reasonable compensation and reimbursement for reasonable expenses. The payment, if any is taken, comes from the property the custodian manages for the beneficiary. If this concerns you, check out your state's laws or see a lawyer. (See Chapter 17, "If You Need Expert Help," Section D.)

5. Choosing a Custodian

In most cases, you should name as custodian the person who will have physical custody of the minor child. That's almost always one of the child's parents. If the beneficiary is your child, name the child's other parent, unless you have serious reservations about that person's ability to handle the property for the child.

Only one person can be named as custodian for one beneficiary. You can, however, name an alternate custodian to take over if your first choice is unable to serve. And you can name different custodians for different beneficiaries.

Example

Elaine, in her living trust, leaves property to two young nephews, Jerry and Mark, and one young niece Reyna. She names Jerry and Reyna's mother, Alice, as custodian for their gifts. She names Mark's mother, Angela, as custodian for his gift. 🍂

chapter 10

PREPARING YOUR LIVING TRUST DOCUMENT

*N*ow it's time to actually prepare your own living trust document. This chapter explains how to do it, step-by-step, when you use one of the trust forms in this book.

**CHECKLIST FOR PREPARING
YOUR LIVING TRUST DOCUMENT**

- Remove the form you need from the Appendix.
- Fill in the form by following the step-by-step instructions in this chapter.
- Have the completed form typed, and proofread the final version.
- Sign your trust document in front of a notary public in the state where you live.
- Store your trust document in a safe place. (See Chapter 12, "Copying, Storing and Registering Your Trust Document.")

Please read this entire chapter carefully so you understand the choices you will make. Take your time and reread as much as you need to.

A. Choosing the Right Trust Form

The Appendix contains three fill-in-the-blanks living trust forms:

- **Form 1:** Basic probate-avoidance living trust for one person.

- **Form 2:** Basic probate-avoidance shared living trust, for a couple (married or not) with shared ownership property.

- **Form 3:** AB trust, for a couple (married or not) who want to save on overall estate taxes and avoid probate.

Generally, you should use only one trust. However, in a few special situations you may decide it's preferable to use more than one living trust. (See Chapter 4, "What Type of Trust Do You Need?" for a discussion.)

B. Getting Started

Once you've selected the appropriate trust form, you may want to photocopy it, so you have a clean copy (or several) to use if you need to prepare more than one draft. One draft is all many people need to prepare the final version of their trust for typing. But having extra copies of the form certainly can't hurt, and may be useful if you make many corrections or changes.

Use a pencil (to make corrections easier), and go through the form slowly and carefully, filling in the blanks, or crossing them out if the information required doesn't apply to you.

C. Making Changes in a Trust Form

These Nolo trusts are intended to be used as printed, except for minor, common-sense variations, or where the directions specifically allow you a choice of what to include. Generally, it's risky to make changes in the trust forms, particularly Form 3, an AB trust. Changes can create the possibility of confusion and even contradictions regarding what you intend with your trust. If you want to make many changes in the form, this should alert you to the fact that our form does not suit you, and you need to see a lawyer.

As previously discussed, you may need to make minor word changes. If you want to name co-successor trustees, you'll need to change the word "trustee" to "trustees" at various places in the form. Just be clear on your draft form what minor changes you've made.

Be very cautious about making changes. You will have to use your common sense to decide whether or not changes in the form are needed. But do be very careful. Don't stray far from the language of the form, especially with an AB trust. You certainly don't want to risk making a change that could cost you your estate tax savings. Be sure you understand the effect of any changes you make.

D. Step-by-Step Instructions

Important: *These instructions are keyed to numbers on the trust forms. For example, Step 1 tells you how to fill in your name(s) and how to name your living trust. On the trust form, each time your name, or names, are called for, you'll see a* ①.

The steps are set out in the most logical order. However, the circled numbers on the forms do not always proceed sequentially; for example, number ①, the name of your trust, appears at the beginning of the form and also later, after other circled numbers. This is because the information called for is needed in more than one place in your trust form. Other numbers appear out of sequence because the information called for is necessary only for that one form, so the number given comes after the numbers and information common to all forms. Just remember the basic principle: The circled number refers you to the specific step in this section that explains how to fill in this blank.

Some simple information you must fill in is not keyed to a circled number because no instructions seem necessary. For instance, where you see a blank and "he/she" printed underneath, put in either "he" or "she," depending on whether the person referred to (which will be clear in the context) is male or female. Similarly, where you see a blank with "your state" printed underneath, fill in the state where you live.

When you have completed the form, proofread it carefully. Then proceed, as explained in Sections E through G, below, to finish your trust document.

For couples. For the most part, the same decisions must be made whether you're preparing a living trust for one person or for a couple, so the instructions are just about the same. However, some instructions apply only to the two shared living trusts. They are identified by this symbol:

SPECIAL INSTRUCTIONS FOR UNMARRIED COUPLES

Forms 2 and 3 are written in terms of a married couple. Therefore, an unmarried couple will need to change some wording in these forms. For example, the printed forms use the terms "spouse" or "surviving spouse" and, in Form 3, "Surviving Spouse's Trust." You can use "mate," "surviving mate," "partner," "lover" or whatever words seem most suitable to you. Once you have selected a word or words, stick with them throughout the trust. And, of course, be sure you've read the trust document carefully, to make all the necessary substitutions.

Aside from words like "spouse" in the text, you'll see a number of blank lines to be filled in, with words below the line, such as

_____

wife's name

or

_____

husband's name

The words that appear below the lines will be deleted from your final trust. But of course, you need to fill in the appropriate member of the couple's name, not a (nonexistent in your case) wife's or husband's name.

Though making these word changes does require some extra work, it's really just a matter of cross-outs and substitutions, which you shouldn't find difficult or onerous.

Step 1: Name Your Living Trust

A living trust must be given a name. Normally, you simply use your own name—for example, "The Denis Clifford Living Trust." It's legal to use more inventive names, for reasons ranging from a desire for privacy to nostalgia. (I once had a client who created the "Rue de Rivoli Trust.") Also, if you create more than one trust, you will want to distinguish them. One way to do this is to use numbers, particularly Roman numerals, to prevent any confusion in a basic shared trust, which splits into Trust #1 and Trust #2 on the death of a spouse. For example, "The Denis Clifford Living Trust #I," "The Denis Clifford Living Trust #II," and so on. Generally, it's more preferable to sign the trusts on different days and identify each trust by the date signed—for example, "The Denis Clifford Living Trust, 3/19/1996"; "The Denis Clifford Living Trust, 4/7/96."

Use only one name per person; don't enter various versions of your name joined by "aka" (also known as).

If you go by more than one name, be sure that the name you use for your living trust is the one that appears on the ownership documents for property you plan to transfer to the trust. If it isn't, it could cause confusion later, and you should change the name on your ownership documents before you transfer the property to the trust.

Example

You use the name William Dix for your trust, but own real estate in your former name of William Geicherwitz. You should prepare and sign a new deed, changing the name of the real estate owner to William Dix, before you prepare another deed to transfer the property from you (William Dix) to your living trust.

Married couples who make a basic shared living trust or an AB trust normally use both their names to identify their trust—for example, "The Kay and Ornette Lewison Living Trust" or "The Cynthia Duffy and Mike O'Mally Living Trust." As with a trust for an individual, a couple can give their shared trust a fanciful name.

Unmarried couples can simply use both their names—for example, "The Natalia Williams and Andrew Johnson Living Trust" or "The Lillian Perry and Sandra Bick Living Trust."

If you use your name or names for your trust, insert it every time there is a ① on the living trust form.

If you don't use your own name, you'll need to determine, each time you see a ①, whether your own name or the trust's name is required. For example, when naming the original trustees, you'll put in your own name(s), not the trust's name.

Step 2: Decide How Many Property Schedules Your Trust Needs

By this time, you should have decided which items of your property you will place in your living trust and which you will leave by other means. (See Chapter 6, "Choosing What Property to Put in Your Living Trust.") Now you need to list all property that you will transfer to the trust on a document called a "schedule" or "schedules," which will be attached to your trust document. How to list the property on a trust schedule is explained in Step 3.

As you can see by looking at the trust forms, a trust schedule is nothing more than a blank sheet of paper. For an individual trust, there's only one "Schedule A." For a couple, there are these:

- "Schedule A, Shared Property Placed in Trust";

- "Schedule B, Wife's Separate Property Placed in Trust"; and

- "Schedule C, Husband's Separate Property Placed in Trust."

First, you must decide how many trust schedules you want to use. If you're creating a trust for one person (Form 1), you will use only one schedule, "Schedule A," even if several—or many—different types of property will be transferred to the trust.

Example

Mrs. Johnson wants to transfer her house, two cars, stock accounts and jewelry to her living trust. She lists all this property on one trust schedule, Schedule A.

The shared trust forms (Forms 2 and 3) have three schedules, A, B and C. Schedule A is for the couple's shared ownership property, B is for the wife's separate property, and C is for the husband's separate property. If you have shared property and each spouse has separate property, you will use all three schedules.

Example

Mrs. and Mr. Andrezly, in their 60s, have been married for 15 years. Each has children from a former marriage. When they got married, each owned property which they agreed would remain each's separate property. Since they married, they have acquired shared property, including a home. In their basic shared living trust, each wants his or her separate property to go to the children from the first marriage; their shared property goes to the surviving spouse.

They list their property in the basic shared living trust by using three schedules: Schedule A for the shared property, Schedule B for Mrs. Andrezly's separate property, and Schedule C for Mr. Andrezly's separate property.

If the Andrezlys created three separate trusts—a basic shared living trust for the shared marital property and two individual living trusts for each spouse's separate property—they would use only Schedule A of the shared trust for their shared marital property.

If one, or both, spouses does not have separate property, you won't use Schedule B, Schedule C or both of them. You'll also need to delete references in the trust document to that spouse's (or both spouse's) separate property. The paragraphs you may need to change are listed below.

Example

Tau and Lien Yu prepare a basic shared living trust. They own shared property. Lien has separate property; Tau does not. So they omit Schedule C from their draft trust and edit the trust form following the instructions below.

CHANGES TO TRUST FORM IF SEPARATE PROPERTY NOT INCLUDED

If either spouse doesn't transfer separate property to the trust, you'll need to make appropriate changes on Form 2 or 3 by deleting the irrelevant material from the following sections:

- Section II, Paragraph A, refers to Schedules A, B and C.
- Section II, Paragraph B(1), refers to the wife's separate property.
- Section II, Paragraph B(2), refers to the husband's separate property.
- Section II, Paragraph D(2), refers first to the wife's separate property on Schedule B and the husband's separate property on Schedule C.
- Section IV refers to Schedules A, B and C.

Instructions for making changes are included on the forms.

• Section V refers to Schedules A, B, C [handwritten]

Below I show a sample Form 2. One spouse owns separate property, one does not. This draft shows the changes that are necessary to prepare the final draft when Schedule C is not used.

Step 3: List Your Trust Property on the Trust Schedule(s)

After you've decided how many schedules to use, list your trust property on them. Listing the trust property on a schedule does not give that property to beneficiaries. You list the property to make clear what property you have transferred to the trust and is owned by the trust. Then, in your trust document, you name your beneficiaries—that is, specify who will inherit the trust property after your death (Step 7, below).

Transferring property to the trust. To complete the transfer of property to the trust, you also must re-register title to that property in the trustee's or trustees' name(s). This absolutely essential process is explained in detail in Chapter 11, "Transferring Property to Your Trust."

When listing trust property on a trust schedule, generally you can use the same wording you used on the worksheet in Chapter 6. Just describe each item clearly enough so that the surviving spouse or successor trustee can identify it and transfer it to the right person. No magic legal words are required. Remember, this isn't a document that will be picked over by lawyers and courts. It's a document for the real world; what's important is that your successor trustee, family and other inheritors are clear on what you've done and what you want.

Think about who will ultimately inherit the property. If you're leaving everything to one person, or a few major items to be parceled out among a few people, there's less need to list property in great detail. But if there will be a number of trust beneficiaries, and objects could be confused, be more precise about each one. When in doubt, err on the side of including more information.

When you name the beneficiaries for the trust property in your trust document (Step 7), your gifts must, of course, be consistent with the property listed on the schedule. You can't leave someone something that isn't listed on a trust property schedule. But the schedule does not have to be as detailed as your gifts. For example, on a schedule you could list "the house, furnishings and personal possessions at [street address]." You can leave all this property to one beneficiary, or you could divide it, naming one beneficiary for the house and another for the furnishings and possessions, or break it down still further into many separate gifts.

IDENTIFYING OWNERSHIP OF TRUST PROPERTY

Don't use "my" or "our" when listing trust property on a schedule. For example, don't enter "my books" or "my stereo system." That's because once the property is in the living trust, technically it doesn't belong to you anymore—it belongs to the living trust, and is held in the name of the trustee.

If you need to refer to yourself or your property in a trust schedule, do so in the third person, by calling yourself "the grantor" or "grantors" rather than using "I" or "we." Sometimes, to clarify what property is owned by the trust, it helps to state on the schedule that identified property was "formerly" or "previously" owned by the grantor.

For example, on a trust schedule, you list: "The 3/4-carat diamond bracelet formerly owned by the grantor."

A variation of this is to identify and list property "in the possession of the grantor," for example, "All compact disks and videos in the possession of the grantor."

Sample Form 2: Basic Shared Living Trust

The ① _____ Tau and Lien Yu _____ Living Trust

~~your names~~

DECLARATION OF TRUST

I. TRUST NAME

This trust shall be known as The ① _____ Tau and Lien Yu _____

~~— your names~~

Living Trust.

II. TRUST PROPERTY

(A) Property Placed in Trust

① Tau and Lien Yu _____ , called the "grantors"

~~— your names~~

or "trustees," declare that they have set aside and hold in The

① _____ Tau and Lien Yu _____ Living Trust all their interest in

~~— your names~~

the property described in the attached Schedules A, B and ~~C.~~ ②

The trust property shall be used for the benefit of the trust beneficiaries, and shall be administered and

distributed by the trustees in accordance with this Declaration of Trust.

(B) Rights Retained by Grantors

As long as both grantors are alive, both grantors retain all rights to all income, profits and control of the

trust property listed on Schedule A of The ① _____ Tau and Lien Yu _____

~~— your names~~

Living Trust.

(1) As long as _____ Lien Yu _____ is alive, she shall retain all

~~wife's name~~

rights to all income, profits and control of her separate property listed on Schedule B of The

① _____ Tau and Lien Yu _____ Living Trust.

~~your names~~

~~(2) As long as _____ is alive, he shall retain all~~

~~— husband's name~~

~~rights to all income, profits and control of his separate property listed on Schedule C of The~~

~~① _____ Living Trust.~~

~~— your names~~

(C) Additional or After-Acquired Property

Either grantor, or both, may add additional or after-acquired property to the trust at any time, and shall describe such property on the appropriate schedule.

(D) Character of Property Placed in Trust

While both grantors are alive, property transferred to this trust shall retain its original character. If the trust is revoked, the trustee shall distribute the trust property to the grantors based on the same ownership rights they had before the property was transferred to the trust, as specified below.

(1) Shared Property

All trust property listed on Schedule A:

④   is community property _____

identify the character of shared property listed in Schedule A

_____

_____

_____ .

(2) Separate Property

The trust property listed on Schedule B shall retain its character as the separate property of

_____ Lien Yu _____. ~~The trust property listed on Schedule C~~

wife's name

~~shall retain its character as the separate property of~~ _____ .

_____

husband's name

~~[Make appropriate deletions if wife and/or husband has no separate property.]~~

[Section 2, Paragraphs E-F, and Section 3 omitted for this example.]

IV. BENEFICIARIES

(A) Husband's Primary and Alternate Beneficiaries

Upon the death of _____ Tau Yu _____, trust property

husband's name

owned by _____ Tau Yu _____, as his share of the trust property

husband's name

listed on Schedule A and any separate property listed on Schedule C shall be distributed as specified to the beneficiaries named in this section.

1. Real Estate

A house can be listed by its street address—for example, "The house and real estate at 10001 Lakeway Drive, Seaview, Florida." Similarly, unimproved property can usually be listed by its common name: "The lots previously owned by the grantor on 50 to 80 Alligator Road, Seaview, Florida."

Usually, the street address is enough. It's not necessary to use the "legal description" found on the deed, which gives a subdivision plat number or a metes-and-bounds description. But if the property has no street address or common name—for example, if it is undeveloped land, off road, out in the country, you need to designate exactly what land you're referring to. So carefully copy the full legal description, word for word, from your deed.

If you own a house and several adjacent lots, it's a good idea to indicate that you are transferring the entire parcel to your living trust by describing the land as well as the house.

Example

The house at 390 Normal Road, Montclair, New Jersey, and all unimproved land between 390 Normal Road and 320 Normal Road.

Real estate often contains items that are properly classified as personal property. For instance, farms are often sold with tools and animals. If you intend to leave both real estate and personal property together to a beneficiary, make clear what this "together" consists of. It's best to specify the large-ticket items (tractor, cattle) and refer generally to the rest of the items as "personal property."

- *"240-acre truck farm on Route 11, in Whitman County, Iowa, with all tools, animals, tractors, threshers and other machines and other personal property located there."*
- *"Fishing cabin on the Wild River in Washington County, Maine, with all the fishing gear, furniture, tools and other personal property found there."*
- *"The house at 442 Wanaha Bay Road, Island of Hawaii, Hawaii, and all personal possessions and household furnishings in the house."*
- *"The mobile home permanently located at E-Z motor camp, Kalispell, Montana, and all possessions and furnishings contained in it."*

If you own real estate with someone else and are transferring only your share to the trust, you don't need to specify how big a share you own. Just describe the property. The trust schedules then state that you are transferring all your interest in the property, whatever share that is, to the living trust.

Examples

Rhea owns a one-fifth interest in an apartment house located in Atlanta, Georgia. She prepares a deed transferring her one-fifth interest to her living trust's name. On the trust schedule, she simply writes *"The interest in the apartment house at 434 Madison Street, Atlanta, Georgia, previously owned by the grantor."*

Time-shares. A time-share in a house or apartment is real estate and can be transferred to the trust like any other real estate. You can describe your interest as: *"the grantor's share in ___(address)___,"* or *"the grantor's right to three weeks per year use of ___(address)___."*

2. Furnishings and Household Items

Household furnishings can be generally listed:

- *"The house and real estate at 12 High St., Chicago, Illinois, and all household furnishings and personal possessions in it."*
- *"All the grantor's household goods and personal possessions located at 82 West Ave., Chicago, Ill."*

Or you can get more specific:

- *"All the furniture normally kept in the house at 44123 Derby Ave., Ross, KY."*
- *"All furniture and household items normally kept in the house at 869 Hopkins St., Great Falls, Montana."*

You can also list individual items, if you plan to leave them separately.

- *"The antique brass bed in the master bedroom in the house at 33 Walker Ave., Fort Lee, New Jersey."*
- *"Daumier print captioned 'Les beaux jours de la vie.'"*
- *"Two Victorian rocking chairs in the living room at 75 Washington Street, Jefferson, Montana."*

3. Bank and Money Market Accounts

You can list bank accounts by any means sufficient to identify them. Generally, it makes sense to list the account number:

- *"Bank account # 78-144212-8068 at Oceanside Savings, Miami, Florida, Market St. Branch."*
- *"Savings Account No. 9384-387, Arlington Bank, Arlington, MN."*
- *"Money Market Account 47-223 at Charles Schwab & Co., Inc., San Francisco, CA."*

4. Cash

You cannot transfer cash to a living trust simply by stating a dollar figure on the schedule. For example, if you list "$25,000" on Schedule A, this doesn't transfer that amount of cash to the trust, because no source for these funds is given. Instead, list a specific source of cash. You can then make specific cash gifts from this source when you name your trust beneficiaries. Here are some examples:

- *"Bank account #33-931007-6214 at Bonanza Thrift, Miami, Florida."*
- *"$25,000 from the grantor's stash in his desk."* This is obviously risky. If the money is moved from the desk, technically it is no longer owned by the trust.

5. Securities

Securities, including mutual fund accounts, need to be listed clearly enough so there is no question what property is referred to:

- *"Mutual fund account #6D-32 2240001, at International Monetary Inc., Chicago, Illinois."*
- *"All stock and any other assets in account #144-16-4124, at Smith Barney & Co., New York City, branch at 58th St./6th Ave."*
- *"100 shares of General Motors common stock."*
- *"Mutual funds in account # 55-144-2001-7, Calvert Social Responsibility Fund, Boston, MA."*

6. Sole Proprietorship Business Property

With a sole proprietorship business that has not been incorporated, the proprietor is the legal owner of all assets of the business, including the business name and any "good will." So you can simply list all assets of that business as a single item of trust property.

- *"All assets of the grantor doing business as Mulligan's Fish Market, 44 Wellington St., Wymouth, Kentucky."*
- *"All assets of the grantor doing business as Fourth Street Records and CDs, 10 Piper's Lane, Hoboken, NJ."*

- *"All assets of the grantor doing business as Jim Pine Plumbing, 477 Market Street, Fort Lauderdale, Florida."*

You can also divide up the business assets if you're leaving different parts to different people. For example:

- *"All accounts receivable of the business known as Garcia's Restaurant, 988 17th St., Atlanta, GA."*
- *"The business name, good will, lease and all food and food preparation and storage equipment, including refrigerator, freezer, hand mixers and slicer used at Garcia's Restaurant, 988 17th St., Atlanta, GA."*

(See Chapter 6, "Choosing What Property to Put in Your Living Trust," Section C.)

7. Shares in a Closely-Held Corporation

- *"The stock of ABC Hardware, Inc., formerly owned by the grantors."*

(See Chapter 6, Section C.)

8. Partnership Interest

Because a partnership is a legal entity that can own property, you don't need to list items of property owned by the partnership. Just list your partnership interest:

- *"All the grantor's interest in the Don and Dan's Bait Shop Partnership, Belmore, Oregon."*

(See Chapter 6, Section C.)

9. Shares in a Solely-Owned Corporation

- *"All shares in the XYZ Corporation."*
- *"All stock in Fern's Olde Antique Shoppe, Inc., 23 Turnbridge Court, Danbury, Connecticut."*

10. Life Insurance Proceeds

- *"The proceeds of Acme Co. Life Insurance Policy #9992A."*

(See Chapter 6, Section B.)

11. Miscellaneous Items of Personal Property

There are various ways you can list items of personal property on a trust schedule, depending primarily on whether you want to leave separate items to different beneficiaries, or all of one type of item to a sole (or group of) beneficiaries.

For items of significant monetary or sentimental value, you may want to list them individually.

- *"The Macintosh SE30 computer (serial number 129311) with keyboard (serial number 165895)."*
- *"The medical textbooks in the grantor's office at 1702 Parker Towers, San Francisco, CA."*
- *"The photograph collection usually kept at 321 Glen St., Omaha, NE."*
- *"The collection of European stamps, including [describe particularly valuable stamps], usually kept at 440 Loma Prieta Blvd., #450, San Jose, CA."*
- *"The Martin D-35 acoustic guitar, serial number 477597."*
- *"The signed 1960 Ernie Banks baseball card kept in safe deposit box 234, First National Bank of Augusta, Augusta, IL."*
- *"The Baldwin upright piano kept at 985 Dawson Court, South Brenly, Massachusetts."*
- *"Gold earrings with small rubies in them, purchased from Charles Shreve and Co. in 1971."*

If you are like most people, you have all sorts of minor personal possessions you don't want to bother itemizing. To deal with them, you can group a number of items in one category:

- *"all tools"* (or *"all carpenter's tools, including power saws, in possession of the grantor"*),
- *"all dolls"*
- *"baseball cards"*
- *"records, tapes and compact disks"* or

- *"machines and equipment."*

Of course, some items without large monetary value can have great emotional worth to you and your family: a photo album, an old music box, a treasured chair. These can be separately listed as you desire.

If you're leaving all these groups of personal items to one beneficiary, there's no need to separately list them, even as groups. You can simply conclude your list with one catch-all item, such as "all personal property previously owned by the grantor."

Sample Schedule A for Shared Property

Below is a sample of a draft Schedule A for shared property for Form 2, a basic shared trust. When the final trust form is typed, the schedule is likewise typed, eliminating the printed instructions on the form. The final typed schedule is attached to the trust document.

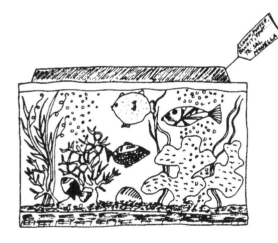

Sample

SCHEDULE A

Shared property placed in trust:

The house and real estate at 428 Dubuque Drive, Alameda, California.

All shares of stock in the Mo-To Corporation, Alameda, California.

The grand piano located at 428 Dubuque Drive, Alameda, California.

The Diebenkorn painting located at 428 Dubuque Drive, Alameda, California.

All other household possessions and furnishings located at 428 Dubuque Drive, Alameda, California.

Money market account #7033372, Working Assets, Boston, MA.

Certificate of Deposit No. 10235, Lighthouse Savings and Loan Association, Oakland, CA.

All copyrights and rights to royalties previously owned by the grantors in these books, currently published by Fly High Press, Berkeley, California:

Dunk It: How You Can Learn to Dunk a Basketball

Winning Through Whining, a Self-Help Guide

Watch It! How to Survive Urban Life

Step 4: Identify the Nature of Shared Trust Property (Forms 2 and 3 only)

If you and your spouse are creating a trust together, you should state in the trust document that all shared property transferred to the trust (listed on Schedule A) retains the legal character it had before. That means that it stays community property if you live in a community property state. If you live in a common law state, all shared property transferred to the trust should be owned equally by the couple as tenants in common, not as joint tenants or tenants by the entirety. (See Chapter 11, "Transferring Property to Your Trust," Section A. See also Chapter 6, "Choosing What Property to Put in Your Living Trust," for a discussion of community property states and common law states.)

If you don't share ownership 50-50, be sure to list each person's percentage of ownership.

If you are an unmarried couple who owns property together, you can likewise state that shared ownership property on Schedule A be returned to the couple in 50-50 ownership if the trust is ever revoked.

To define the nature of shared trust property, insert one of the following clauses in the living trust form where you see: "All trust property listed on Schedule A," followed by a line with ④:

- If you live in a common law state:

  "was co-owned equally by the grantors as tenants in common and shall retain that character after being transferred to this trust. If the trust is revoked, this property shall be returned to the grantors as co-owned equally by them as tenants in common."

- If you live in a community property state:

  "was community property of the grantors and shall retain that character after being transferred to this trust. If the trust is revoked, this property shall be returned to grantors as their community property."

- If you are an unmarried couple:

"was co-owned equally by the grantors as tenants in common. Any power reserved to the grantors to alter, amend, modify or revoke this trust, as to the property listed in Schedule A, must be exercised by both grantors, in writing, to be effective. If this trust is revoked, this property shall be returned to the grantors as co-owned equally by them as tenants in common."

As I've discussed, you are free to change ownership of trust property if you wish—for example, to convert one spouse's separately-owned property to shared or community property or vice versa.

Step 5: Decide If You Want Management of Trust Property If You Become Incapacitated

Form 1 provides that the successor trustee takes over management of the trust if you (the grantor) become incapacitated and are unable to manage trust property. These provisions eliminate any need for court proceedings to appoint a guardian or custodian for trust property if you become incapacitated.

The basic shared trust (Form 2) and an AB trust (Form 3) provide that if both spouses become incapacitated, or if the survivor becomes incapacitated after one spouse dies, the trust property is managed by the successor trustee for the grantor's benefit.

It's sensible and standard to provide for management of trust property if you become incapacitated. If you want this, simply leave the clause where you see ⑤ as is. If for some very unusual reason you don't want this, delete the clause where you see the ⑤.

The term "incapacitated" is not defined in the trust document. It doesn't need to be; the trust states that physical or mental incapacity must be determined by a doctor, in writing. That is the conventional way of determining incapacity.

Your successor trustee won't have legal authority over property that's not in your living trust. To give someone that power, you need a document called a Durable Power of Attorney for Finances.

If you don't prepare a Durable Power of Attorney, and you become incapacitated, property not transferred to your living trust will need to be managed by a court-appointed conservator or guardian.

For this reason (and because you may receive other property or income in the future that doesn't make it into the trust), I strongly suggest that you also create a Durable Power of Attorney for Finances. See Chapter 15, "A Living Trust as Part of Your Estate Plan," Section E.

Step 6: Name Your Successor Trustee

In the blanks with the ⑥ on the trust forms, name your successor trustee and your alternate successor trustee. (Choosing your successor trustee is discussed in Chapter 7, "Trustees.") You've already named yourself as the original trustee.

Naming Co-Successor Trustees

If you name more than one successor trustee or more than one alternate successor trustee, you need to specify in your trust document how the authority of the co-trustees is to be shared. Clearly, this is your personal decision, depending on how well the co-trustees get along, and whether or not you think it's safe to let any of them act individually for the trust. So, depending on your needs, immediately after you name your successor trustees and alternate successor trustees, you'll insert one of the following clauses from the form:

- *"Any of the successor trustees has full and independent authority to act for and represent the trust."*

  or

- *"All the successor trustees must agree in writing to any transaction involving the trust or trust property."*

If you have only one successor trustee and don't use co-successor trustees, you'll need to delete all this material from the form.

LISTING SPECIFIC TRUSTEE POWERS

The trust forms provide that the trustee has "all authority and powers" your state's laws allow. But the trust forms also list specific powers, including the power to sell trust real estate, buy or sell stocks and several other detailed powers. All of these specific powers are normally included in the general authority conferred on a trustee under state law. But banks, title companies, stock brokerage companies and other financial institutions frequently insist that a trustee be specifically authorized by the trust document to engage in a transaction involving their institution. So spelling out these powers often makes the successor trustee's work much easier in the real world.

Bond

The forms provide that no trustee has to post a bond. A bond is basically an insurance policy guaranteeing that a person will honestly carry out his or her duties; it pays off up to a stated amount if he or she doesn't. Bonding companies, which are normally divisions of insurance companies, issue a bond in exchange for a premium, usually about 10% of the face amount of the bond.

If you select a trustworthy successor trustee, there's no reason for a bond. In almost all situations, the question never comes up. Since the successor trustee handles the trust outside any court system, there's no forum where a demand for a bond could be raised. But just in case the question is somehow raised in a lawsuit (very unlikely), it's sensible to have waived any bond requirement. The cost of a bond would have to be paid for by your estate, and your beneficiaries would then receive less. Also, it's difficult for an individual to even get a bond in many states.

Requiring a successor trustee's bond. If you do want your successor trustee to post a bond, see a lawyer.

Step 7: Name the Primary and Alternate Trust Beneficiaries

Now you enter the names of your trust beneficiaries, naming who gets what.

With a trust for an individual (Form 1) or a basic shared living trust (Form 2), insert their names, and descriptions of property given them, in the blanks where you see ⑦. You can make as many separate gifts as you need to. The forms have spaces for five; if you have more, use another sheet of paper.

Reminder for Unmarried Couples: If you are an unmarried couple and use either Form 2 or 3, you'll need to change the printed form's references to spouses. Thus "Husband's Beneficiaries" or "Wife's Beneficiaries" must be changed to the appropriate individual's name. Example: "Al Smith's Beneficiaries" instead of "Husband's Beneficiaries."

With an AB trust (Form 3), each spouse can make up to three separate gifts to primary beneficiaries, outside of the AB trust property, and can list alternates for these gifts. Of course, it isn't required that you make such gifts; many couples simply leave everything to each other. (See Chapter 5, "The Tax-Saving AB Trust," Section D.)

With Form 3, each spouse will also name his or her final beneficiaries, to receive the marital trust property after the surviving spouse dies, and alternate final beneficiaries. See Step 8B, below.

1. How to Enter Beneficiaries' Names

Many people worry that some precise, technical language must be used in living trusts to identify their beneficiaries, or their gifts won't be legally binding. Fortunately, this isn't true. You simply need to give the name that clearly identifies a beneficiary, so that your successor trustee understands to whom the gift is made. You don't have to worry about using a person's "legal" name, such as the full name on her birth certificate. Nor do you need to list the beneficiary's address or Social Security number.

If you name an institution (charitable or not) to inherit property from your trust, enter its complete name. It may be commonly known by a shortened version, which could cause confusion if there are similarly-named organizations. Call to ask if you're unsure. (An institution that stands to inherit some of your money will be more than happy to help you.) Also, be sure to specify if you want a specific branch or part of a national organization to receive your gift—for example, a local chapter of the Sierra Club.

Gifts to charities. A few states (the District of Columbia, Florida, Georgia, Idaho, Mississippi, Montana and Ohio) restrict your ability to make large gifts to charities. These laws, holdovers from centuries past, were enacted primarily to discourage churches and other charitable organizations from using unfair means, such as promising elderly people a place in heaven, to fill their own coffers at the expense of a surviving family. If you're leaving a relatively small percentage of your estate to a charity, you needn't worry about these restrictions. But if you desire to leave a large part of your estate (certainly more than half) to charity, especially if you believe your spouse or children will object, or that you may not have too long to live, check with an attorney.

2. Identifying Property Left to Beneficiaries

There are three basic approaches to identifying property in a beneficiary clause:

1. Use exactly the same words you used on your property schedule. For example, if you listed "Money Market Account #60-32 2240001 at International Money Inc., Boston, MA" on your schedule, use exactly the same words in the beneficiary clause.

2. Group items left to a certain beneficiary. If you listed and specifically identified a number of similar items on a schedule (for example, five bank accounts, ten valuable paintings, four automobiles) and you wish to leave all items in a particular group to the same beneficiary, it's sufficient to say "all bank accounts listed on Schedule A" or "all paintings listed on Schedule A."

3. Be more specific than your trust schedule. For example, suppose on Schedule A you listed "all books in possession of the grantor," to indicate that ownership of all your books is transferred to your living trust. However, you don't wish to leave all these books to one beneficiary. When making gifts, you could state:

- *"Beth Ruveen shall be given all books by F. Scott Fitzgerald in the possession of the grantor."*

- *"John Advale shall be given all books in French in the possession of the grantor."*

- *"Jim Horton shall be given all books in the possession of the grantor, except those left or given by this trust document to Beth Ruveen and John Advale."*

Shared property. On Forms 2 and 3, each spouse can give away only his or her half-interest in shared property, not all of it. So, when naming a beneficiary or beneficiaries for property listed on Schedule A of a shared living trust, it must be clear that each spouse is giving away only his or her share of the co-owned property. To accomplish this, when you leave a gift from property on Schedule A, add an identifying phrase to the beneficiary clause. Here are two examples; the language you must add is in italics:

If property left to one beneficiary:

Karen Zombanski shall be given all _Lonnie Zombanski's_
beneficiary

interest in the house listed on Schedule A.
property identified

If property left to more than one beneficiary:

Charles Berry shall be given 50%, and
beneficiary

Le Petite Richard and _B. Diddly_
beneficiary   beneficiary

each shall be given _25% of all Jackson Smith's interest in the_

the stock account at Smith Barney, NYC, #177-4N-2044,

as listed on Schedule A.

3. Naming Children or Young Adults as Beneficiaries

You name a child or a young adult as a beneficiary exactly as you do an adult beneficiary, entering the child's name and identifying the trust property left to him or her.

Later in the trust document, you can arrange for an adult to manage property left to a young beneficiary. (See Steps 10 and 11.)

4. Leaving All Trust Property to One Beneficiary or Group of Beneficiaries

If you are using Form 1 or 2 and you want to leave all of your trust property to one person or to be shared by several, you can use just one beneficiary clause. Here are some examples:

- For a basic shared trust:
  All property to your spouse: *"John Andrews shall be given all grantor Mary Andrews' interest in the property listed on Schedule A and Schedule B."*

- For an individual trust:
  All property equally to children: *"Steve Cronin, Elizabeth Cronin and Roarke Cronin shall be given all property listed on Schedule A in equal shares."*

5. Leaving Property to Several Beneficiaries to Share

You may want to leave an item of trust property to be shared among several beneficiaries. This is fine, as long as you use language that clearly identifies what share each beneficiary is to receive. This is best done by using percentages. Be sure you modify the language of the beneficiary clause, because you are not giving "all" your interest in the property to any one person. (Shared gifts are discussed in detail in Chapter 8, "Choosing Your Beneficiaries," Section D.)

Example

From a stock account transferred to his living trust, Jim Denniston makes the following gifts:

- *"Melinda Denniston shall be given 20% from the trust's stock account #660134-N, Dean Witter Co."*
- *"Mike Denniston shall be given 30% from the trust's stock account #660134-N, Dean Witter Co."*
- *"Roger Denniston shall be given 5% from the trust's stock account #660134-N, Dean Witter Co."*
- *"Margo Denniston shall be given 35% from the trust's stock account #660134-N, Dean Witter Co."*
- *"Cerrita Gibbs shall be given 10% from the trust's stock account #660134-N, Dean Witter Co."*

6. Naming Beneficiaries of Proceeds from a Life Insurance Policy

If you have named your living trust as the beneficiary of a life insurance policy, you can simply name, within the trust, a beneficiary, or beneficiaries, for any insurance proceeds payable to the trust. Remember, you don't need to list the policy on a trust schedule, because the trust never owns the policy; it is simply the beneficiary of it.

Example

"The grantor's children, Zack Philson and Zelda Philson, shall be given, in equal shares, all life insurance proceeds on the grantor's life paid to the trust."

If the beneficiaries you name are minors or young adults, you can arrange for someone to manage property, including insurance proceeds that they inherit while still young. (See Steps 10 and 11.)

7. Explanations and Commentary Accompanying a Gift

There are times, particularly in family situations, when explaining the reasons for your gifts can help avoid hurt feelings or family fights. If you wish, you can provide a brief commentary when making a gift. There are two ways to do it: in the trust document itself, or in a separate letter.

In the trust document. You'll need extra space for your comments. For your rough draft, you can simply write out your comments on a separate piece of paper and attach it to the trust form, with a note on where they should be inserted in the trust document. When you have your final trust typed, your comments will be integrated into the trust form.

Examples

- *"The grantor's business associate, Mildred Parker, who worked honestly and competently with her over the years, and cheerfully put up with her occasional depressions, shall be given $40,000 from the Money Market Fund #166-SJ-4111, Parnassus Mutual Funds, San Francisco, California."*
- *"The grantor's best friend, Hank Salmon, whom the grantor enjoyed fishing with for so many years, shall be given the cabin and boathouse on Lake Serene and the boat and outboard motor in the boathouse."*

- *"Theodore Stein shall be given 40% of Alfred Stein's interest in the house at 465 Merchant St., Miami, Florida.*

  "Sandra Stein Rosen shall be given 40% of Alfred Stein's interest in the house at 465 Merchant St., Miami, Florida.

  "Howard Stein shall be given 20% of Alfred Stein's interest in the house at 465 Merchant St., Miami, Florida.

  "I love all my children deeply and equally. I give 20% to Howard because he received substantial family funds to go through medical school, so it's fair that my other two children receive more of my property now."

- *"Matt Jackson shall be given my bank account #41-6621-9403 at First Maple Bank.*

  "I love all my children deeply and equally. I leave more of my property to Matt than my other children because Matt is physically disadvantaged and is likely to need special care and attendants throughout his life."

Notice that here you can refer to yourself in the first person, as "I," not "the grantor." It just sounds too awkward to express deep feelings as "the grantor." Besides, this type of wording isn't making a gift, but explaining it, so it's hard to imagine that any trouble could possibly arise from referring to yourself as "I" when speaking of your love for your kids.

In an accompanying letter. Another approach is to write a letter stating your views and feelings and attach it to your living trust document. Many people prefer this approach because it allows personal sentiments to be kept private. The living trust will have to be shown to people in various institutions, from banks to title companies to brokerage offices to county records offices. Many people don't want their personal feelings exposed to strangers in the business world. A letter can simply be removed from the trust document when showing the trust to any outsider. Also, if you have a lot to say, a letter is generally better than trying to express all your sentiments in the trust document itself.

Your letter isn't a legal part of your trust document, and it has no legal effect. It is prudent for you to state in your letter that you understand this, to eliminate any possibility someone could claim you intended the letter to somehow modify the terms of your trust.

The scope of your remarks is limited only by your imagination, short of libel. (If you write something so malicious (and false) that you libel someone, your estate could be liable for damages.) Some writers have expressed, at length and in their own chosen words, their love for a mate, children or friend. By contrast, Benjamin Franklin's will left his son William, who was sympathetic to England during our Revolution, only some land in Nova Scotia and stated, "The fact he acted against me in the late war, which is of public notoriety, will account for my leaving him no more of an estate that he endeavored to deprive me of."

8. Imposing a Survivorship Period

When you leave property to a primary beneficiary, you can specify that if the beneficiary doesn't survive you by some specified period of time, the gift will go to the alternate beneficiary, if you name one, or the residuary beneficiary if you don't name an alternate. The pros and cons of survivorship periods are discussed in Chapter 8, "Choosing Your Beneficiaries," Section F.

If you want to add a survivorship period, simply insert a specific time period after naming a primary beneficiary.

Example

"___*Hester Dinsdale*___ shall be given the grantor's
     primary beneficiary's name

interest in the antique doll collection located at

61 Hawthorn Lane, Gabels, Massachusetts .
     property

"If ___*Hester Dinsdale*___ doesn't survive the grantor by
          beneficiary

30 days, that property shall be given to ___*Pearl Dinsdale*___."
                              alternate beneficiary

9. Naming Alternate Beneficiaries

As discussed, you are not required to name an alternate beneficiary for a gift. Some people, understandably, don't wish to contemplate the chance of an inheritor, usually someone younger, dying before they do. But most people name an alternate beneficiary for each gift to a primary beneficiary if they wish to. After all, there is always the chance that the primary beneficiary may not survive you, and you won't be able to amend your trust in time.

With Form 1 or Form 2, if you don't name an alternate, the property that beneficiary would have received will be distributed to the person or institution you name as your "residuary beneficiary." (See Step 8A, below.)

With an AB trust (Form 3), you can name alternate beneficiaries only for any specific gifts you make (up to three). If the primary beneficiary and alternate predecease you, that gift becomes part of the A or B trust property.

You can name more than one person or institution as alternate beneficiaries. These "co-alternate beneficiaries" share the property equally, unless you specify otherwise.

Example

Sherry names her husband as beneficiary of her interest in their house, which they have transferred to their basic shared living trust. As alternate beneficiaries, she names their three children, Sean, Colleen and Tim, to share equally.

Sherry's husband dies just before she does, leaving his half of the house to Sherry. Under the terms of the trust document, it stays in the living trust. At Sherry's death, because her husband (the primary beneficiary) is no longer alive, the house goes to the three children. All three own equal shares in all of it.

For shared gifts, it's easiest to name the other surviving beneficiaries to receive a deceased beneficiary's share. You can accomplish this by using or adapting the following language, which may require some minor changes in the printed portion of a beneficiary clause:

"_Gwen Riordan, Richard Riordan and Martha Riordan Ling_ shall be given _____ _Jack Riordan's_ _____
beneficiaries   grantor's name
interest in the house at _41 Sussex Road, Needles, Arizona_, in equal shares. If any of these beneficiaries doesn't survive _____ _Jack Riordan_ _____, the deceased beneficiary's interest shall be shared equally by the surviving beneficiaries."

You can also name different alternates for each beneficiary of a shared gift. For example, an older person who leaves a shared gift to his children may list each child's children (or spouse) as alternate beneficiaries for that child's share of the gift.

"_Gwen Riordan, Richard Riordan and Martha Riordan Ling_ shall be given all Jack Riordan's interest in _the house at 41 Sussex Road, Needles, Arizona_.
"If Gwen Riordan doesn't survive Jack Riordan, her children, Mike Riordan James and Tracy Riordan James, shall be given the interest in the property she would have received.

"If Richard Riordan doesn't survive Jack Riordan, Richard's child, Sean Riordan, shall be given the interest in the property she would have received.

"If Martha Riordan Ling doesn't survive Jack Riordan, her husband, Patrick Ling, shall be given the interest in the property she would have received."

Step 8A: Name Your Residuary Beneficiary (Forms 1 and 2 only)

If you are preparing an AB trust (Form 3), skip to Step 8B. If you are preparing a trust for one person (Form 1) or a basic shared living trust (Form 2), the next step is to name your residuary beneficiary or beneficiaries.

You must name one or more residuary beneficiaries for your living trust, where you see the (8A).

The residuary beneficiary of your living trust is the person or organization who will receive:

- any trust property designated for primary and alternate beneficiaries who die before you do

- any trust property that you didn't leave to a named beneficiary (this could include property you transferred to the trust later but didn't name a beneficiary for)

- any property you leave to your living trust through a pour-over will (Because property left through a pour-over will doesn't avoid probate, there's usually no reason to use one. See Chapter 16, "Wills," Section D.)

- any property that you actually transferred to your living trust but didn't list in the trust document.

Sometimes the residuary beneficiary of a basic living trust doesn't inherit anything from the trust, because all trust property is left to primary beneficiaries, with alternates. In this situation, naming a residuary beneficiary can be just a back-up measure, to guard against the extremely small chance that both a primary and alternate trust beneficiary do not survive you.

You may, however, deliberately leave the residuary beneficiary trust property by:

- Not naming specific beneficiaries for most trust property. Everything not left to a specific beneficiary will go to your residuary beneficiary. It's common, for example, for a grantor to leave much of his estate to his children as residuary beneficiaries.

- Adding property to the trust later and not amending your trust document to name a specific beneficiary to receive it after your death.

- Using a pour-over will to leave property to your living trust and not naming a specific beneficiary in the trust document to receive property that passes through the will.

Co-residuary beneficiaries. If you name more than one residuary beneficiary (or alternate residuary beneficiary), you need to state, in the clause, what portion or percentage each residuary beneficiary will receive. It's common, especially if one's children are the residuary beneficiaries, to state that they each receive an equal share.

Example

"The residuary beneficiaries…shall be Rachel Weinstock and Alan Weinstock, each to receive 50% of all trust property not specifically and validly disposed of…."[by earlier gifts]

Of course, you can also specify that residuary beneficiaries receive unequal shares. In that case, you must specify what percentage of the property each residuary beneficiary will receive.

Example

Zane Jilconty names three siblings—Lucy, Jill and Warren—as his residuary beneficiaries. For several reasons, he wants to leave them unequal amounts. So he provides, in his residuary clause, that his residuaries are: *"Lucy Jilconty, 50% of the residuary property; Jill Jilconty Jackson, 30% of the residuary property and Warren Jilconty, 20% of residuary property."*

Alternate residuary beneficiaries. You should also name an alternate residuary beneficiary, or beneficiaries, to be sure you have one final backup to receive trust property if all other beneficiaries, including your residuary beneficiary, predecease you and you can't amend your trust in time. (True, this is a remote possibility, but remote possibilities are lawyers' stock-in-trade, and even we at Nolo can't bring ourselves to completely jettison concern for such unlikely contingencies.)

Step 8B: Name Your Final Beneficiaries (Form 3 Only)

If you are preparing an AB trust, it's vital that each spouse name a final beneficiary or beneficiaries, and normally alternate final beneficiary(ies), where you see ⑧Ⓑ. Each spouse names his or her own final beneficiary or beneficiaries. Often these are the same people for both spouses, most commonly their children. But spouses can name different final beneficiaries if they want to. (See Chapter 5, Section B.)

The final beneficiaries will receive all property remaining in the A trust after the surviving spouse (the life beneficiary) dies. (See Chapter 5, "The Tax-Saving AB Trust," Section D.) The final beneficiaries might also receive any of the specific gifts the deceased spouse may have made, if both the specific beneficiary and the alternate beneficiary for a specific gift predecease that spouse. (A remote possibility, surely, but not impossible.) In that case, the specific gift becomes part of the Trust A property.

Each spouse's final beneficiaries also serve as the primary beneficiaries of Trust B, the surviving spouse's trust. As you know, after one spouse dies, the surviving spouse's trust remains revocable. But if he or she does not amend that trust and name new beneficiaries, the property in that trust (again, except for up to three specific gifts) will go to the final beneficiaries he or she named in the original trust document.

Charities as final beneficiaries. If you name a charity as a final beneficiary, and federal estate taxes are due, the IRS will take all the taxes from other gifts you've made. This may diminish the value of these gifts substantially, or even wipe some out. To avoid this, you can specify that any taxes be paid from the property inherited by the charity. Then the charity gets whatever is left. The math calculations here can get complex and confusing because the size of the charitable contribution depends on the amount of estate taxes, and vice versa. If you want to know how the exact figures work out, see a knowledgeable estate tax accountant or lawyer.

Step 9: Provide for Payment of Debts and Taxes

There are three ways to handle payment of debts and taxes after your death:

- leave it up to the successor trustee
- designate certain trust assets to be used
- direct that they be paid from what the residuary beneficiary receives. (This cannot be done with an AB trust.)

For many people, payment of debts and taxes is not a serious concern. Their estates are now well under the minimum estate tax threshold, so they don't expect that federal taxes will be due, and their debts are relatively minor—perhaps a few personal bills, credit card charges, household utilities and any unpaid bills from the last illness or funeral/burial costs.

1. Leave the Decision to the Trustee

You do not have to specify how your debts and taxes are to be paid. Many people prefer to leave this decision to their successor trustee, who will know what the real financial situation is when these debts must be paid. You can, at best, make only a reasonable guess now. If you direct that a specific asset or assets be used to pay any debts or estate taxes, it can cause problems later on. If you've also left the asset to a specific beneficiary, the provision for payment of debts and taxes takes priority, so that beneficiary may receive little or nothing from your gift. Also, if the property you identified isn't sufficient to pay all your debts and taxes, your successor trustee will still have to decide how to pay any balance due.

If allowing the trustee to make the decision makes sense to you, for an individual trust or basic shared living trust, where you see the ⑨, delete all language after the first sentence of the section, as shown in the example below.

DECIDING ABOUT DEBTS AND TAXES

(C) Payment by Trustee of the Grantor's Debts and Taxes

The grantor's debts and death taxes shall be paid by the trustee. ~~The trustee shall pay these from the following trust property:~~

⑨ _____

_____

_____ .

For an AB trust (Form 3), you need only delete the language after the first sentence from the first paragraph, because the second paragraph is not part of this trust form.

2. Designate Specific Assets

If you decide you want to make specific provisions for payment of your debts and taxes from trust property, write in the specific items you want used to pay them in the blank where you see the ⑨ on the trust forms. And do your best to be sure these assets will actually be sufficient to pay all your debts and taxes.

Example

"The grantor's debts and death taxes shall be paid by the trustee from the following trust property:

- *First, from the bank account #99-8062144, Wells Fargo Bank, Berkeley, California.*

- *Second, from stock account #82-304, Smith Barney & Co., San Francisco, California."*

Remember that any property you specify to pay your debts and taxes must be owned by your trust. That means you must list it on a property schedule and transfer title into the trustee's name. (That process is explained in Chapter 11, "Transferring Property to Your Trust.")

In a basic shared living trust or an AB trust, each spouse can specify the property to be used to pay his or her debts and death taxes.

Example

Sid and Ellen Wall want each's debts and taxes paid from a shared stock account. In their basic shared living trust, they provide:

"1. Wife's Debts

"Ellen Wall's debts and death taxes shall be paid by the trustee from her interest in stock account #0014463, Smith Barney & Co.

"2. Husband's Debts

"Sid Wall's debts and death taxes shall be paid by the trustee from the following trust property: his interest in stock account #0014463, Smith Barney & Co."

With an AB trust, the property a spouse specifies to be used to pay debts and taxes will normally be part of Trust A. So primarily what's accomplished by specifying assets to pay debts is to protect the specific gifts from being used to pay any debts and taxes.

3. Use Residuary Property

Yet another approach here is to specify that all your last debts and taxes be paid from any property that goes to the residuary beneficiary. Of course, you will want to be sure that those assets will cover any possible debts and taxes.

This method can't be used with an AB trust, because no property goes to a residuary beneficiary when the first spouse dies. There are only some specific gifts (if that spouse made any), and the property in Trust A.

Step 10: Create Children's Subtrusts

In the blank with the ⑩ on the trust forms, you establish children's subtrusts by listing each person (minor or young adult) you want to name as beneficiary of a child's subtrust. This may include minors and young adults you've named as alternate beneficiaries. Be sure not to list as children's subtrust beneficiaries any persons you want to make gifts to using the Uniform Transfers to Minors Act. You'll do that in Step 11. You cannot leave a gift to a minor by both the Uniform Transfers to Minors Act and a child's subtrust.

For each trust beneficiary you list here where you see the ⑪, you also state the age at which you want that beneficiary to receive his or her trust property. If you die before the beneficiary reaches the age you specify, the beneficiary's property will be retained in a child's subtrust until the age is reached. (See Chapter 9, "Property Left to Minor Children or Young Adults," Section B.) If you don't specify an age, each listed beneficiary will receive the trust property outright on becoming 35 years old.

Step 11: Create Custodianships Under the Uniform Transfers to Minors Act

If you want to make a gift to a child using your state's Uniform Transfers to Minors Act (UTMA), complete the custodianship clause where you see an ⑪. The form contains three blank clauses for individual beneficiaries, but you can add as many additional clauses as you want.

To complete the UTMA clause, begin by listing the state where you live (after doublechecking the list in Chapter 9, "Property Left to Minor Children or Young Adults," Section B, to be sure your state has adopted the UTMA). Then, to make an individual gift, you fill in the beneficiary's name, the custodian's name and the age the beneficiary will receive the property outright. You can also use an UTMA clause to leave gifts to other minors, such as grandchildren, if they live in a state that has an UTMA law.

The age a child will receive the gift outright depends on state law; Chapter 9, Section B, lists each state's termination age. In some states, you are given a limited choice of when the custodianship ends. For example, you can choose any age from 18 to 21 in Maine, and 18 to 25 in California. But most states allow you no choice. The gift must end at the age set by the state. So to complete the age provision of an UTMA gift clause in states where you have no choice, all you need do is fill in the age from the list in Chapter 9.

Examples

In California, where age can be varied from 18 to 25:

"All property Ned Clark becomes entitled to under this trust document shall be given to Mary Clark as custodian for Ned Clark under the California Uniform Transfers to Minors Act until Ned Clark reaches age 24."

In New Hampshire, where age cannot be varied from 21:

"All property Luisa Brookside shall become entitled to under this document shall be given to Nancy Curtis as custodian for Luisa Brookside under the New Hampshire Uniform Transfers to Minors Act until Luisa Brookside reaches age 21."

IF YOU DO NOT CREATE A CHILD'S SUBTRUST OR MAKE GIFTS USING THE UNIFORM TRANSFERS TO MINORS ACT

If you do not create a child's subtrust or make any gifts under the Uniform Transfers to Minors Act, simply cross out the blank section(s) before your final trust is typed. These clauses have been placed at the end of the trust form so that you do not have to renumber other trust clauses if you delete both of them.

If you create children's subtrusts but do not make gifts under the Uniform Transfers to Minors Act, simply delete that later clause. Again, no renumbering of clauses is required.

However, if you do not create any children's subtrusts but do make gifts under the Uniform Transfers to Minors Act, you must delete the children's subtrust clause and renumber the Uniform Transfers clause. To do this, simply change the clause number for gifts under the Uniforms Transfers to Minors Act:

- From "X" to "IX" in the Living Trust for One Person
- From "XI" to "X" in the Basic Shared Living Trust or AB Trust.

Step 12: Decide About Reports to Final Beneficiaries (Form 3 Only)

You have a choice regarding reports the surviving spouse (as trustee) must give the final beneficiaries about an operational A trust.

The trust form provides, where you see the ⑫ (in Section V(C)6), that the surviving spouse doesn't have to provide any accountings, except that the spouse must give the final beneficiaries copies of the trust's annual federal income tax return.

Some couples, understandably, feel that even providing tax returns is an intrusion into their financial privacy—that just because they've established a trust to save on estate taxes for their children is no reason they must reveal details of their finances to them yearly. If you feel this way, simply delete the final portion of this accounting clause, so that it reads:

"No accounting of the Trust A shall be required of the trustee."

Another version is to provide that no accounting is required as long as the surviving spouse serves as trustee, but when the successor trustee takes over, accountings are required. If you decide on this approach, here is the clause to use when you see the ⑫ (Part V(C)6):

"No accounting of Trust A shall be required as long as the surviving spouse serves as trustee. When any successor trustee serves as trustee of Trust A, the final beneficiaries shall be provided with copies of the annual trust income tax return."

Unless the surviving spouse becomes incapacitated and cannot serve as trustee for a while, the successor trustee will take over only when the surviving spouse dies. So usually, this last clause will require the successor trustee to provide only the one final trust income tax return to the beneficiaries. The trust property should be rapidly transferred to the final beneficiaries, and the last trust income tax return is just one part of closing down the trust.

E. Prepare Your Final Trust Document

When you have completely filled in the trust form, proofread it carefully. Check to be sure you have:

- included all property you want to leave through the trust
- clearly and accurately identified all property (doublecheck account and serial numbers, for example)
- included all beneficiaries to whom you want to leave property
- spelled beneficiaries' (including alternate and residuary beneficiaries) names correctly and consistently

- made adequate arrangements for management of trust property that young beneficiaries might inherit.

When preparing the final trust, you want a document that looks as much like a conventional lawyer's living trust as possible. So don't include any of the following material from your draft form in your final version:

- The top caption of the form, such as "Form 2, Basic Shared Living Trust." You can leave the heading of the trust schedules as printed. For example, if you use a Schedule C, "Schedule C, husband's separate property placed in trust," this does not need to be crossed out or changed.

- Instructions

- Circled numbers

- Any printed material on the form that doesn't apply to you. This may include:

- blank beneficiary clauses, if you don't have as many beneficiaries as the forms provide space for

- the alternate beneficiary provision of a beneficiary clause, if you decided not to name alternates for a specific gift

- all material relating to subtrusts for minor beneficiaries, if you didn't create any

- all material relating to the Uniform Transfers to Minors act, if you didn't make any gifts using it.

Cross out all material you want to eliminate before the final trust document is typed.

The ① _____ Living Trust 　　　　　your name	The ~~①~~ *Denis Clifford* Living Trust 　　　　~~your name~~	The Denis Clifford Living Trust

Once you're satisfied that your trust form is fully completed, have the final document, including all trust schedules, prepared from your draft. You can either type it (or have it typed) or use a word processor. The final version should be prepared on good quality (bond) 8-1/2" x 11" typing paper. Although not required by law, obviously it makes sense to use non-erasable paper.

Be sure the pages of the final document are consecutively numbered correctly. You may well have to change the numbering from that on the form. For instance, if you add material (such as commentary about gifts), or have quite a number—say 16—of primary beneficiaries, you'll have to renumber the pages of your final document. Similarly, if you deleted material (such as the sections on children's subtrusts or gifts under the Uniform Transfers to Minors Act), you'll need to renumber the pages of your final document.

After the final trust document has been typed, carefully proofread it.

F. Consider Having Your Work Checked by a Lawyer

Once you are sure your final trust document is clear and correct, consider whether or not, in your circumstances, it makes sense to have your living trust checked by a lawyer who is familiar with living trusts. If you have any questions or doubts about your trust, it can be wise to have a lawyer review it. If your estate is large enough to be subject to estate tax (at least $625,000), this can be a particularly good idea. Also, if you have a long list of property and a number of beneficiaries and alternate beneficiaries, you may wish to have an experienced person review it. On the other hand, if your desires are clear and straightforward, and you're confident your trust unambiguously transfers your property to your named beneficiaries, a lawyer's review is unlikely to be necessary.

Unfortunately, it often is not easy to find a lawyer who will accept the responsibility to review a trust you've prepared. (See Chapter 17, "If You Need Expert Help,"

Section A.) So, while you might consider lawyer review a prudent idea, don't count on it until you've found a willing lawyer.

G. Sign Your Living Trust in Front of a Notary

It is essential that you sign your trust document and have your signature notarized by a Notary Public in the state where you live, even if you work in another state. Normally, no witnesses watch you sign a living trust. Because of this, it's always possible that after your death someone could claim that the signature wasn't genuine. As you won't be around to verify it then, you should do it now. The best way to remove any question of whether or not the signature on the document is authentic is to sign it in front of a notary.

Special Florida requirements. In Florida, it is customary, though not legally required, to have your living trust witnessed by two witnesses. It's safest to go along with this custom. Since the notary counts as one, you must have at least one other. Use the special Florida Witnessing Form 4, in the Appendix.

The signature line on the trust form is preceded by a provision entitled "Certification by Grantor(s)." Here you state that you've read the trust document and approve of it. This is a bit of legalese, included to make your trust look more like ones with which most financial institutions are familiar.

A notarization form is included with each living trust form in the Appendix. If your notary prefers to use a different form, fine—the important thing is to get the notarization done.

Both spouses must sign a basic shared trust or AB trust, and both spouses must appear before a notary.

Don't stop now. Even after your trust document is signed and notarized, you're not done. You must transfer the property you listed in the trust schedules into the name of the trust. Do it as soon as possible. Chapter 11, "Transferring Property to Your Trust," shows you how. 🦃

chapter 11

TRANSFERRING PROPERTY TO YOUR TRUST

*A*fter you sign your living trust document, you have a valid living trust. But the trust is of absolutely no use to you until the property you listed in the trust document (on the property schedules) is actually transferred into the trust. Lawyers call this "funding" the trust.

Transferring your property to your living trust is crucial, and takes some time and paperwork, but it's not difficult. You should be able to do it yourself, without a lawyer.

WE'RE COUNTING ON YOU: MAKE SURE YOU DO IT

Many lawyers who prepare living trusts insist on doing all the property-transfer work themselves, because they claim their clients cannot be trusted to do this work themselves. In other words, lawyers get paid hundreds of dollars per hour to do paperwork and won't allow their clients to do it.

This book, and Nolo Press, rest on the belief that people can be trusted to understand basic legal forms and do the work required to make the forms work. It is absolutely essential that you do the work necessary to formally transfer your property to your trust. If you don't, your trust will not work and, perhaps worse, you'll be proving that those lawyers who say people just can't be trusted to do basic tasks correctly are, sadly, sometimes correct. So, study this chapter carefully and be absolutely sure you've properly transferred all trust property into the trust's name.

A. Paperwork

For property without a document of title (ownership document), you don't need to do anything but prepare your trust document, including listing the property on a trust schedule. A document of title is a formal ownership paper, such as a deed, pink slip on a car or bank account registration form. Property without a document of title includes most furniture, clothing, books, appliances and other household goods, as well as some more valuable items, like jewelry, art works, furs, precious metals, electronic and computer equipment and most farm equipment.

If you want to be extra cautious, you can prepare a written "Assignment of Property" of these kinds of property to the trust, using Form 5 or 6, but this is not required. It's merely an option some conservative lawyers use to provide additional written proof that these items of property have been transferred to the trust. While it's not necessary, preparing an Assignment of Property form can't hurt.

For items that have a title document that shows ownership—real estate, bank accounts, securities and many more—you will have to prepare new documents to establish that the trust owns the property. This chapter shows you how to accomplish this.

For certain types of property without a title document, but that seem to require formal transfer because they are property owned in paper form—such as promissory notes or deeds of trust—you can use an Assignment form to make absolutely clear that this property is transferred to the trust.

Finally, trademarks, patents and copyrights have special transfer forms and are discussed in Sections K, L and M, below.

Don't delay. This matter is so vital, I'll give you one more warning, at the risk of redundancy. Failing to transfer property to the trust is the most serious mistake people can make when creating a living trust. If you don't get around to preparing, signing and filing (where required) these new documents, your trust document will have no effect on what happens to any of your property after your death. Instead, that property will go to the residuary

 TRANSFERRING JOINT TENANCY PROPERTY IF YOU LIVE IN A COMMON LAW STATE

If you are a couple and live in a common law state—that is, all states except Arizona, California, Idaho, Louisiana, Nevada, New Mexico, Texas, Washington and Wisconsin—transfers of property held in "joint tenancy" or "tenancy by the entirety" require an extra step more than transfers of other shared property. If your deed or title document lists you as "tenants-in-common owners" (or lists ownership as "tenants in common"), or simply lists your two names, you can safely go ahead and prepare a deed or title document transferring the property from you to the trust.

Before you transfer joint tenancy property to your trust, you'll need to prepare and execute an additional deed or title document, transferring that property from you as "joint tenants" (or tenants by the entirety) to you as "tenants in common, in equal shares." Then you prepare a second deed or document of title, transferring the property from you as "tenants in common" into the trust.

Why is this rigmarole necessary? Because some lawyers argue that joint tenancy property transferred to a living trust in common law states (somehow) retains its character as joint tenancy property, even if the trust declares

otherwise. Worse, the IRS could argue the same. You do not want any risk of having joint tenancy property in your trust. Joint tenancy property must go to the surviving joint tenant, your spouse. This may be what you want; indeed, if it is, consider leaving the property in joint tenancy. (See Chapter 15, Section B.) But if you want to leave some of that property to someone other than your spouse, or you want to name alternate beneficiaries for your share of the property, you want to be sure no one can assert, after a spouse dies, that the trust property is, in legal reality, still joint tenancy property.

With an AB trust, you could face even worse problems. If the joint tenancy property had to go to the surviving joint tenant, the surviving spouse, Trust A might have relatively little money or property in it. Most property of the deceased spouse would be owned outright by the surviving spouse—exactly what you don't want.

So, to be absolutely safe, prepare the extra deed or document of title wherever your present ones list you as owning the property as "joint tenants" or as "tenants by the entirety."

beneficiary named in your back-up will. (See Chapter 16, "Wills.") If you don't have a will, that property will go to certain close relatives, according to state law. Either way, it will probably go through probate.

B. Technical Ownership

To transfer ownership of property with a document of title to your living trust, list the new owner(s) as your name, or names, followed by "as trustee(s) for the [your name(s)] Trust." It's common to include the date the trust was signed and notarized.

Examples

Denis Clifford creates a living trust and transfers real estate to it. On a new real estate deed, he lists the new owner as "Denis Clifford, as trustee of the Denis Clifford Living Trust, dated July 10, 1995."

Denise and Fred Gulekston create a shared living trust and transfer their home, a money market account and a stock brokerage account to the trust. On each title document, they name the new owners as "Denise and Fred Gulekston, as trustees of the Denise and Fred Gulekston Living Trust, dated October 14, 1992."

Formally, the property is owned by the trustee(s), not the trust itself. The reason for holding technical ownership in the trustee(s)' name(s), and not the trust's, is that some title companies and a few other financial institutions have been known to insist that the trust itself cannot own property. This position is at best dubious, but why risk a quarrel between your beneficiaries and some financial company? It makes sense to hold your trust property in the technical form least likely to bother financial institutions.

Including the date your living trust was signed and notarized isn't necessary, but may make your documents appear more lawyer-like, and therefore more acceptable to banks, title companies and other financial institutions.

(It also avoids confusion over subsequent trusts with the same name, if there are any.)

Another form of dating a living trust is to include the letters "UTD" (for Under Trust Dated) and then give the date. For example, "Denis Clifford, as trustee of the Denis Clifford Living Trust, UTD 10/12/94."

1. Property You Acquire Later

If, after your trust has been created, you acquire property you want to be part of the trust, you can simply take ownership in the trustee's name directly. There's no reason to buy the property in your personal name and then transfer it to you as trustee.

Example

Mr. and Mrs. Siqueiros buy a new house. They take title in their names, listing the new owners as "Juan and Luisa Siqueiros, as trustees of The Juan and Luisa Siqueiros Living Trust, dated September 20, 1994."

2. Problems With Financial Institutions

I've received a few reports, from readers of other Nolo books and from lawyers, that some banks, mutual funds or other financial institutions (usually in more remote parts of the country) have balked at re-registering trust property in the trustee's name. People have been told, "You can't do that. Only our trust department does that," or "You need a federal tax ID number."

If this happens to you, simply insist that it is absolutely legal, and essential, for you to re-register your property in the trustee's name, and that this can be done without a new taxpayer ID. If you have to, go higher up in the institution's bureaucracy until you find someone who understands what the law is now, not what it may have been 20 years ago (when a federal tax ID number was required).

C. An Abstract of Trust

An "abstract of trust" is a kind of shorthand version of the trust document. You may find one useful when transferring your property. The purpose of an abstract of trust is to show that the trust exists, without revealing the heart of it—what property is in it and who will inherit. Some people do not want to reveal this core information to institutions that require proof of the trust's existence, such as stock brokerage companies and title companies. So they submit an "abstract of trust," rather than a copy of the entire trust.

In the great majority of states, there's no one set form for an abstract of trust. Ask first, to see what's wanted. Some institutions accept a copy of the first and last (signature) pages of the trust. Another method is simply to remove the property and beneficiaries provisions from a copy of the trust and call what's left an abstract. You do not need to re-sign or re-notarize this document. A photocopy of the original signature(s) and notarization suffices. Or, the grantor can sign a statement swearing he has created the trust. However an abstract of trust is prepared, the following are usually included:

- that the trust was created (the first page of the trust document will do)

- who the original trustees are

- the date the trust was created (the date the trust document was signed)

- what the trustees' powers are (this can be quite a bit of verbiage)

- the signature of the grantor(s) and

- the notarization of the trust document.

There's one example of an "abstract of trust," below. The signature and notarization are simply copies from the original trust.

Some states have their own forms. Two states, California and Minnesota, have adopted statutes that require certain specific information to be in an abstract of trust. (More legislative tinkering, more work for lawyers.) So, if you live in one of these states, don't use the general form. Check with the financial institution involved and use the form they require.

ABSTRACT OF TRUST
THE NORINE AND PAUL LOMBARDI
DECLARATION AND INSTRUMENT OF TRUST

I. TRUST NAME

This trust shall be known as The Norine and Paul Lombardi Trust.

II. TRUST PROPERTY

(A) Norine and Paul Lombardi, wife and husband, called the "grantors" or the "trustees," declare that they have set aside and hold in The Norine and Paul Lombardi Trust, all their interest in that property listed in attached Schedules A and B. The trust property shall be used for the benefit of the trust beneficiaries, and shall be administered and distributed by the trustees in accordance with this trust document.

. . . .

IX. TRUSTEE'S POWERS AND DUTIES

(A) Powers Under State Law

To carry out the provisions of this Declaration of Trust and to manage the trust property of The Norine and Paul Lombardi Living Trust, The Marital Life Estate Trust and The Surviving Spouse's Trust, and any child's subtrust created under this Declaration of Trust, the trustee shall have all authority and power allowed or conferred under New York law, subject to the trustee's fiduciary duty to the grantors and the beneficiaries.

(B) Specified Powers

The trustee's powers include, but are not limited to:

1. The power to sell trust property, and to borrow money and to encumber property, specifically including trust real estate, by mortgage, deed of trust or other method.

2. The power to manage trust real estate as if the trustee were the absolute owner of it, including the power to lease (even if the lease term may extend beyond the period of any trust) or grant options to lease the property, to make repairs or alterations and to insure against loss.

3. The power to sell or grant options for the sale or exchange of any trust property, including stocks, bonds, debentures and any other form of security or security account, at public or private sale for cash or on credit.

4. The power to invest trust property in property of any kind, including but not limited to bonds, debentures, notes, mortgages and stocks.

5. The power to receive additional property from any source and add to any trust created by this Declaration of Trust.

6. The power to employ and pay reasonable fees to accountants, lawyers or investment experts for information or advice relating to the trust.

7. The power to deposit and hold trust funds in both interest-bearing and non-interest-bearing accounts.

8. The power to deposit funds in bank or other accounts uninsured by FDIC coverage.

9. The power to enter into electronic fund transfer or safe deposit arrangements with financial institutions.

10. The power to continue any business of either grantor.

11. The power to institute or defend legal actions concerning the trust or the grantors' affairs.

12. The power to execute any documents necessary to administer any trust created in this Declaration of Trust.

13. The power to diversify investments, including authority to decide that some or all of the trust property need not produce income.

. . . .

Certification by Grantors

We certify that we have read this Declaration of Trust and that it correctly states the terms and conditions under which the trust property is to be held, managed and disposed of by the trustee and we approve the Declaration of Trust.

Dated: July 6, 1997

Norine Lombardi

Norine Lombardi

Paul Lombardi

Paul Lombardi
Grantors and Trustees

State of New York

County of Duchess

On July 6, 1997, before me, _____Ilana Weinstock_____, a notary public for the State of New York, personally appeared Norine Lombardi and Paul Lombardi, known to me to be, or proved to me on the basis of satisfactory evidence to be, the trustees and grantors of the trust created by the above Declaration of Trust, and to be the persons whose names are subscribed to the Declaration of Trust, and acknowledged that they executed it as grantors and trustees.

IN WITNESS WHEREOF, I have set my hand and affixed my official seal the day and year first above written.

/s/_____Ilana Weinstock_____
NOTARY PUBLIC

D. Property That Names the Living Trust as a Beneficiary

If you have named your trust as beneficiary of a life insurance policy or pension plan, you do not re-register title to the policy or plan. For example, if you want your living trust to receive the proceeds of your life insurance policy at your death, all you need to do is properly designate your trust as the beneficiary of that policy. You do not transfer ownership of the policy into the trust's name.

While you live, the trust is not the legal owner of the insurance policy; you personally remain the legal owner. The trust is simply the entity you've named to receive the life insurance proceeds payable on your death. Because the trust never owned the insurance policy, this asset was not listed on a trust schedule. You do, of course, name one or more beneficiaries and alternate beneficiaries for the proceeds in the trust document. For example, a wife could name her husband as beneficiary, and her two minor children as alternate beneficiaries. If the children received the proceeds while minors, the money would be held in children's trusts.

E. Real Estate

The term "real estate" includes land, houses, condominiums, cooperatives, "time shares" and any other interest in what lawyers call "real property." To transfer title of a piece of real estate to a living trust, you prepare and sign a deed listing the trustee or trustees of the trust as the new owner. You can fill out the new deed yourself; it's not difficult. Then you sign the deed in front of a notary public and record a copy of it with the county land records office. You don't have to prepare a second document transferring your mortgage; that liability follows the asset, the real estate.

Co-op apartments. If you own a co-op apartment, you can't simply use a deed to transfer your shares in the co-op. You will have to check the co-op corporation's rules

to see if the transfer is allowed, Some co-ops resist such transfers because they are afraid a living trust isn't a proper shareholder in the corporation. You can probably overcome any resistance you encounter by reminding the powers that be that, for all practical purposes, you and the trust are the same—you have the same tax identification number, for example.

1. Preparing the Deed

First, locate your existing deed. Then get a deed form in common use in the state where the real estate is located. The technical requirements for real estate deed forms vary from state to state, so you must get one from the appropriate state.

FINDING DEED FORMS AND INSTRUCTIONS

You can use a "quitclaim" or "grant" deed form. The type of deed isn't important when you're transferring property to your own living trust. Deed forms vary from state to state. If you're in California, you can find deed forms and instructions for filling them out in *The Deeds Book*, by Mary Randolph (Nolo Press). Much of its information is valid in other states as well, but it's best to use a deed form that's in common use in your area.

In many places, you can find blank deed forms in stationery or office supply stores, or perhaps from a local title company. If you live in a small town and can't find a deed in a local store, try calling a stationery store in a major city, because deed forms are the same throughout a state. Or go to a local law library; look for books on "real property" that have deed forms you can photocopy.

Although deed forms vary somewhat, they all require the same basic information. Using a typewriter, fill out your deed like the sample shown below. Type in:

- **The recording information, at the top left of the document.**

- **The date.**

- **The current owners' names.** If you are the sole owner, or if you and someone else co-own the property and you are transferring just your share, only your name goes here. If you are transferring only a portion of ownership, you can specify what portion (for example, "1/3 ownership of ..." or simply state "all his/her interest in..."). If you and your spouse own the property together and are transferring it to a shared marital trust or an AB trust, type in both of your names. Use exactly the same form of your name as is used on the deed that transferred the property to you and you used in your living trust document.

    As you can see from the sample completed document, you may have to type in the correct ending of some printed words, like "part...." If you are a couple, you add "ies" to make this "parties." If you are a single person, you add a "y" to make it "party."

- **The new owner's name.** Fill in the trustee's name or trustees' names as specified above, and add the date of notarization of the trust if you wish. (See Section B, above.)

- **The "legal description" of the property.** This is usually something like, "From a point 12 degrees South of... Map 4, Book 6," etc. Copy the description exactly as it appears on the previous deed.

Depending on the form you use, you may need to cross out, as shown in the sample deed, inappropriate printed language, such as words stating the transfer is "forever," or that the property is also transferred to the second party's (here, the trust's) "assigns, etc."

After everything is filled in, sign and date the deed in front of a notary public for the state in which the property is located. Everyone listed as a current owner, who is transferring his or her interest in the property to the trust, must sign the deed.

Below is a completed quitclaim deed transferring a home to a living trust. As you'll see, this deed contains bunches of legalese ("...appurtenances thereunto belonging or appertaining..."). I'm no fan of the legalese it uses, but it's typical of a deed you're likely to get at a stationery store.

2. Recording the Deed

After the deed is signed and notarized, you must "record" it—that is, put a copy of the notarized deed on file in the county office that keeps local property records. Depending on the state, the land records office is called the County Recorder's Office, Land Registry Office or County Clerk's office.

Just take the original, signed deed to the land records office. (You can probably mail it in, if you wish. Call the land records office to find out the correct procedure.) For a small fee, a clerk will make a copy and put it in the public records. You'll get your original back, stamped with a reference number to show where the copy can be found in the public records.

3. Transfer Taxes

In most places, you will not have to pay a state or local transfer tax when you transfer real estate to a revocable living trust. Most real estate transfer taxes are based on the sale price of the property and do not apply when no money changes hands. Others specifically exempt transfers where the real owners don't change—as is the case when you transfer property to a revocable living trust you control.

Before you record your deed, you can get information on transfer tax from the county tax assessor, county recorder or state tax officials.

Sample Deed

Quitclaim Deed

This Indenture made the ......twenty-first............................... day of
........April.................... one thousand nine hundred and ...eighty-eight.................

Between ....Jane .and .Gordon .McCann..
.... the part..ies of the first part,
and .Jane .and .Gordon .McCann, .as .trustees .of .the .Jane .and .Gordon .McCann .Living .Trust,..
.......dated April 12, 1988.. the part .y... of the second part,

Witnesseth: That the said part ..ies.... of the first part,XXXXXXXXXXXXXXXXXXX
XXXXXXXXXXXXXXXXXXXXXXXXXXXXXXXXXXXXXXXXXXXXXXXXdollars,
XXXXXXXXXXXXXXXXXXXXXXXXXXXXXXXXXXXXXXXXXXXXXXXXXXX
XXXXXXXXXXXXXXXXXXXXXXXXXXXXXXXXXXX do .... hereby
release and XXXXXXXQUITCLAIM unto the part y......... of the second part, XXXXXXXXXXXX
XXXXXXXXXall that........ certain lot........., piece........... or parcel......... of land situate in
the ...City .of .Chicago.......................... County of ....Cook.................
State of ......Illinois.............................., and bounded and described as follows, to-wit:

Commonly known as 47 Greene Street, and more particularly described as:

(Legal description, exactly as given in previous deed)

Together with the tenements, hereditaments, and appurtenances thereunto belonging
or appertaining, and the reversion and reversions, remainder and remainders, rents, issues,
and profits thereof.

To have and to hold the said premises, together with the appurtenances, unto
the part .y........ of the second part, XXXXXXXXXXXXXXXXXXXXXXXXXXXXX

In Witness Whereof the part ...ies.... of the first part have........ executed this
conveyance the day and year first above written.

Signed and Delivered in the Presence of

_____

[notarized]

CALIFORNIA PROPERTY TAXES

In California, transferring real estate to a revocable living trust does not trigger a reassessment for property tax purposes. Similarly, transfers from the trustee back to the original owner don't cause reassessments. (Cal. Rev. & Tax. Code § 62(d).) You may, however, have to file a form called a Preliminary Change of Title Report with the county tax assessor. If you do, you sign this form with your name, as trustee for your trust.

EXAMPLE

Erin Quake signs a Preliminary Change of Title Report as "Erin Quake, Trustee, the Erin Quake Living Trust dated November 7, 1992."

4. Due-on-Sale Mortgage Clauses

Many mortgages contain a clause that allows the bank to call ("accelerate") the loan—that is, demand that you pay the whole thing off immediately—if you transfer the mortgaged property. Fortunately, in most instances lenders are forbidden by federal law to invoke a due-on-sale clause when property is transferred to a living trust. The lender can't call the loan if the borrower is a trust beneficiary and the transfer is "unrelated to occupancy" of the premises. (Garn-St. Germain Act, 12 U.S.C. §§ 1464, 1701.) Also, it's doubtful that the transfer of any real estate to your trust is the type of transfer that would legally permit a bank to call a loan. (See Chapter 3, "Common Questions About Living Trusts," Section I.)

5. Home Insurance

Your home insurance policy should not be changed simply because your home has been placed in your living trust. You do not need to notify your insurance company (or any title company) of the transfer of owner-occupied property. (Why disturb a bureaucracy if you don't have to?) If you own other real estate, besides your own home, that you're transferring to your trust, it can be prudent to notify your insurance company so it can't balk later on.

6. Transferring Deeds of Trust

One type of real estate asset is called a "deed of trust." It is similar to a mortgage. If you lend money to someone, you may receive a deed of trust, making real estate collateral for a loan—that is, if the borrower defaults, you can foreclose on the real estate to collect what's owed you. Because a deed of trust is an interest in real estate, it should be recorded.

To transfer a deed of trust to your living trust, you can prepare a "Notice of Assignment" transferring it from you to your trust. You then record that document. Use Form 5 or 6 in the Appendix.

7. Real Estate Outside the United States

There doesn't seem to be much point to transferring foreign property to a U.S. living trust. That property wouldn't go through U.S. probate anyway, and U.S. courts don't have authority to order transfer of real estate in another country.

Each country has its own rules and laws regarding real estate. (When I lived in Ireland, I had to visit a lawyer—a "solicitor"—and sign a fancy legal document to rent an apartment.) If this is important to you, hire someone in that other country to learn what you can do. After all, if you own real estate in a foreign country, that's fortunate, so spending a little money to learn how to transfer that property after your death isn't a disaster.

F. Bank Accounts and Safe Deposit Boxes

It should be simple to re-register ownership of a bank account in your name(s) as trustee(s) of your living trust or open a new account in the trustee's name. Just ask the bank what paperwork you need to submit.

The bank will be concerned with the authority granted to the trustees to act on behalf of the trust. Depending on the kind of account, the bank may want to know whether or not the trustees have the power to borrow money, put funds in a non-interest-bearing account or engage in electronic transfers. (The trust forms in this book include all these powers.)

To verify your authority, the bank may want to see a copy of your trust document or have you fill out its own form, often called a Trust Certification.

If you want to transfer title to a safe deposit box to your trust, you'll have to re-register its ownership, too. The bank will have a form for you to fill out.

Estate planning note. Instead of transferring a bank account to a living trust, you may want to turn the account into a pay-on-death account. It's another, even easier, way to avoid probate of the money in the account. (See Chapter 15, "A Living Trust as Part of Your Estate Plan.")

G. Securities

How you transfer stocks, bonds, mutual funds and other securities to your living trust depends on whether or not you hold your stocks in a brokerage account or keep the actual certificates yourself. (For stocks in closely-held corporations, see Section I3, below.)

1. Brokerage Accounts

If, like most people, you hold your stocks, bonds or other securities in a brokerage account, either change the account to the trustee's name or open a new account in the trustee's name. Simply ask your broker for instructions. The brokerage company may have a straightforward form that you can fill out, giving information about the trustees and their authority.

Tell them you want the account to keep the same account number as when it was in your name. If they don't want to, insist (politely). If they still refuse, you've got a technical problem, because the account number listed in your trust document isn't the same as the new number of that account in the trustee's name. You'd have to revise a trust schedule to get the new account number in it. So, you can see why you want to insist the account keep your original number.

If the brokerage company doesn't have its own form, you will probably need to send the broker:

- a copy of the trust document or an "abstract of trust," and

- a letter instructing the holder to transfer the brokerage account to the trustee's name or open a new account in the trustee's name.

After you've submitted your request, get written confirmation that the account's ownership has in fact been put in the trustee's name.

2. Stock Certificates

If you have the actual stock certificates or bonds in your possession—most people don't—you must get new certificates issued, showing the trustee as owner. Ask your broker for help. If the broker is unwilling or unable to help, write to the "transfer agent" of the corporation that issued the stock. You can get the address from your broker or the investor relations office of the corporation. The transfer agent will give you simple instructions.

You will probably have to send in:

- your certificates or bonds

- a form called a "stock or bond power," which you must fill out and sign

- a copy of the trust document or an "abstract of trust," showing your notarized signature, and.

- a letter requesting that the certificates be reissued in the trustee's name.

The stock or bond power may be printed on the back of the certificates; if not, you can probably find a copy at a stationery store.

3. Government Securities

To transfer government securities—for example, Treasury bills or U.S. bonds—have your broker contact the local Federal Reserve Bank, or do it yourself. Also, local banks may have the necessary transfer forms.

4. Mutual Fund Accounts

Mutual funds should be re-registered in the name of the trustee of your living trust by communicating with the company and meeting its requirements. You'll probably just need to send a letter of instructions (or a form the company provides) and a copy of the trust document.

H. Vehicles and Boats

Most people don't transfer vehicles such as cars, mobile homes or trailers to a living trust, for reasons discussed in Chapter 6, "Choosing What Property to Put in Your Living Trust," Section B.

If you want to put a vehicle in trust, you must fill out a change of ownership document and have title to the vehicle reissued in the trustee's name. The title certificate to your vehicle may contain instructions. If you have questions, call your state's Motor Vehicles Department.

Transferring a boat to your living trust may require you to re-register title with the Coast Guard. This bureaucracy isn't familiar with living trusts, so you may have to do some explaining to convince them that what you are doing is fully legal.

I. Business Interests

How you transfer small business interests to your living trust depends on the way the business is owned.

TRADEMARKS AND SERVICE MARKS

If you have a registered trademark or service mark, you must re-register ownership in the name of the trustee of the living trust. For sample forms, see *Trademark: How to Name Your Business & Product,* by Kate McGrath and Steve Elias (Nolo Press).

---

1. Sole Proprietorships

An unincorporated business that you own by yourself is the easiest to transfer to a trust. You should have listed the business, by name, as an item of property on a trust schedule—for example, "The Dish Restaurant." That transfers the name and whatever customer goodwill goes with it, to your living trust.

Because you own the business assets in your own name (a sole proprietorship, unlike a corporation, is not an independent entity that can own property), you transfer them to your living trust like you would any other valuable property. For many businesses, this simply means listing those business assets on the appropriate trust schedule—for example, "…all property and assets used in the grantor's business Jim Dimes Hardware." Because there is no ownership document for the business, nothing further is required.

2. Solely Owned Corporations

If you own all the stock of a corporation, you shouldn't have any problem transferring it to your living trust. Follow these steps:

Step 1. Fill out the stock transfer section on the back of the stock certificate.

Step 2. Mark the certificate "canceled" and place it in your corporate records book.

Step 3. Reissue a new certificate in the name of the trustee of the living trust.

Step 4. Show the cancellation of the old certificate and the issuance of the new certificate on the stock ledger pages in your corporate records book.

3. Closely-Held Corporations

Normally, you can transfer your shares in a closely-held corporation to your living trust by following corporate bylaws and having the stock certificates reissued in the name of the trustee of the trust. But first, check the corporation's bylaws and articles of incorporation, as well as any separate shareholders' agreements, to see if there are any restrictions on such transfers. If an agreement limits or forbids transfers, it will have to be changed before you can put your shares in your living trust.

4. Partnership Interests

To transfer your partnership interest to your living trust, you must notify your business partners and modify the partnership agreement to show that your partnership interest is now owned by the trustee of your living trust. If there is a partnership certificate, it must be changed to substitute the trustee as owner of your share.

REVISING A PARTNERSHIP AGREEMENT

You can revise your partnership agreement by using *The Partnership Book,* by Denis Clifford and Ralph Warner (Nolo Press), or *Nolo's Partnership Maker, a* software program (DOS).

J. Limited Partnerships

Limited partnerships are a form of investment, governed by securities laws. Contact the partnership's general partner to find out what paperwork is necessary to transfer your interest to a living trust.

K. Copyrights

If you want to transfer your interest in a copyright to your living trust, list the copyright on a trust schedule. Then sign and file, with the U.S. Copyright Office, a document transferring all your rights in the copyright to the trustee of the living trust. Sample transfer forms are in *The Copyright Handbook,* by Stephen Fishman (Nolo Press).

L. Patents

If you own a patent and want to transfer it to your living trust, you should prepare a document called an "assignment" and record it with the U.S. Patent and Trademark Office in Washington, D.C. There is a small fee for recording. Assignment forms and instructions are in *Patent It Yourself,* by David Pressman (Nolo Press, available as a book or software).

M. Royalties

Your rights to receive royalties—from sales of a book, copies of photos, residuals for TV ads, whatever—can be transferred to your trust with technical ownership held by the trustee. It's best to transfer any royalty rights by preparing an Assignment of Property (Form 5 or 6), although legally, just listing these rights on a trust schedule would suffice. But with an Assignment of Property form, you can clearly specify, in a separate, distinct document, exactly what royalty rights are transferred to the trust.

It is sensible to give a copy of the Assignment of Property form to whatever company pays you the royalty rights. Let them know, of course, that they are to keep making payments to you while you live. It can help get these payments to your beneficiaries without great hassles if you give the company some warning that your royalty rights will be transferred by your successor trustee out of your living trust when you die. ❧

chapter 12

COPYING, STORING AND REGISTERING YOUR TRUST DOCUMENT

*A*fter you've completed your living trust and signed all documents necessary to transfer property to the trust, you're almost done. There are just a couple of minor tasks left to accomplish.

A. Making Copies

You will probably need some copies of your completed trust document. Some lawyers advise stamping or writing the word "COPY" on each duplicate, so none can ever be mistaken for an original. While you can certainly do this, it seems a bit overcautious to me. Photocopies of your original trust are different from the original—your signature is not in ink on the copy, nor is the notary stamp original. But then again, that's not always so easy to determine these days, with better and better quality photocopying, so if you want maximum security, go ahead and write or stamp "COPY" on each copy, or even on each page of each copy.

You may well need copies to transfer certain types of property—stocks, for example—to your trust. (See Chapter 11, "Transferring Property to Your Trust," Section F.) If a broker, bank or other institution wants to see your trust document, use a photocopy of the original.

You may want to give a copy of your trust document to your successor trustee so that person knows what is in your trust well in advance of actually serving as trustee. Keep the original, which your successor trustee will need after your death or incapacity.

Finally, you should instruct your successor trustee to give copies after your death to any custodian you named for trust property inherited by a young beneficiary.

There's no requirement that you give copies to any beneficiaries. Indeed, there can be drawbacks to this. If you later revoke or amend the trust but don't collect all the old copies, there will be outdated copies of your trust document floating around. Someone who is given less (or nothing) in the new document may cause trouble later on. Also, the property in the trust may substantially change later if the trustee must dip into or even deplete the trust because of a grantor's illness or other unexpected expenses. Why set up expectations that may not be fulfilled even with the best of intentions?

On the other hand, if you doubt the trust property will change much, and if there are only a few beneficiaries and you trust them all—as is true for many families—why not let your beneficiaries know now what they'll receive? What's wrong with revealing your generosity?

Sign only one trust document. It is important not to prepare another "original" document—that is, to sign a second copy of your living trust form. This is because each trust document you actually sign becomes, legally, a distinct trust document (even it if isn't notarized). If you revoke or change one original, that does not revoke or change other originals. Clearly, you don't want any duplicate original trust documents floating around.

B. Storing the Trust Document

Store your living trust document where you keep other important papers, such as your financial records, will or durable power of attorney. A fireproof box in your home or office is fine. If you want to be extra careful, a safe deposit box is a good choice, but only if the successor trustee has access to it. Many people keep their living trust document in a locked drawer in a home desk or file cabinet. (After all, it's very unlikely anyone would steal a trust document, since it has no value to anyone but you. But this doesn't deal with the risk of fire or other disaster.)

Make sure your successor trustee (or spouse, if you made a basic shared living trust or a living trust with marital life estate) knows where the original trust document is and can get hold of it soon after your death or incapacity. The new trustee will need it to manage or distribute trust property. (The new trustee will also need to know the information in Chapter 14, "After a Grantor Dies," to carry out his or her duties.)

C. Registering the Trust

**STATES THAT PROVIDE FOR
REGISTRATION OF LIVING TRUSTS**

Alaska	Maine
Colorado**	Michigan
Florida*	Missouri
Hawaii	Nebraska*
Idaho	North Dakota

*Not mandatory.

** Registration of a revocable living trust not required until the grantor's death; no registration required if all trust property is distributed to the beneficiaries then.

Some states require that the trustee of a trust register the trust with the local court. But there are no legal consequences or penalties if you don't, which, in effect, means this is an optional requirement. (The only exception is that if a court demands that a trustee register a trust, and the trustee refuses, the trustee can be removed.)

Registration of a living trust doesn't give the court any power over the administration of the trust, unless there's a dispute. Registration serves to give the court jurisdiction over any disputes involving the trust—for example, if after your death a beneficiary wants to object to the way your successor trustee distributed the trust property. But if you don't register your trust, the result is the same: the court still has jurisdiction if a disgruntled relative or creditor files suit.

To register a revocable living trust, the trustee must file a statement with the court where the trustee resides or keeps trust records. The statement must include at least the following:

- the name(s) of the grantor(s)
- the name(s) of the original trustee(s)
- an acknowledgment of the trusteeship (that is, a written acceptance by the trustees of their role)
- the date of the trust document.

A trust can be registered in only one state at a time. ❦

chapter 13

LIVING WITH YOUR LIVING TRUST

*T*his chapter discusses what you need to know after your living trust is up and running, and how to change your trust document if your circumstances change.

As a day-to-day, practical matter, it makes no difference that your property is now owned by your revocable living trust. As you know by now, you have no special paperwork to prepare, tax forms to file or other duties to perform as the trustee of your own revocable living trust. Nor do you have any legal responsibilities to any of the beneficiaries you named in the trust document. They have no rights over any trust property while you are alive.

Some lawyers urge you to have your trust reviewed and updated by a lawyer every year. There's no need for this whatsoever. Indeed, there's no need for you to review your trust yourself every year. Review your trust if something major has changed, or you want to make a major change. But for many, probably most, people who create a living trust, there's very little or no change that affects the trust from the time they create it to the time it goes into effect.

A. If You Move to Another State

Your living trust is still valid if you prepare it in one state and then move to another. When you prepare a trust using the forms in this book, you declare the state of your legal residence and state that the law of this state applies to any disputes about disposition of the property. So no matter where you are living at your death, the successor trustee generally will only have to deal with one state's law.

You may, however, need to take some actions after your move:

- Your new state may require you to register your living trust document with the local court. (See Chapter 12, "Copying, Storing and Registering Your Trust Document," Section C.)

- If you made a gift using your old state's version of the Uniform Transfers to Minors Act (UTMA) and your new state hasn't adopted this law, you'll need to amend your trust, deleting the UTMA gift and creat-

ing a child's subtrust for it. (See Chapter 9, "Property Left to Minor Children or Young Adults," Sections C and D.)

- You may want to amend the trust document if you are married and the new state's laws differ on marital property rights. (See Chapter 6, "Choosing What Property to Put in Your Living Trust," Section D.)

- If you acquire real estate in your new state, that real estate is governed by the new state's laws. For instance, if the new state is a community property state, that law governs the real estate.

B. Adding Property to Your Living Trust

The living trust forms in this book specifically give you the right to add property to your trust. If you acquire valuable items of property after you create your living trust, you should promptly add them to the trust so that they won't have to go through probate at your death.

There are four steps to adding property to your trust:

Step 1. Type a revised Property Schedule A, B or C of your trust document, adding the new property. (If you made an individual trust, you have only one schedule, Schedule A. If you and your spouse made a basic shared living trust or an AB trust, Schedule A lists your co-owned property, Schedule B lists the wife's separate property, if any, and Schedule C lists the husband's separate property, if any.)

Step 2. Remove the old schedule from your trust document and attach the new one.

Step 3. Place title of the property in the trustee's name. If, acting in your capacity as trustee, you originally purchased the property in the trustee's name, you don't need to bother about this, because, obviously, you've already done it. But if you acquire the property in your own name—for example, an inheritance—you need to prepare the appropriate title document. (See Chapter 11, "Transferring Property to Your Trust.")

Example

Rose and Michael have prepared an AB trust. Later on, they buy a new house, and they want it to be in their living trust. So, on the deed, they take title in the name of "Rose Morris and Michael Morris, trustees of the Rose Morris and Michael Morris Living Trust, dated January 13, 1996." They then type a revised Schedule A (which lists shared property) of their trust document and replace the old Schedule A.

Step 4. Amend the trust document if you need to name a beneficiary for the new property. You won't need to amend the trust document if you've left all your trust property to one person or if you want the property to go to your residuary beneficiary.

Example

Mercedes adds a new money market account to her living trust. She wants to leave this account to her brother, Neil, who is not her residuary beneficiary. Mercedes must prepare an amendment of her trust, listing Neil as the beneficiary for this new property. (See Section F, below.)

Usually, you won't need to amend the trust document of an AB trust if you put new property in the trust. That property will be subject to the trust provisions creating the AB trust. Only if you want the new property to go to someone other than your spouse do you need to amend the trust.

C. Selling or Giving Away Trust Property

You have complete control over the property you have transferred to the living trust. If you want to sell or give away any of it, simply go ahead, using your authority as trustee. This means you (or you and your spouse, if you made a basic shared marital trust or AB trust) sign ownership or transfer documents (the deed, bill of sale or other document) in your capacity as trustee of the living trust.

Example

Martin transfers ownership of his house to his living trust, but later decides to sell it. He transfers the house to the buyer by signing the new deed as "Martin Owens, trustee of the Martin Owens Living Trust dated June 18, 1992."

If you and your spouse made a basic shared living trust or an AB trust, either trustee (spouse) has authority over trust property. That means that either spouse can sell or give away any of the trust property—including the property that was co-owned or was the separate property of the other spouse before it was transferred to the trust. In practice, however, both spouses will probably have to consent to transfer real estate out of the living trust. Especially in community property states, buyers and title insurance companies usually insist on both spouses' signatures on transfer documents.

If for any reason you want to take property out of the trust but keep ownership of it, you can transfer the property to yourself. So if Martin, in the previous example, wanted to take his house out of his living trust but keep ownership in his own name, he would make the deed out from "The Martin Owens Living Trust dated June 18, 1992, Martin Owens, trustee" to "Martin Owens." He would sign the deed "Martin Owens, trustee of the Martin Owens Living Trust, dated June 18, 1992."

Unless this change will be for a brief period (for example, only for the time necessary to obtain refinancing of your home loan), you should modify the property schedule of your trust document to reflect the change. If you don't, the schedules will still show that the property is owned by the trust. Legally, the trust no longer owns it, and the discrepancy could be confusing to the people who carry out your wishes after your death.

Example

Wendy and Brian, a married couple, made a basic shared living trust several years ago. Wendy transferred a valuable antique dresser, which she inherited from her grandfather before she was married, to the living trust. It's listed on Schedule B of the trust document. The trust document provides that the dresser will go to her son at her death. But she's changed her mind and decided to give the dresser to her daughter while she's alive.

After Wendy gives the dresser to her daughter, she prepares two documents. First, she prepares a new Schedule B, deleting the dresser from the list of property, and replaces the old Schedule B attached to her trust document. Second, she prepares a Trust Amendment, stating that the paragraph that left the dresser to her son is no longer in effect. (See Section F, below.)

D. When to Amend Your Living Trust Document

One of the most attractive features of a revocable living trust is its flexibility: you can change its terms, or end it altogether, at any time. This section discusses several events that should be red flags, alerting you that you may need to amend your living trust.

In most circumstances, you will want to amend your living trust document, not revoke it. At first glance, it might seem easier to revoke it and start again, as is usually done with a will. But if you revoke your living trust and create another one, you must transfer all the trust property out of the old living trust and into the new one. This means preparing new documents of title and all the

other paperwork required to transfer property to your original trust. (Section G, below, discusses when it is advisable to revoke your living trust and make another.)

As explained in Section C, above, you may need to amend your trust document if you add property to the trust, or sell or give away property from it. Following are other events that normally require amendment of a trust.

1. You Marry or Have a Child

If you get married or have a child, you'll almost certainly want to amend your trust document to provide for your new spouse or offspring. And remember that your spouse or minor child may be entitled, under state law, to a certain portion of your property. (See Chapter 8, "Choosing Your Beneficiaries," Section H.)

2. You Move to Another State

Although your living trust is still valid if you move to another state, you may want to change your living trust in response to your new state's laws. Here are several aspects of your trust, and overall estate plan, that may be affected by a move to a new state.

a. Marital Property Laws: Who Owns What

As previously discussed, if you are married and move from a common law state to California, Idaho or Washington, property you acquired during marriage may become "quasi-community property," and so owned by both spouses, however it was originally owned. See Chapter 6, "Choosing What Property to Put in Your Living Trust," Section D.

b. Property Management for Young Beneficiaries

Your state's law determines the choices you have when it comes to arranging for property management for young trust beneficiaries. In all states, you can create a child's subtrust for any beneficiary who might inherit trust property before he or she is 35. But state law determines whether or not you have another option: Appointing someone to be the "custodian" of trust property inherited by a young beneficiary who isn't yet 18 to 21 (25 in Alaska, California and Nevada). (See Chapter 9, "Property Left to Minor Children or Young Adults," Section C.)

c. Rights of a Surviving Spouse to Inherit

Different states entitle surviving spouses to different shares of a deceased spouse's estate. If you prepare a shared basic living trust and you plan to leave at least one-half of your total estate to your spouse, you don't have to worry about this. And, as previously mentioned, this doesn't apply to an AB trust. But if you want to leave your spouse less than one-half, and you're concerned that your spouse might challenge your estate plan and demand the "statutory share" of your property after your death, you'll want to know what your new state's laws say. (See Chapter 8, "Choosing Your Beneficiaries," Section H.)

3. Your Spouse Dies

If you and your spouse made a basic shared living trust, when one spouse dies the other will probably inherit some, if not all, of the deceased spouse's trust property. The surviving spouse may want to amend his or her trust to name beneficiaries for that property.

If you and your spouse made an AB trust, the surviving spouse cannot amend the A trust, which is created when the first spouse dies. And there's often no reason the surviving spouse needs to amend his or her trust, which remains revocable. (This is explained in Chapter 5, "The Tax-Saving AB Trust.") The surviving spouse would amend her B trust only if she independently now wants to change who she will leave her own property to.

4. A Major Beneficiary Dies

If you left much or all of your trust property to one person, and that person dies before you do, you may well want to amend your trust document. If you named an alternate beneficiary for the deceased beneficiary, there's not an urgent need; the alternate will inherit the property. But it still makes sense to amend the trust so that you can name another alternate beneficiary, who will receive the property if the former alternate (now first in line) dies before you do.

Example

Maria and Carlos make a basic shared living trust together. Maria leaves all her trust property to Carlos, but he dies before she does. Because she named her daughter Teresa as alternate beneficiary for her husband, she has already planned for the possibility of Carlos's death. But it still makes sense for her to amend her trust to name Teresa as the beneficiary and then to name an alternate beneficiary for Teresa.

Remember that your trust document has another back-up device built into it: the residuary beneficiary. If both the primary and alternate beneficiary die before you do, the residuary beneficiary will inherit the trust property.

With an AB trust, if a final beneficiary dies before either spouse dies, the spouses can amend their trust to name a new final beneficiary, or they can leave the trust as is, allowing the alternate(s) named for the deceased final beneficiary to inherit that beneficiary's share of the AB trust property. (If they were cautious, the couple might still amend the trust, to name new alternate final beneficiaries, since the previous alternates for the deceased final beneficiary have become the final beneficiaries themselves.)

Also, as I've frequently stated, with an AB trust, the surviving spouse can amend her own revocable surviving spouse's trust to name a new final beneficiary, if she desires to, as long as she is competent.

5. Changing Ownership of Trust Property

Sometimes couples decide, for various reasons, to change shared property into property owned separately by one spouse or the other. Or a spouse may decide to change his or her separate property into shared ownership property. The legal term for this is "transmutation of property."

If after you've placed property in a trust you want to make this type of change, you'll need to:

- write out the appropriate written declaration of change of ownership. If real estate is involved, new deeds reflecting the changed ownership must be prepared.

- revise the appropriate trust schedules, so the changed property is deleted from the old schedule and placed on the now correct one.

Example

Soon after they get married, Felicity and Russell Jones create a basic shared living trust. They live in a home in New Jersey that is Felicity's separate property, and is listed as such on Schedule B of their trust. After several happy years together, Felicity decides she wants to place the house in shared ownership with Russell. So she lists the house on Schedule A, the shared property schedule of their trust, removing it from Schedule B. As trustee, Felicity executes a deed transferring the house to herself, as her separate property. She then executes a second deed, identifying the property as co-owned equally between her and her husband. The house is now owned by the couple as trustees of their trust.

Since each spouse owns half the house, they'll need to revise their beneficiary provisions, unless each simply left all his or her property to the other spouse.

E. Amending a Living Trust Document

Who can amend the terms of a living trust document depends on the kind of trust you created.

1. Individual Living Trusts

If you created an individual living trust, you (the grantor) can amend any of its provisions at any time, as long as you are mentally competent.

2. Basic Shared Living Trusts and AB Trusts

While both spouses are alive, both must agree to amend any provision of the trust documents—for example, to change a beneficiary, successor trustee or the management set up for a young beneficiary.

After one spouse dies, a basic shared living trust is split into two trusts. The deceased spouse's trust can no longer be amended. The surviving spouse can, of course, amend his own revocable trust.

Similarly, with an AB trust, when a spouse dies, the trust is split into two distinct trusts. Trust A, which contains the property of the deceased spouse, becomes irrevocable. The surviving spouse has no power to amend it. But again, the surviving spouse can amend or revoke her own trust, Trust B, as long as she is competent.

3. Someone Acting on Your Behalf

A trust document created from a form in this book cannot be amended by someone acting on a grantor's behalf, unless the grantor has given that authority in another document.

In reality, this means no one can amend your trust unless you specifically authorized someone to do it in a document called a Durable Power of Attorney for Finances (this person is called your "attorney-in-fact"). Or, in rare cases, a court can appoint someone (a conservator or guardian of the estate), with power to amend your living trust. (Durable Powers of Attorney for Finances are discussed in Chapter 15, "A Living Trust as Part of Your Estate Plan," Section E.)

To stress that point, if you want to give your attorney-in-fact authority to amend your living trust, you must specifically grant this authority in your Durable Power of Attorney for Finances. Why would you want to give this authority? Frankly, I think most people wouldn't. But I can certainly imagine unusual situations where someone might want to grant it, perhaps some unstable family or economic situation where a grantor wanted a trusted person (his attorney-in-fact, who was also his successor trustee) to be able to make last minute changes in a trust if that seemed wise and the grantor was incapacitated and unable to make the change herself. Or the grantor might have an ongoing annual gifting program of money from his living trust, designed to reduce eventual estate taxes. And the grantor might want this program continued, even if he becomes incapacitated.

F. How to Amend Your Trust Document

It's simple to amend your trust document to change a beneficiary, successor trustee or custodian named in it, or change any other provision. Simply complete the appropriate amendment form from the Appendix, sign it and have the form notarized, and then attach it to your original trust document. If you have an individual trust, use Form 7; if you have either a shared living trust or an AB trust, use Form 8.

With an AB trust, you can't change the life beneficiary (the other spouse) while both spouses are alive. To do so defeats the whole point of this kind of trust. Otherwise, any term of the trust can be changed while both spouses live.

A sample draft amendment of an AB living trust, ready for final typing, is shown below.

Example

Jim and Toni created their AB trust three years ago. Jim named his sister Eileen as a specific beneficiary for some stock in the Wyche Co. (he named no alternate beneficiary) that Jim transferred to the trust. But since then, Jim and his sister have had a falling out. He wants to amend the trust document to leave the stock to his brother Aaron.

All Jim and Toni need to do is use Form 8 to prepare a trust amendment. The amendment deletes the paragraph in the Declaration of Trust that left the stock to Eileen. It also adds a paragraph leaving the stock to Aaron and stating that if Aaron doesn't survive him, that it should go to his nephew David.

If they eliminated Eileen as a beneficiary but didn't name a new beneficiary for the stock, it would eventually become part of the AB trust (if Jim dies first) or the surviving spouse's trust (if Toni predeceases Jim).

Their draft trust amendment form (before typing, with appropriate cross-outs in the form) is shown on the following page.

You can similarly amend your trust document if you change your mind about who you want to serve as:

- **Successor trustee.** The person who handles the trust, and any children's subtrusts, after your death or the surviving spouse's death if a shared trust was created.

- **Alternate successor trustee.** The person who takes over as trustee if your first choice can't serve.

- **Custodian of a child's trust property.** The person who manages a young beneficiary's trust property under the terms of the Uniform Transfers to Minors Act, if it's available in your state.

- **Alternate custodian.** The person who serves as custodian if your first choice can't serve.

Example

Geoffrey creates a living trust and names his brother as successor trustee. His brother moves to Europe two years later, so Geoffrey prepares a Trust Amendment to his trust document, naming his friend Brad as successor trustee instead.

Sample Form 8: Amendment to Basic Shared Living Trust or AB Trust

AMENDMENT TO LIVING TRUST

This Amendment to The ①_____ Jim and Toni Nance _____ Living Trust

your names

dated _____ July 1, _____, 19 _91_ , is made this _30th_ day of ___ November _____, 19_92_ ,

date Declaration of Trust signed

by ___ Toni Nance and Jim Nance _____, the grantors and trustees of the trust. Under the power

your names

of amendment reserved to the grantors by Section II, Paragraph (F), of the Declaration of Trust, the grantors

amend the trust as follows:

    1. The following is added to the Declaration of Trust:

        in Section IV, Paragraph A(1), Aaron Nance shall be given all Jim Nance's interest

        in the Wyche Co. stock

    2. The following is deleted from the Declaration of Trust:

        in Section IV, Paragraph A(1), Eileen Nance Jones shall be given all Jim Nance's

        interest in the Wyche Co. stock

    [Repeat as needed]

    In all other respects, the Declaration of Trust as executed on _____ July 1 _____, 19 _91_ , by

the grantors is hereby affirmed.

    Executed at _____ Fairview _____, _____ Ohio _____, on

city   state

_November 30 _____, 19 _92_ .

date

_____

Grantor and Trustee

_____

Grantor and Trustee

Do not change the original trustees of the living trust. You (and your spouse, if you made a basic shared living trust or AB trust) must be the original trustees of your living trust. If you aren't, the tax treatment of the trust changes. (See Chapter 7, "Trustees," Section A.)

G. Revoking Your Living Trust

You can revoke your living trust at any time, but you probably won't want to. After all, the reason(s) you established a trust wont go away, and revoking a living trust (unlike revoking a will) requires some work. The revoked trust ceases to exist and cannot own property. That means you must transfer ownership of all the trust property out of the living trust, back into your own name (or names) or into the name of a new living trust.

1. Who Can Revoke a Living Trust

Who can revoke your living trust depends on the kind of trust you created.

a.   Individual Living Trust

If you create an individual living trust, you (the grantor) can revoke it at any time. The trust document does not allow the trust to be revoked by someone acting on your behalf (your attorney-in-fact, for example) unless you have specifically granted that authority in another document. (See Section E, above.)

b.   Basic Shared Living Trust or AB Trust

Either spouse can revoke either of these trusts, wiping out all terms of the trust. The trust property is returned to each spouse according to how they owned it before transferring it to the trust.

Example

Yvonne and André make a basic shared living trust. Each transfers separately owned property to the trust. They also transfer their house, which they own together equally, as tenants in common, to the trust. Later Yvonne, anticipating a divorce, transfers the trust property she owned back to herself, and the property her husband owned back to him. The co-owned house goes back to both of them, who own it as tenants in common like before. She then revokes the trust.

The reason either spouse can revoke either a basic shared or AB trust, but it takes both to amend one, is that revocation simply returns both spouses to the status quo. By contrast, in the event of divorce or bitter conflict, it's risky to allow one spouse to amend a trust that governs both spouse's property.

2.   When to Revoke Your Living Trust

If you're like most people, amending your living trust will take care of your changing circumstances over the years, and you will never need to revoke your trust. But here are two situations in which you might need to revoke a living trust and start over.

a.   You Want to Make Extensive Revisions

If you want to make very extensive revisions to the terms of the trust document, you should revoke it and start fresh with a new trust document. If you don't, you risk creating inconsistencies and confusion.

b.   You Get Divorced

If you divorce, you should revoke your living trust, and you and your ex-spouse should make new, separate ones. In Florida and Tennessee, the provisions of your living trust that affect your spouse are automatically revoked by divorce, but you shouldn't rely on these laws.

3. How to Revoke Your Living Trust

To revoke your living trust, you must do two things:

Step 1. Transfer ownership of trust property from the trust back to yourself. Basically, you must reverse the process you followed when you transferred ownership of the property to the trust's name. (See Chapter 10, "Preparing Your Living Trust Document.") You can make the transfer because of your authority as trustee of the trust.

Step 2. Use Form 9 to prepare a simple document called a Revocation of Living Trust. Have the form typed, deleting all extraneous material from the final version. Sign the typed revocation in front of a notary. ❦

chapter 14

AFTER A GRANTOR DIES

The benefit of a revocable living trust doesn't come until after a grantor's death, when trust property is transferred to beneficiaries, or placed in an AB trust, without probate. The all-important responsibility of handling that transfer falls to your surviving spouse, if you made a basic shared living trust or an AB trust, or to your successor trustee, if you made an individual living trust.

The successor trustee or surviving spouse does not have to file any reports with, or be supervised by, any government agencies or court.

A. Who Serves as Trustee After the Grantor's Death

With a basic shared marital trust or AB trust, the surviving spouse serves as sole trustee after one spouse's death. With an individual trust, or when the surviving spouse dies, the successor trustee is in charge.

WHO SERVES AS TRUSTEE AFTER GRANTOR'S DEATH?

Individual Living Trust

1. Successor trustee(s)
2. Alternate successor trustee(s)

Basic Shared Living Trust or AB Trust

1. Surviving spouse
2. Successor trustee(s)
3. Alternate successor trustee(s)

---

1. More Than One Successor Trustee

If more than one person is named in the trust document as successor trustee, they all serve together. Whether each must formally agree on any action taken with regard to the living trust property, or they can act independently, depends on the terms of the trust document.

If one of the trustees cannot serve, the others remain as trustees. The person named as alternate successor trustee does not take over unless all the people named as successor trustees cannot serve.

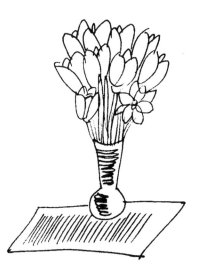

2. If a Trustee Resigns

A trustee can resign at any time by preparing and signing a resignation statement like the one shown below. The ex-trustee should deliver the notice to the person who is next in line to serve as trustee.

NOTICE OF RESIGNATION

I, Lucia Freni, current trustee of The Robert Ambruzzi Living Trust dated March 3, 1992, resign my position as trustee, effective immediately.

Date: November 19, 1993

Lucia Freni

[notarization]

Under the terms of Nolo living trusts, any trustee, including the last acting trustee, can appoint someone else to take over if no one named in the trust document can serve.

Normally, it would be the last, or alternate, successor trustee who named someone else to act as trustee if the need arises. The appointment must be in writing, signed and notarized. The trustee making the appointment can prepare a simple document like the one shown below.

APPOINTMENT OF TRUSTEE

I, Lucia Freni, Trustee of The Robert Ambruzzi Living Trust dated March 3, 1990, appoint Clarence Ryan as trustee, effective immediately. This appointment is made under the authority granted in the Declaration of Trust.

Date: November 19, 1993

Lucia Freni

[notarization]

---

3. Removing a Trustee

Very rarely, a beneficiary becomes seriously unhappy with the way a trustee handles trust property. For example, the beneficiary of a child's subtrust might complain that the trustee isn't spending enough of the trust property's income on the beneficiary's education. If the dispute can't be worked out, the beneficiary can file a lawsuit to try to force the removal of the trustee.

B. The Trustee's Duties

The trustee's job depends on whether you made an individual living trust, a basic shared living trust with your spouse, or an AB trust.

One step, however, is required in all three situations: The execution and recording of a document establishing that the successor trustee can act for the trust. The trustee may need such proof, particularly for transactions involving real estate, since there are no court proceedings to officially give the trustee authority. The accepted convention is to record a document called "Affidavit of Assumption of Duties by Successor Trustee" at the county land record's office. There is no set form for this affidavit. It should always include:

- the name of the trust
- the date the trust document was signed, and
- the name of the person becoming successor trustee.

A certified copy of the grantor's death certificate should be attached. Certified copies can be obtained from your county or state's vital records department.

A sample completed draft Affidavit of Assumption of Duties by Successor Trustee, ready for final typing, is shown below. A fill-in-the-blanks version is in the Appendix, Form 12.

Form 12: Affidavit of Successor Trustee

AFFIDAVIT OF ASSUMPTION OF DUTIES BY SUCCESSSOR TRUSTEE

State of _____Illinois_____, County of _____Cook_____.
                state   county

_____Ida Beilengeur_____, of legal age, first being duly sworn, declares:
        successor trustee's name

On _____March 23_____, 19_91_, _____Rosa and Vladimir Rostop_____ created
            date   name(s) of grantor(s)

the _____Rosa and Vladimir Rostop_____ Living Trust.
            name(s) of grantor(s)

On _____Sept. 2,_____, 19_94_, _____Vladimir Rostop_____ died, as
            date   grantor's name

established in the attached certified copy of the Certificate of Death.

[for a shared or AB trust, add:]

On _____Jan. 3,_____, 19_96_, _____Rosa Rostop_____ died, as
            date   second grantor's name

established in the attached certified copy of the Certificate of Death.

The Declaration of Trust creating the _____Rosa and Vladimir Rostop_____ Living Trust
                                            grantor(s) name(s)

provides that upon the death of the grantors, I, _____Ida Beilengeur_____,
                                                        successor trustee's name

become the trustee of the trust.

I hereby accept the office of trustee of the trust, and am now acting as trustee of the trust.

Dated: _____

_____
Successor Trustee
                [notarized]

1. Individual Trust

When the grantor, who is also the trustee, dies, the successor trustee named in the trust document takes over as trustee. The new trustee is responsible for distributing the trust property to the beneficiaries named by the grantor in the trust document.

It is not the trustee's responsibility to sell or manage trust property.

Example

Jamie is Elliot's successor trustee. Elliot's trust leaves his house to his children, Clarence and Grace. Elliot dies. Jamie, as trustee, deeds the house from the trust to Clarence and Grace, who can do with it what they wish—live in it, rent it or sell it. Jamie does not sell the house and divide the proceeds between the beneficiaries—that's not his decision to make.

Normally, the trust continues to exist only as long as it takes the successor trustee to distribute trust property to the beneficiaries. In many cases, a living trust can be wound up within a few weeks after a grantor's death. No formal termination document is required. Once the trust property has been distributed, the trust ends.

The successor trustee is also in charge of managing any property left to a young beneficiary in a child's subtrust. A subtrust will exist until the beneficiary reaches the age specified in the trust document, so if there's a subtrust the successor trustee may have years of work ahead. (See Chapter 9, "Property Left to Minor Children or Young Adults.")

If trust property inherited by a young beneficiary is to be managed by a custodian under the Uniform Transfers to Minors Act, instead of in a child's subtrust, the person named as custodian will receive that property and be responsible for it. The successor trustee may also have been named as the custodian for a young beneficiary's property.

THE SUCCESSOR TRUSTEE'S DUTIES: INDIVIDUAL TRUST

- Distribute trust property to beneficiaries named in the trust document.
- Manage trust property left in a child's subtrust, if any.
- File federal and state estate tax returns, if necessary (this is also the responsibility of the executor of the estate, if there was a will).

---

2. Basic Shared Living Trust

When a spouse dies, a basic shared living trust automatically splits into two separate trusts:

- Trust 1 contains the deceased spouse's share of trust property, excluding any trust property he or she left to the surviving spouse. The terms of Trust 1 cannot be changed, and it cannot be revoked.

- Trust 2 contains the surviving spouse's trust property, including any of the deceased spouse's share of the trust property that is left to the surviving spouse. The surviving spouse remains free to amend the terms of Trust 2, or even revoke it.

The survivor is sole trustee of Trust 1, Trust 2 and any children's subtrusts set up for the deceased spouse's young beneficiaries.

The two new trusts can be identified by adding "Trust 1" or "Trust 2" and the date these trusts came into existence (the date the first spouse dies), to the original basic shared living trust's name.

Example

Debra and Timothy Zeltzer create a basic shared living trust. Timothy dies. Debra can refer to her trust as "The Debra and Timothy Zeltzer Trust, Trust 2, dated June 11, 1990," and to her husband's trust, now irrevocable, as "The Debra and Timothy Zeltzer Trust, Trust 1, dated June 11, 1990."

It's the surviving spouse's job to distribute the property in Trust 1 to the beneficiaries the deceased spouse named in the trust document. If, as is common, much of the trust property is left to the surviving spouse, that spouse will have little to do. The trust property he or she inherits is already in the revocable trust (Trust 2), and remains there. The trust document provides that trust property left to the survivor does not go to the surviving spouse outright but instead stays in the living trust and becomes part of the property in Trust 2. If it did not contain such a provision, the property would have to be transferred from the living trust to the spouse and then, if the surviving spouse wanted it to avoid probate, back to her living trust again.

When all the property in Trust 1 has been distributed to the beneficiaries, that trust ceases to exist. No formal termination document is required.

Trust 2 contains only the surviving spouse's property and remains revocable. The surviving spouse is free to change it as he or she wishes.

Example

Edith and Jacques create a basic shared living trust. They transfer their house, which they own together, into the trust, and name each other as beneficiaries. Edith names her son as alternate beneficiary.

When Jacques dies, Edith inherits his half-interest in the house. Because of the way the trust document was worded, she doesn't have to change the trust document to name a beneficiary for the half-interest in the house that she inherited from her husband. Both halves will go to her son at her death. She may, however, want to amend the trust to make her son the primary beneficiary and name someone else to be alternate beneficiary.

When the second spouse dies, the successor trustee named in the trust document takes over as trustee. The process of winding up the living trust is the same as that for an individual trust. (See Section 1, above.)

Example

Harry and Maude, a married couple, set up a basic shared living trust to avoid probate. They appoint Maude's cousin Emily as successor trustee, to take over as trustee after they have both died. They transfer ownership of much of their co-owned property—their house, savings accounts and stocks—to the trust. Maude also puts some of her family heirlooms, which are her separate property, in the living trust.

In the trust document, Maude leaves her heirlooms to her younger sister. She leaves her half of the trust property she and Harry own together to Harry.

When Maude dies, Harry becomes the sole trustee. Following the terms of the trust document, he distributes Maude's heirlooms (from Trust 1) to her sister, without probate. Maude's half of the property they had owned together stays in the trust (in Trust 2); no transfer is necessary. After Maude's death, Harry decides to amend the trust document to name his nephew, Burt, as successor trustee instead of Maude's cousin Emily. When Harry dies, Burt will become trustee and distribute the property in Trust 2 according to Harry's written gifts made in the trust document. When all the property is given to Harry's beneficiaries, the trust ends.

THE SURVIVING SPOUSE'S DUTIES: BASIC SHARED LIVING TRUST

- Distribute the deceased spouse's share of the trust property to beneficiaries named in the trust document.
- Manage property left in a child's subtrust, if any.
- File federal and state estate tax returns, if necessary (this is also the executor's responsibility, if there is a will).
- Amend Trust 2 to reflect changed circumstances, if necessary or desired.

3. AB Trust

With an AB trust, both spouses are the original trustees. When a spouse dies, the surviving spouse becomes sole trustee. The living trust splits into two trusts: the irrevocable Trust A (of the deceased spouse) and Trust B, the revocable surviving spouse's trust.

The surviving spouse, as trustee, must first distribute any trust property the deceased spouse left to specifically named beneficiaries. (Remember, each spouse can make specific gifts of trust property to beneficiaries other than the other spouse.) Then the trustee must maintain the rest of that property in the ongoing Trust A.

THE SURVIVING SPOUSE'S DUTIES: AB TRUST

- Create and maintain Trust A. Divide property between this trust and the surviving spouse's Trust B.
- Distribute any specific gifts of the trust property made by the deceased spouse.
- Administer Trust A. File trust tax return each year, and, if required by trust document, give copies to final beneficiaries.
- Manage property left in a child's subtrust, if any.
- File federal and state estate tax returns, if necessary. (This is also the executor's responsibility if there is a will.)
- Amend the surviving spouse's trust, Trust B, to reflect changed circumstances, if necessary or desired.

As I've said before, determining the most financially desirable way to divide the living trust property between the A trust and the surviving spouse's B trust is often not a simple task. (See Chapter 5, "The Tax-Saving AB Trust," Section D.) Any allocation of equally owned trust property is valid, as long as each trust gets 50% of the total worth. But each item of property does not have to be split, with half going to each trust. For example, a house,

worth (net) $300,000 can be placed in Trust A, as long as other co-owned property with a total worth of $300,000 is placed in Trust B.

Determining the wisest division of property between the A, marital life estate, trust and the B, surviving spouse's, trust can be tricky. Hiring an expert tax and financial planner is often a wise investment here; it can sometimes result in far larger estate tax savings later on, after both spouses die. Since this book is primarily a living trust preparation book, I don't go through all the permutations and possibilities regarding this property division. If you have any questions, see an expert.

The IRS might want to know, at some point, which property was placed in the A trust and which was maintained in the B, or surviving spouse's, trust. So it's always a good idea for the successor trustee to prepare a list of property placed in each trust, and the net value of each item of property, as of the date of division.

To establish the A trust, the survivor does not need to create a new trust document. But property must be clearly identified as being owned by Trust A or Trust B. This usually requires some re-registering of title of some of the living trust property in the name of Trust A. For example, if you decide that it is wisest to put all of a shared ownership house in the Trust A, a new deed should be prepared to reflect this, listing the new owner as, for example, "The Moira and Joseph O'Sullivan Living Trust, A, dated 10/12/93." The deed is signed by the surviving spouse, as trustee.

In addition to a name, as just described, Trust A needs a federal taxpayer ID number. The surviving spouse must keep appropriate trust financial records and file a federal trust tax return every year. The IRS will want it clear which trust owns what. Annual state trust tax returns may also be required, in states with income taxes.

If the trust document requires it, the trustee is required to give copies of the trust's annual federal trust income tax return to the final beneficiaries.

The spouse as trustee manages the property in Trust A and, as life beneficiary, receives any income it generates.

The surviving spouse's trust, Trust B, goes on as before. It remains revocable and can be changed at any time. No new property documents are required. No tax return needs to be filed for this trust.

After the death of the surviving spouse, the successor trustee winds up both A and B trusts by distributing all property (except for any specific gifts made by the surviving spouse) of both trusts to each trust's final beneficiaries. The successor trustee must file a final tax return for Trust A. The successor trustee also manages any property left in a child's subtrust and files a closing income tax return for the second spouse.

C. Transferring Property to Beneficiaries

The procedure for transferring trust property to the beneficiaries who inherit it depends on the kind of property you're dealing with.

- Property of a basic shared living trust left by a deceased spouse to the surviving spouse remains in the trust, and no action is required.

- Property left to Trust A must be clearly identified as Trust A property. (See Section B, above.)

- Trust property left to adult beneficiaries must be actually transferred to them.

- Property left to a young beneficiary in a child's subtrust stays in the subtrust until the child reaches the age to receive that trust property outright.

- Property left to a custodian under the Uniform Transfers to Minors Act must be given to the custodian named in the trust document.

To obtain the trust property, generally the trustee will need a copy of the grantor's death certificate (both grantors' death certificates, if both are dead and the trust property was originally co-owned) and a copy of the trust document. (The trustee should be prepared to show the original trust document in case anyone doubts the copy's authenticity.) Frequently an Affidavit of Assumption of Duties by Successor Trustee will also be needed. And finally, in some cases, the trustee will need to prepare some other paperwork, such as a specific form of a brokerage company or a new deed for real estate.

Specific requirements for transferring property vary slightly from place to place, and the trustee may have to make inquiries at banks, stock brokerages and other institutions about current procedures, but here are the general rules. A trustee who runs into difficulties has the authority to get help—from a lawyer, accountant or other expert—and pay for it from trust assets.

For California residents, *How to Probate an Estate*, by Julia Nissley (Nolo Press), contains forms and instructions on transferring the property of a decedent, including living trust property.

Terminology. This section refers to whoever takes over as trustee after a grantor's death as the "trustee." To remind you, if you made an individual trust, the trustee is the person you named as successor trustee. If you made a shared marital trust, or an AB trust, the trustee is the surviving spouse or, after both spouses have died, the successor trustee.

1. Property Without Title Documents

For trust property that doesn't have a title document—furniture, for example—the task of the trustee is quite simple. The trustee must promptly distribute the property to the beneficiaries named in the trust document. If the trustee thinks it's a good idea, it's appropriate to have the recipient sign a receipt. But in many family situations, where all trust each other, this formality isn't necessary.

2. Bank Accounts

It should be simple for the trustee to transfer the funds in a bank or savings and loan account, already held in the name of the living trust, to the beneficiary. Financial institutions are familiar with living trusts and how they work, and the bank probably has the trust document (or a bank form with information about the trust) already on file.

The trustee will need to show the bank or savings and loan:

- a certified copy of the trust grantor's death certificate

- a copy of the living trust document, if the bank doesn't already have one (again, being prepared to show the original trust document, if demanded), and

- proof of his or her own identity, perhaps including an Affidavit of Assumption of Duties by Successor Trustee.

3. Real Estate

The trustee needs to prepare and sign a deed transferring ownership of real estate from the trust to the beneficiary. The trustee signs the deed, in her capacity as trustee.

Example

"Jane Adanski, Trustee of The Robert Whilhite Living Trust, dated October 25, 1992."

The signed and notarized deed should also be filed (recorded) with the county land records office. In most places, recording costs no more than a few dollars per page. It's unlikely, but depending on local and state law, there may be a transfer tax to pay. (Deeds, recording and transfer taxes are discussed in Chapter 11, "Transferring Property to Your Trust," Section E.)

Example

The deed to Evelyn Crocker's house shows that it is owned by Evelyn Crocker, as trustee of her living trust. The living trust document states that Evelyn's daughter, Amanda, is to inherit the house when Evelyn dies. Amanda is also the successor trustee of the trust.

After Evelyn's death, Amanda prepares and signs a new deed, transferring ownership of the house from the trust to herself. She signs the deed in her capacity as trustee of the trust, and records the deed in the county land records office, along with an Affidavit of Assumption of Duties by Successor Trustee.

A title company, before it will issue title insurance to the new owners, will probably want a copy of the trust document and a certified copy of the death certificate of the trust grantor.

4. Stocks and Bonds

How to transfer stocks or bonds from a trust to the beneficiary depends on whether they were held in a brokerage account or separately.

Stock in closely-held corporations. See Section 6, below.

a. Brokerage Accounts

The trustee should contact the broker and ask for instructions. The brokerage company will almost surely already have either a copy of the living trust document or a form that includes relevant information about the trust. (These are necessary to transfer the account to the living trust in the first place.)

If not, the trustee will probably need to send the broker:

- a copy of the trust document or an "abstract of trust" (the first, last and other relevant pages of the trust document, showing the notarized signature—see Chapter 11, "Transferring Property to Your Trust," Section C, for a sample "Abstract of Trust"), and

- a letter instructing the holder to transfer the brokerage account to the beneficiary's name.

b. Stock Certificates

If the deceased grantor kept the stock certificates or bonds in his or her possession—most people don't—the trustee must get new certificates issued, showing the beneficiary as the new owner.

The trustee will have to send the securities' transfer agent several documents. It's a good idea to write the transfer agent and ask exactly what is needed. Usually, the name and address of the transfer agent appear on the face of the stock or bond certificate. But because transfer agents change occasionally, the first thing the trustee should do is write or call (or check with a stock brokerage firm) to verify the name and address of the current transfer agent.

The trustee will probably have to send in:

- A certified copy of the grantor's death certificate

- The certificates or bonds

- A document called a "stock or bond power," which the trustee must fill out and sign, with the signature guaranteed by an officer of a bank or brokerage firm (the stock or bond power may be printed on the back of the certificates; if not, stationery stores carry them)

- A copy of the trust document or an "abstract of trust" if the transfer agent did not receive one when the securities were transferred into the trust

- An Affidavit of Domicile (a form available from banks and stock brokers) signed by the trustee, showing what the trust grantor's state of residence was

- A letter of instructions requesting that the certificates be reissued in the beneficiary's name.

Also, the trustee may be required to have his signature "guaranteed" by a stock broker. If neither the trustee nor the deceased grantor have, or had, a stock account with a brokerage company, this too may cause trouble. The trustee will have to locate a broker—maybe one who handles a friend's account—to "guarantee" your signature.

The trustee may be required to produce "certified copies" of the living trust, although the transfer agent isn't sure what agency "certifies" documents. Your best bet here is to file the original document with your local county records office and have them "certify" copies for you.

BUREAUCRATS, BUREAUCRATS

In rare instances, the trustee can encounter odd and difficult problems, depending on the narrowness and obstinacy of the transfer agent. For example, one successor trustee was told by two transfer agents that he must obtain a written statement from a lawyer or bank that the trust hadn't been modified since it was signed. This was an irrational and unreasonable requirement. The grantor was dead, and no lawyer or bank was involved in preparing his trust. Eventually, after considerable persistence, the trustee succeeded in persuading the transfer agents that he knew of no amendment to the trust, and it was ridiculous for them to demand impossible proof that no amendment existed, so the stock transfers were approved.

Moral: Be persevering if you must, and eventually you'll get the stock transfer approved by the transfer agent.

---

c. Government Securities

To transfer government securities—Treasury bills or U.S. bonds, for example—the trustee should ask the broker to contact the issuing government agency, or contact the government directly.

5. Mutual Funds or Money Market Accounts

For mutual funds or money market accounts owned in the trust's name, the trustee should ask the company what it requires to re-register ownership of the account in the beneficiary's name. Generally, the trustee must send the company proof of his or her own identity, a copy of the grantor's death certificate, a letter of instructions (or a form that the company provides) and a copy of the trust document.

6. Small Business Interests

How a trustee transfers small business interests owned by a living trust depends on the way the business was organized.

Trademarks. A registered trademark or service mark of a small business must be reregistered in the name of the beneficiary. See *Trademark: How to Name Your Business and Product*, by Kate McGrath and Steve Elias (Nolo Press).

a. Sole Proprietorships

The trustee must transfer business assets to the beneficiary like he or she would transfer any other trust property. The name of the business itself, if owned by the living trust, does not have a title document, so the trustee doesn't need to do anything to transfer it to the beneficiary.

b. Solely-Owned Corporations

Corporation officers must prepare the appropriate corporate records to show that ownership has been transferred to the beneficiary. This will depend on the incorporation papers and company bylaws. Often a resolution by the board of directors is required. Additional paperwork may include such documents as "Notice of Special Meeting of Board of Directors" and "Waiver of Notice of Time Re-

quirements to Hold Special Meeting of Board of Directors." Then the trustee must have the stock certificates reissued in the beneficiary's name.

c. Closely-Held Corporations

The stock certificates owned by the trust will have to be reissued in the beneficiary's name. The trustee should contact the officers of the corporation; the other shareholders may have the right, under the corporation's bylaws or a separate shareholders' agreement, to buy back the shares.

d. Partnership Interests

The trustee should contact the deceased grantor's partners, who may have the right to buy out the grantor's share. If the beneficiary wants to enter into the partnership, the partnership agreement must be changed to add the beneficiary. See *The Partnership Book*, by Denis Clifford and Ralph Warner (Nolo Press).

7. Copyrights

To transfer an interest in a copyright to a beneficiary, the trustee should sign and file, with the U.S. Copyright Office in Washington, D.C., a document transferring all the trust's rights in the copyright to the beneficiary. Sample transfer forms are in *The Copyright Handbook*, by Stephen Fishman (Nolo Press).

8. Patents

To transfer a patent from a living trust, the trustee should prepare a document called an "assignment" and record it with the U.S. Patent and Trademark Office in Washington, D.C. There is a small fee for recording. Sample assignment forms and instructions are in *Patent It Yourself* and *Patent It Yourself* software, by David Pressman (Nolo Press).

9. Other Property With Title Documents

If an item of trust property has a title document that shows ownership in the name of the trust, the trustee must prepare and sign a new title document transferring ownership to the beneficiary. Usually, the trustee will need a copy of the trust document and of the trust grantor's death certificate if the property is in someone else's possession.

If a vehicle was owned by the trust, the trustee should contact the state Department of Motor Vehicles to get the forms required to transfer it to the beneficiary.

D. Preparing and Filing Tax Returns

Depending on the circumstances, the successor trustee may have to file several tax returns:

- Federal estate tax return for the deceased grantor, if the value of the estate is large enough

- State death tax return for the deceased grantor, if state law requires it

- Final federal income tax return (and state return, if there's a state income tax) for the deceased grantor

- Final federal income tax return (and state return, if there's a state income tax) for the A trust after both spouses die.

Legally, filing these returns is the responsibility both of the successor trustee and of the executor named in the deceased grantor's will. The same person usually serves as both executor and successor trustee.

Generally, the state and federal income tax returns are due April 15 of the year following the grantor's death. The federal estate tax return is due nine months after the grantor's death.

The trustee is entitled, by the terms of the trust document, to pay for professional help out of the trust assets. And that help may well be necessary, because tax matters—particularly estate tax matters—can get quite tricky.

For assistance with the estate tax return, the successor trustee can get a helpful set of instructions, "Instructions for Form 706," from the Internal Revenue Service. Another useful IRS publication is called "Federal Estate and Gift Taxes" (Publication 448).

E. Administering a Child's Subtrust

If, in the trust document, the deceased grantor set up a child's subtrust, the trustee will have to manage that property if the beneficiary isn't old enough to receive it outright. A child's subtrust comes into being only if, at the grantor's death, the beneficiary has not yet reached the age the grantor specified.

Example

Carl sets up a living trust and names his two young children as beneficiaries. He specifies that if either child is younger than 30 when he dies, the property that child is to inherit from the trust should be kept in a separate child's subtrust.

When Carl dies, one child is 30; the other is 25. The 30-year-old receives her trust property with no strings attached. But a child's subtrust is created for the 25-year-old. The successor trustee is responsible for managing the property and turning it over to the child when he turns 30.

The trustee's duties in managing a child's subtrust are explained in Chapter 9, "Property Left to Minor Children or Young Adults," Section C.

F. Administering a Custodianship

Someone who is appointed in the trust document to be the custodian of trust property inherited by a young beneficiary has roughly the same management responsibilities as the trustee of a child's subtrust. (See Chapter 9, "Property Left to Minor Children or Young Adults," Section D.) The specifics of the custodian's duties are set out in the Uniform Transfers to Minors Act, as adopted by the particular state's legislature. ❧

chapter 15

A Living Trust as Part of Your Estate Plan

*a*revocable living trust can accomplish most people's main estate planning goal: leaving their property to their loved ones while avoiding probate and perhaps saving on estate taxes as well. But it is not, by itself, a complete estate plan. For example, in most states, parents of young children can't use a living trust to appoint a personal guardian to care for their minor children. To do this, you need a will. A living trust also can't take care of property you buy or inherit shortly before you die and don't get around to transferring to the trust.

This chapter provides an overview of estate planning methods that you may want to explore in addition to a living trust. Basically, estate planning includes:

- Deciding who will inherit your property when you die

- Deciding who will take care of your children and their finances if you die while they are young

- Setting up procedures and devices to minimize probate fees at your death

- If your estate is large, planning to reduce federal estate taxes (and state death taxes, if your state has them); with the exception of an AB trust, the trust forms in this book don't afford any estate tax savings

- Arranging for someone to make financial and health care decisions for you in case at some time you can no longer do so yourself.

A. Using a Back-Up Will

Even though you create a living trust, you need a simple back-up will, too. Like a living trust, a will is a document in which you specify what is to be done with your property when you die.

Having a will is important for several reasons:

- A will is an essential back-up device for property that you don't get around to transferring to your living trust.

- In a will you can name someone to be the personal guardian of your minor child, in case you and the child's other parent die while the child is still under

18. In most states, you can't do that in a living trust. (A few states' laws can be construed to permit appointing a child's personal guardian in a living trust, but it's prudent to be conventional and appoint the guardian in a will, the normal way.)

- If you want to disinherit your spouse or a child, you must make your wishes clear in a will. (State law may restrict your freedom to disinherit a spouse; see Chapter 8, "Choosing Your Beneficiaries.")

Instructions for preparing a back-up will are in Chapter 16, "Wills," and sample will forms are in the Appendix, Forms 10 and 11.

B. Other Probate-Avoidance Methods

A living trust is not the only way to transfer some kinds of assets without probate, and it's not the best in all circumstances. For example, it's usually cumbersome to have your personal checking account held in the name of your living trust, because businesses may be reluctant to accept your checks.

Fortunately, you can mix and match probate-avoidance techniques. Just put whatever property you want in your living trust, and choose other transfer methods—ones that also avoid probate—for the rest of your property.

You might, for example, want to put your checking account into joint tenancy with your spouse; at your death, your spouse would automatically take sole ownership of the account. Some helpful probate-avoidance methods are summarized below.

1. Pay-on-Death Accounts

Setting up a pay-on-death account, also called an informal bank account trust or revocable trust account, is an easy way to transfer cash at your death, quickly and without probate. All you do is designate, on a form provided by the institution, one or more persons you want to receive any money in the account when you die.

OTHER NOLO PRESS ESTATE PLANNING RESOURCES

Plan Your Estate, by Denis Clifford and Cora Jordan, covers all the estate planning methods briefly discussed in this chapter, and more. It contains extensive discussion about probate avoidance methods and estate tax reduction techniques from gift-giving to generation-skipping trusts, including estate and gift taxes, ongoing trusts and probate-avoidance methods.

WillMaker®, Nolo's computer will program, enables you to prepare a comprehensive will, including a simple trust for your minor children, allowing you to choose the age at which your children inherit property you leave them.

Living Trust Maker, Nolo's computer living trust program, lets you make a probate-avoidance living trust. It does not cover tax-reducing trusts for couples with large estates.

Nolo's Simple Will Book, by Denis Clifford, is an in-depth explanation of how to prepare a will that covers all normal needs, including simple trusts for your minor children.

The Quick & Legal Will Book, by Denis Clifford, enables you to prepare a basic will easily and effectively.

How to Probate an Estate (California), by Julia Nissley, enables Californians to handle a normal probate without an attorney.

The Deeds Book (California), by Mary Randolph, explains how to use deeds to transfer real estate for estate planning.

Beat the Nursing Home Trap: A Consumer's Guide to Choosing and Financing Long-Term Care, by Joseph Matthews, discusses how to finance and choose long-term care.

Social Security, Medicare and Pensions, by Joseph Matthews, is an excellent resource about rights and benefits of older Americans.

All these books and software are good in every state but Louisiana.

You can use any kind of bank account, including savings, checking or certificate of deposit accounts. You can also register ownership of certain kinds of government securities, including bonds, Treasury bills and Treasury notes, in a way that lets you name a beneficiary to receive them at your death.

Example

Terry opens a savings account in her name, and names Lynn Harris as the pay-on-death (P.O.D.) beneficiary. When Terry dies, whatever money is in the account will go to Lynn.

During your life, the beneficiary has absolutely no right to the money in the account. You can withdraw some or all of the money, close the account or change the beneficiary, at any time. When you die, the beneficiary can claim the money simply by showing the bank the death certificate and personal identification.

Like other bank accounts, a pay-on-death account may be temporarily frozen at your death, if your state levies death taxes. The state will release the money to your beneficiaries when shown that your estate has sufficient funds to pay the taxes.

COMMON PROBATE-AVOIDANCE METHODS

Method	Advantages	Disadvantages
Revocable living trust	Flexible, private. Easy to create. You keep control over property during your life.	Some paperwork involved. May need attorney if yours is a complicated estate.
Pay-on-death accounts (revocable trust accounts)	Easy to create, using a form provided by the bank or agency.	Limited to bank accounts and some government securities.
Naming beneficiary of pension plan or retirement account	Easy to do. Beneficiary inherits all funds in the account at your death.	None, unless particular program imposes limits.
Life insurance	Good way to provide quick cash for beneficiaries or to pay estate taxes. Proceeds don't go through probate.	Family members may not need much immediate cash if they don't rely on you to support them, so expense of policy may not be justified.
Joint tenancy with right of survivorship	Easy to create.	Restricted in a few states. If you don't already own property in joint tenancy, you may not want to add another owner, who could sell his share. (For larger estates, there are negative gift tax consequences, too.) Can be a problem if a co-owner becomes incapacitated. No probate avoidance if all joint owners die at once.
Tenancy by the entirety	Easy to create.	Available only in some states; limited to married couples. Can be a problem if one spouse becomes incapacitated.
Community property with right of survivorship	All the benefits of community property ownership plus probate-avoidance when one spouse dies.	Available only to married couples in four states: Arizona, Nevada, Texas and Wisconsin.
Gifts of property made while you're alive	Reduces amount of property in your estate, which avoids both probate and estate taxes.	You lose control over property given away while you're alive. Large gifts use up part of your federal gift/estate tax exemption. Insurance policies must be given away at least three years before death, or proceeds are included in your taxable estate.
State laws that allow simplified probate proceedings	Exempts certain property from formal probate.	Applies only to small estates; you may still need an attorney to explain the technicalities of your state's laws.
Transfer-on-death designation for motor vehicles	Easy to do. All you do is name, on your registration form, someone to inherit your vehicle.	Currently available only in California and Missouri, but other states are considering similar programs.
Transfer-on-death registration for securities	Easy to do. All you do is name, on the registration form, someone to inherit the securities at your death.	Not available in a number of states. See list in Chapter 6, "Choosing What Property to Put in Your Living Trust," Section C.

Most banks have forms for setting up this kind of account, and they don't charge more for keeping your money this way. Before you open a pay-on-death account, ask your bank if there are any special state law requirements about notifying the beneficiary. In a few states, a pay-on-death provision isn't effective unless you have notified the beneficiary that you've set up the account. Your bank should be able to fill you in on your state's rules.

2. Pension Plans and Retirement Accounts

Retirement accounts such as IRAs and Profit Sharing Plan accounts weren't designed to be probate avoidance devices, but if you have any money left in such accounts when you die, they can easily be used that way. All you have to do is name a beneficiary to receive the funds still in your pension plan or retirement account at your death, and the funds will not go through probate.

After age 70½, however, federal law requires you to withdraw at least a certain amount every year or face a monetary penalty. The amount is refigured every year, based on your current life expectancy and, to some extent, that of your beneficiary.

3. Life Insurance

As life insurance agents will be delighted to explain, life insurance is a good way to provide surviving family members with quick cash for debts, living expenses and, in larger estates, estate taxes. And because you name the beneficiary in the policy itself, not in your will, life insurance proceeds don't go through probate.

The only circumstance in which life insurance proceeds are subject to probate is if the beneficiary named in the policy is your estate. That's done occasionally if the estate will need immediate cash to pay debts and taxes, but it's usually counterproductive. It's almost always a better idea to name your spouse, children or another beneficiary who can take the money free of probate and use it to pay debts and taxes.

Although the proceeds of a life insurance policy don't go through probate, they are included in your estate for federal estate tax purposes. If you think your estate will be liable for federal estate taxes, you can reduce the tax bill by giving away the policy to the beneficiary, another person or an irrevocable life insurance trust (discussed below in Section C2).

For help with choosing a life insurance policy from the bewildering array now available, see *Consumer Reports Life Insurance Handbook: How to Buy the Right Life Insurance Policy at the Right Price* (Consumer Reports Books).

LIFE INSURANCE TO PROVIDE FOR YOUR CHILDREN

If you have young children but not much money, consider buying a moderate amount of term life insurance, which would provide cash to support your children if you died while they were still young. Because term life insurance pays benefits only if you die during the covered period (often five or ten years), it's far cheaper than other types of life insurance. You can stop renewing the insurance when, by the end of the current term, the children will be on their own or your estate would be large enough to support them until they are.

4. Joint Tenancy

Joint tenancy is one of the more commonly used probate-avoidance devices. It's an efficient and practical way to transfer some kinds of property in some situations, but for most kinds of property, a living trust is usually a better choice.

a. How Joint Tenancy Works

Joint tenancy is a way two or more people can hold title to property they own together. It is available in almost all states (see list below).

For estate planning purposes, the most important characteristic of joint tenancy is that when one joint owner (called a joint tenant) dies, the surviving joint owners automatically get complete ownership of the property. This is called the "right of survivorship." The property doesn't go through probate court—there is only some simple paperwork to fill out to transfer the property into the name of the surviving owner.

Example

Evelyn and her daughter own a car in joint tenancy. When Evelyn dies, her half-interest in the car will go to her daughter without probate. Her daughter will need only to fill out a simple form to transfer ownership of the car into her own name.

Joint tenancy certainly has the virtue of simplicity. To create a joint tenancy, all the co-owners need to do is pay attention to the way they are listed on the document that shows ownership of property, such as a deed to real estate, a car's title slip or a card establishing a bank account. In the great majority of states, by calling themselves "joint tenants with the right of survivorship," the owners create a joint tenancy. In a few states, additional specific words are necessary. If you want to set up a joint tenancy and aren't sure how to word a title document, ask a real estate lawyer or someone at a land title company. All joint tenants must own equal shares of the property.

A joint tenant cannot leave his or her share to anyone other than the surviving joint tenants. So even if Evelyn, in the preceding example, left a will giving her half-interest in the car to her son instead of her daughter, the daughter would still get the car.

STATE LAW RESTRICTIONS ON JOINT TENANCY

Alaska	No joint tenancy in real estate, except for husband and wife.
Pennsylvania	No joint tenancy in real estate (but this rule has been questioned in court decisions).
Tennessee	No joint tenancy except for husband and wife.
Texas	No joint tenancy in any kind of property unless there's a written joint tenancy agreement signed by the owners.

This rule isn't as ironclad as it may sound. A joint tenant can, while still alive, break the joint tenancy by transferring his or her interest in the property to someone else (or, in most states, to himself, but not as a "joint tenant"). The new owner isn't a joint tenant with the other original owners.

Example

David, Jan and Loren own property together in joint tenancy. David sells his one-third interest to Paul. Paul is not a joint tenant with Jan and Loren; he is a "tenant in common," free to leave his property to whomever he wants. Jan and Loren, however, are still joint tenants with respect to their two-thirds of the property; when one of them dies, the other will own the two-thirds.

Joint bank accounts. If you and someone else want to set up a joint tenancy account together, so that the survivor will get all the funds, normally you can do it in a few minutes at the bank. Your bank should be able to tell you about any requirements. In a few states, you may need to comply with certain formalities. Texas law, for example, requires a written agreement—not just a signature card—to set up such an account. A dispute over such an account ended up in the Texas Supreme Court. Two sisters had set up an account together, using a signature card that allowed the survivor to withdraw the funds. When the surviving sister withdrew the funds, the estate of the deceased sister sued and won the funds. *Stauffer v. Henderson*, 801 S.W.2d 858 (Tex. 1991).

b. When to Consider Joint Tenancy

Joint tenancy often works well when couples (married or not) acquire real estate or other valuable property together. If they take title in joint tenancy, probate is avoided when the first owner dies.

But there are advantages to transferring the property to your living trust, even if you already own it in joint tenancy. First, a living trust, unlike joint tenancy, allows you to name an alternate beneficiary—someone who will inherit the property if the first beneficiary (your spouse)

doesn't survive you. If you own property in joint tenancy, and you and your spouse die at the same time, the property will go to the residuary beneficiary named in your will—but it will have to go through probate first.

Second, if you transfer joint tenancy property to a living trust, you will avoid probate both when the first spouse dies and when the second spouse dies. With joint tenancy, probate is avoided only when the first spouse dies. The second spouse, who owns the property alone after the first spouse's death, must take some other measure—such as transferring it to a living trust—to avoid probate.

Transferring joint tenancy property in common law states. As discussed in Chapter 11, "Transferring Property to Your Trusts," Section A, if you live in a common law state, when transferring joint tenancy property to a living trust, you need first to transfer the property into "tenancy in common, in equal shares" by preparing a new deed, and then transfer the property to your trust.

c. When to Think Twice About Joint Tenancy

Joint tenancy is usually a poor estate planning device when an older person, seeking only to avoid probate, puts solely owned property into joint tenancy with someone else. Doing this creates several potential problems that don't occur with a living trust:

You can't change your mind. If you make someone else a co-owner, in joint tenancy, of property that you now own yourself, you give up half ownership of the property. The new owner has rights that you can't take back. For example, the new owner can sell or mortgage his or her share. And even if the other joint tenant's half isn't mortgaged, it could still be lost to creditors.

Example

Maureen, a widow, signs a deed that puts her house into joint tenancy with her son to avoid probate at her death. Later, the son's business fails, and he is sued by creditors. His half-interest in the house may be taken by the creditors to pay the court judgment, which means that the house might be sold. Maureen would get the value of her half in cash; her son's half of the proceeds would go to pay the creditors.

By contrast, if you put property in a revocable living trust, you don't give up any ownership now. You are always free to change your mind about who you want to get the property at your death.

There's no way to handle the incapacity of one joint tenant. If one joint tenant becomes incapacitated and cannot make decisions, the other owners must get legal authority to sell or mortgage the property. That may mean going to court to get someone (called a conservator, in most states) appointed to manage the incapacitated person's affairs. (This problem can be partially dealt with if the joint tenant has signed a document called a "Durable Power of Attorney," giving someone authority to manage his affairs if he cannot. See Section E, below.)

With a living trust, if you (the grantor) become incapacitated, the successor trustee (or the other spouse, if it's a shared trust) takes over and has full authority to manage the trust property. No court proceedings are necessary.

Gift taxes may be assessed. If you create a joint tenancy by making another person a co-owner, federal gift tax may be assessed on the transfer. This probably isn't a reason not to transfer property; making a gift can be a sound estate planning strategy. But be aware that if gifts to one person (except your spouse) exceed $10,000 per year, you must file a gift tax return with the IRS. (See Section C, below.) There's one exception: If two or more people open a bank account in joint tenancy, but one person puts all or most of the money in, no gift tax is assessed against that person. A taxable gift may be made, however, when a joint tenant who has contributed little or nothing to the account withdraws money from it.

Surviving spouse misses an income tax break. If you make your spouse a joint tenant with you on property you own separately, the surviving spouse could miss out on a potentially big income tax break later, when the property is sold.

When it comes to property owned in joint tenancy, the Internal Revenue Service rule is that a surviving spouse gets a stepped-up tax basis only for the half of the property owned by the deceased spouse. The tax basis is the amount from which taxable profit is figured when property is sold. You may not face this problem if you live in a community property state. If property held in joint tenancy property is actually community property, it will still qualify for a stepped-up tax basis if the surviving spouse can show the IRS that it was in fact community property. But it's up to you to prove it; when one spouse dies, the IRS presumes that property held in joint tenancy is not community property. When the property is later sold, this means higher tax if the property has gone up in value after the joint tenancy was created but before the first spouse died.

If you leave your solely-owned property to your spouse through your living trust, however, the entire property gets a stepped-up tax basis.

5. Tenancy by the Entirety

"Tenancy by the entirety" is a form of property ownership that is similar to joint tenancy, but is limited to married couples. It is available only in the states listed below.

STATES THAT ALLOW TENANCY BY THE ENTIRETY

Alaska*	Maryland	Ohio
Arkansas	Massachusetts	Oklahoma
Delaware	Michigan*	Oregon*
District of Columbia	Mississippi	Pennsylvania
Florida	Missouri	Tennessee
Hawaii	New Jersey*	Vermont
Indiana*	New York*	Virginia*
Kentucky*	North Carolina*	Wyoming*

*Allowed for real estate only.

Tenancy by the entirety has almost the same advantages and disadvantages of joint tenancy and is most useful in the same kind of situation: when a couple acquires property together. When one spouse dies, the surviving spouse inherits the property. The property doesn't go through probate.

If property is held in tenancy by the entirety, neither spouse can transfer his or her half of the property alone, either while alive or by will or trust. A living spouse must get the other spouse's consent to transfer the property; at death, it must go to the surviving spouse. (This is different from joint tenancy; a joint tenant is free to transfer his or her share to someone else during his life.)

Example

Fred and Ethel hold title to their house in tenancy by the entirety. If Fred wanted to sell or give away his half-interest in the house, he could not do so without Ethel's signature on the deed.

6. Community Property With Right of Survivorship

Married couples in one of these four community property states—Arizona, Nevada, Texas, Wisconsin—have another option that may be useful.

Couples in Arizona, Nevada, or Wisconsin can hold title to their community property "with right of survivorship"—meaning that when one spouse dies, the other automatically owns all the property. (Ariz. Rev. Stat. § 33-431; Nev. Rev. Stat. § 111.064; Wis. Stats. § 766.60.) Texas lets couples make a written agreement that some or all of their community property will have a right of survivorship. (Tex. Prob. Code § 451.)

These arrangements offer all the benefits of community property ownership, plus the important advantage that the property doesn't go through probate when one spouse dies. Instead, the surviving spouse owns it automatically.

Wisconsin law goes even further. It lets married couples avoid probate altogether for their marital property. In a "marital property agreement," they can name a beneficiary—a person, trust or other entity—to inherit their marital property, without probate. And like an AB trust, the agreement can even provide for the disposition of property at the death of the second spouse (though that spouse can amend the agreement after the first spouse's death unless the agreement says otherwise). (Wis. Stats. §§ 766.58, 766.60.)

7. Gifts

If you give away property while you're alive, there will be less property in your estate to go through probate when you die. But if probate avoidance is your goal, usually it's better to use one of the other methods discussed above, which let you keep control over your property while you're alive, than to give away everything before you die.

Making gifts of up to $10,000 per year per person, however, may be a good strategy if you expect your estate to owe federal estate tax after your death, and you want to reduce the eventual tax bite. (See Section C, below.)

8. Simplified Probate Proceedings

Many states have begun, albeit slowly, to dismantle some of the more onerous aspects of probate. They have created categories of property and beneficiaries that don't have to go through a full-blown probate court proceeding. If your family can take advantage of these procedures after your death, you may not need to worry too much about avoiding probate.

Almost every state has some kind of simplified (summary) probate or out-of-court transfer process for one or more of these categories:

Small estates. For "small estates," many states have created an out-of-court procedure that lets people collect the property they've inherited by filling out a sworn statement (affidavit) and giving it to the person who has the property. Typically, the beneficiary must also provide some kind of proof of his or her right to inherit, such as a death certificate and copy of the will. What qualifies as a small estate varies from state to state, from $5,000 to $60,000.

Personal property. In some states, the only property that qualifies for simplified transfer procedures is personal property—that is, anything except real estate.

Property left to the surviving spouse. In some states, if a surviving spouse inherits less than a certain amount of property, no probate is necessary.

Most people leave property that is worth more than can be passed without probate under state probate simpli-

fication laws. In many states, if the value of your entire estate exceeds the maximum set by law for simplified probate, you cannot use simplified probate procedures—even if most of your property is being passed through probate-avoidance devices such as a living trust.

Example

At her death, Jane has an estate worth $300,000. Her major asset is her home, worth $200,000, which she passes to her daughter through a living trust. She also passes $80,000 worth of other property through other probate-avoidance devices. That leaves $20,000 of property. In Jane's state, the maximum total estate (including all property transferred by all methods) for streamlined probate procedures is $25,000. So Jane's heirs can't use the simplified procedures for the last $20,000 of property, because Jane's total estate exceeds the limit.

In some states, however, even if your total estate is too large, you can still make use of the simplified procedures if the amount that actually goes through probate is under the limit. For example, in California, property worth less than $60,000 transferred by will is exempt from normal probate, no matter how large the total estate. So, if Jane lived in California, the $20,000 of property left through Jane's will could be transferred by a simple affidavit.

Every state's simplified probate laws are summarized in *Plan Your Estate,* by Denis Clifford and Cora Jordan (Nolo Press).

C. Federal Gift and Estate Taxes

Some basic federal estate tax rules have been discussed in previous chapters. Here are the basics you need to keep in mind:

- A certain amount of property ($625,000 in 1996, more after that) of property is exempt from tax, no matter who it is given to or left to. (See chart in Chapter 5.)

- All property given or left to a surviving spouse who is a United States citizen is tax-exempt (the marital deduction).

- All property given or left to tax-exempt charities is exempt.

- Gifts of up to $10,000 per year per person (that is, the person who receives the gift) are exempt from gift taxes.

A federal estate tax return must be filed if the gross value of the estate, on death, exceeds the exempt amount. Estate taxes will be due if the net estate exceeds the exempt amount. (The assets in the estate are valued as of the date of death or, as an optional alternative, six months later, if it produces a lesser estate value. An exception is that any asset distributed to beneficiaries or sold at an earlier date must be valued when it is distributed or sold.) Tax must be paid within nine months of death.

Federal estate taxes start at 37% for property worth between $625,000 and $750,000, and rise to 55% for property over $3 million.

Because the federal government taxes substantial gifts made during life or at death, the proper name of the federal estate tax is the "unified gift and estate tax." Congress reasoned that if only gifts made at death were taxed, everyone would give away as much property as they could during their lives. No tax is actually paid on gifts made during your life, however, until your death (unless you give away an enormous amount of property while you're alive), when your combined gift and estate tax liability is calculated.

The federal estate/gift tax won't affect you unless you give away or leave taxable property worth more than the exempt amount.

Example

Susan doesn't make any taxable gifts during her life and leaves $500,000 worth of property at her death, using a living trust and back-up will. Her estate owes no federal gift and estate tax. However, if Susan had made taxable gifts of $450,000 during her life, her combined estate and gift tax property would be $950,000, over the exempt amount.

1. Special Rules for Non-Citizen Spouses

The unlimited marital deduction for property one spouse leaves (or gives while living) to another applies only if the recipient spouse is a citizen of the United States. It doesn't matter that a non-citizen spouse was married to a U.S. citizen or is a legal resident of the U.S. While both are alive, a spouse can, however, give the other, non-citizen, spouse up to $100,000 per year free of gift tax.

The exempt amount, however, remains available, and a citizen can leave a non-citizen spouse property tax-free under this exemption.

Example

Lily Lim, a U.S. citizen, leaves her entire estate worth $800,000 to her husband, Choy Lim, a non-U.S. citizen. Some of the property will be subject to estate tax when Lily dies, because it will be over the exempt amount. By contrast, if Choy were a U.S. citizen, all $900,000 would be free from tax because of the marital deduction.

Special trusts for non-citizen spouses. Congress has provided one exception to this non-citizen spouse rule. Property left by one spouse to a non-citizen spouse in what's called a "Qualified Domestic Trust" is allowed the marital deduction. To create one of these trusts, you'll need to see a lawyer. Indeed, if you're married to a non-citizen and have an estate worth more than the exempt amount, see a lawyer for estate tax planning.

2. Reducing Estate Tax Liability

Avoiding probate does not affect estate tax liability. Property you leave in a living trust or in joint tenancy is still considered part of your estate for federal estate tax purposes. Aside from an AB trust, there are only a few strategies to reduce the tax bill. I discuss the main ones briefly here. All these matters are covered in depth in *Plan Your Estate*, by Denis Clifford and Cora Jordan (Nolo Press).

Get help to reduce your tax bill. If you want to take steps to reduce eventual estate taxes (aside from creating an AB trust), see a knowledgeable attorney.

a. Gifts

If you expect your estate to be liable for estate taxes after your death, and you don't need all your income and property to live on, making sizable gifts while you're alive can be a good way to reduce eventual federal estate taxes.

Tax-exempt gifts. You can give gifts of $10,000 or less annually, tax-free. Each member of a couple can give $10,000 to any one person or a combined total of $20,000 tax free. Only gifts larger than $10,000 made to one person or organization in one calendar year reduce the exempt amount.

Example

Allen and Julia give their two daughters each $20,000 every year for four years. They have transferred a total of $160,000 without ever becoming liable for gift tax.

Other gifts are exempt regardless of amount, including:

* gifts between spouses who are U.S. citizens
* gifts for medical bills or school tuition
* gifts to tax-exempt charitable organizations.

If you make gifts subject to tax during your life, they are counted toward the exempt amount. But though you will have to file a gift tax return, you don't pay any tax when you make a gift unless you give away more than the exempt amount worth of property during your life. Otherwise, your combined gift and estate tax liability is calculated and paid after your death, out of the property in your estate.

Example

Harry gives his daughter $25,000 in one year. Although he must file a federal gift tax return, he does not pay tax on the $15,000 that is not tax-exempt. At his death, if the value of the taxable gifts and the property he leaves exceeds the exempt amount, his estate will have to pay tax.

Gifts made within three years of death. The IRS ignores a few types of gifts made in the last three years of someone's life—that is, they don't qualify as gifts for tax purposes, and the value of the property that was given away is still considered part of the deceased person's taxable estate. The most important, for most people, are gifts of life insurance policies.

How to choose property to give away. It's usually wise to give away property that you think will go up in value substantially before your death. That way, you may avoid gift tax now—if the gift is worth less than $10,000—and you may avoid estate tax later, because the increased value of the property won't be included in your estate when you die. Also, if the recipient (other than a child age 14 or under) is in a lower tax bracket, you may want to give away income-generating property, so that the income will be taxed at the recipient's lower tax rates. Any income over $1,000 per year received by a child 14 years or under from any gift (whether from parents or anyone else) is taxed at the parents' rate.

You may not, however, want to give away property that has already appreciated greatly in value. Usually, it's wiser to hold onto it until death to take advantage of the stepped-up tax basis rules discussed in Section B, above.

Gifts of life insurance. Life insurance policies you own on your own life and give away at least three years before your death are excellent gifts, from an estate planning view. Your gift tax liability is determined by the current value of the policy, which is far less than the amount the policy will pay off at death. For many policies, the present value will be less than the $10,000 annual gift tax threshold, which means that no gift tax will be assessed.

To give away a life insurance policy, you must comply with some fairly technical IRS rules, which should be available from your insurance company. The process of actually transferring ownership is simple. Insurance companies have forms you can use to make the transfer. You must make an irrevocable gift of the policy. If you keep the right to revoke the gift and get the policy back, the proceeds will be taxed as part of your estate.

And if you buy a policy that requires future premium payments, you'll want to make more gifts to the new owner of the policy to cover the payments. As an alternative, you can pay for some kinds of policies all at once; they are called single-premium policies.

Example

Sarah buys three single-premium life insurance policies (that is, she pays the entire premium in advance) for $50,000 each and transfers ownership of the policies to her three children. She must file a gift tax return because the value of the gifts exceeds the $10,000 per person per year tax exemption. The taxable value of all three gifts is $120,000. The gift tax is not due until her death. When Sarah dies, each policy pays $300,000. The $900,000 in proceeds is not taxed as part of her estate; only the $120,000 that exceeded the gift tax exemption is counted toward her exempt amount.

b. Tax-Saving Trusts and Devices

As you know, this book presents one type of estate tax-saving trust: an AB trust. Other types of tax-saving trusts and devices can be used by couples, or in some cases individuals, with larger estates.

Don't try this on your own. If you want to create any of these kinds of trusts or devices, see an experienced estate planning lawyer.

QTIP trusts (for married couples only). A "QTIP" (for "Qualified Terminal Interest Property," pure IRS jargon) trust is a specific type of trust used to postpone payment of estate taxes that otherwise are due when the first spouse dies. A QTIP trust enables the surviving spouse to postpone payment of these taxes until the death of the second spouse.

One drawback of a QTIP trust is that the federal estate taxes eventually paid on the property of the first spouse to die are assessed against what the property is worth when the surviving spouse dies, not what the property was worth when the first spouse died. Usually, that means higher taxes.

Example

Mary Edna, a widow with three grown children, marries Roberto. Her estate, which comprises primarily her house and summer cottage, has a net value of $900,000. Roberto has little property beyond his monthly social security check. Mary Edna wants Roberto to be able to continue to live in both her houses if she predeceases him. After his death, she wants all her property to go to her children.

If Mary Edna creates an AB trust, with Roberto having the life estate, all of her property will be subject to estate tax when she dies. Some tax will have to be paid, because her estate is over the exempt amount. Since neither her estate nor Roberto has much cash, this will necessitate sale of one of her houses. So she creates a QTIP trust. No estate taxes will be assessed against her property until Roberto dies. However, if the worth of the property has risen to $1,300,000 when Roberto dies, estate taxes will be based on this value.

Generation-skipping trusts (for individuals or couples). One of the legal devices traditionally used by the very wealthy to minimize estate taxes has been to leave the bulk of their property in trust for their grandchildren, with the income from the trusts (but not the principal) available to their children. This strategy avoided death taxes several times. Without a trust, taxes would typically be paid when the first grandparent died, then again when the second grandparent died, and then when each of their children died.

Current laws impose a tax on all "generation-skipping transfers" in excess of $1 million. For a generation-skipping trust of $4 million, this means estate taxes are levied on the middle generation for $3 million as if the trust didn't exist.

Generation-skipping trusts can be quite complex. These trusts are designed to have effect for at least two generations after the grantor's life, normally over 50 years, and many contingencies should be considered. Also, there are IRS requirements regarding the age of the trustee and when estate taxes will be assessed.

Disclaimers (for individuals or couples). Using a disclaimer, someone who's inherited a gift declines to accept it. The gift is then given to an alternate beneficiary originally named by the gift-giver. The beneficiary who disclaims the gift does so to make the overall estate tax picture better. Of course, this means she doesn't need the gift she disclaimed to live on. Any beneficiary has an inherit right to disclaim a gift, but often that right is expressly stated in people's estate planning documents.

Example

Jim and Hester, in their 40s, own property together worth $1,040,000. Thus each has an estate worth $520,000. In their estate plan, each leaves their property outright to the other rather than creating an AB trust. However, they worry about what will happen if they acquire considerably more valuable property but don't get around to revising their plan. Suppose their net estate becomes worth, say, $3 million? Then, there will be substantial federal estate taxes when the surviving spouse dies. On the other hand, maybe the surviving spouse will need or want the entire estate if it's much less than $3 million.

Jim and Hester create a trust specifically permitting a disclaimer, authorizing the surviving spouse to decline to accept all or any portion of the deceased spouse's property. All disclaimed property goes to an AB trust, with the couple's children the final beneficiaries.

Life Insurance trusts. An irrevocable life insurance trust is a legal entity you create for the purpose of owning life insurance you previously owned. It becomes operational during your lifetime. An irrevocable trust, like a corporation or any other trust, is a legal entity, distinct from any human being.

Transferring ownership of life insurance from the insured to a new owner—the trust—reduces death taxes, especially federal estate taxes, by removing the proceeds of the policy from your taxable estate.

Why create a life insurance trust, rather than simply transfer a life insurance policy to someone else? One reason is that there may be no one you want to give your policy to. In other words, you want to get the proceeds out of your taxable estate, but you don't want the risks of having an insurance policy on your life owned by someone else. For example, the trust could specify that the policy must be kept in effect while you live, eliminating the risk that a new owner of the policy could decide to cash it in.

Example

Mrs. Brandt is the divorced mother of two children, in their 20s, who will be her beneficiaries. Neither is sensible with money. Mrs. Brandt has an estate of $600,000, plus life insurance that will pay $300,000 at her death. She wants to remove the proceeds of the policy from her estate. If she doesn't, her estate will be subject to federal estate tax. However, there's no one Mrs. Brandt trusts enough to give her policy to outright. With the controls she can impose through a trust, however, she decides it's safe to allow her sister, the person she's closest to, to be the trustee of a life insurance trust for the policy. She creates an irrevocable trust and transfers ownership of the life insurance policy to that trust.

Strict federal requirements govern life insurance trusts. To gain the estate tax savings:

- The life insurance trust must be irrevocable. If you keep the right to revoke the trust, you will be considered the owner of the policy, and the proceeds will be considered part of your estate upon death.

- You cannot be the trustee. You must name either an "independent" adult (that is, someone with no legal ties to you—a spouse or child cannot serve, but a good friend can) or an institution to serve as trustee.

- You must establish the trust at least three years before your death. If the trust has not existed for at least three years when you die, the trust is disregarded for estate tax purposes, and the proceeds are included in your taxable estate.

Charitable remainder trusts. With a charitable remainder trust, you make an irrevocable gift of property to a tax-exempt charity while you're alive. You are entitled to receive certain income from the property as well as continue to use and control it while you're alive, with significant income tax breaks. When you die, the property, of course, must go to the charity—and therefore, no estate tax can be due.

D. State Inheritance Taxes

Twenty-seven states and the District of Columbia have effectively abolished state inheritance taxes. The rest impose inheritance taxes on:

- all real estate owned in the state, no matter where the deceased lived; and

- all property of residents of the state, no matter where it's located.

In most states that have them, death taxes are called inheritance taxes. In a few, they are called estate taxes. Although theoretically different—one's a tax on the person who inherits, the other a tax on the estate itself—the reality is the same. The tax is paid from the deceased's property.

State tax rules. Death tax rules for all states are summarized in *Plan Your Estate*, by Denis Clifford and Cora Jordan (Nolo Press). More detailed information is available from state tax officials.

If you divide your time between a state that doesn't impose inheritance tax (or has a very low one) and one with high death taxes, you'll want to establish your permanent residence in the lower tax state.

Example

A couple divides the year between Florida and New York. Florida effectively has no death taxes. New York imposes comparatively stiff estate taxes, with rates ranging from 3% for $50,000 to $150,000 or less, to 21% for $10,100,000 or more. Other things being equal, it makes sense for the couple to make Florida their legal residence.

To establish your legal residence in a particular state, you should register all vehicles there, keep bank and other financial accounts there and vote there.

Getting your legal residence established. Establishing residence in a no-tax state can be tricky if you also live in a high-tax one, because the high-tax state has a financial incentive to conclude that you really reside there. If you have a large estate, and a complicated two-or-more-state living situation, consult a knowledgeable tax lawyer or accountant.

STATES WITHOUT INHERITANCE TAXES

Alabama	Illinois	South Carolina
Alaska	Maine	Texas
Arizona	Minnesota	Utah
Arkansas	Missouri	Vermont
California	Nevada	Virginia
Colorado	New Mexico	Washington
District of Columbia	North Dakota	West Virginia
Florida	Oregon	Wisconsin
Georgia	Rhode Island	Wyoming
Hawaii		

E. Planning for Incapacity

A living trust can be a big help if you become unable to manage your own affairs, because your successor trustee (or your spouse, if you make a shared trust) can take over management of trust property. That person, however, has no power over any of your other financial or health affairs. For that reason, you should prepare some other documents as well and coordinate them with your living trust.

1. Durable Power of Attorney for Finances

The best way to plan for the management of your property not covered by your living trust is to use a document called a Durable Power of Attorney for Finances. Every state recognizes this document. This document gives a trusted person you choose, called your "attorney-in-fact," the legal authority to manage your finances (except for property owned by your living trust) on your behalf. The document can be worded so that it becomes effective only if you become incapacitated, as certified in writing by a physician.

Unfortunately, there are no self-help materials currently available for Durable Powers of Attorney for Finances. Try a legal supply store to see if they have a form.

2. Durable Power of Attorney for Health Care

In this document, valid in most states, you give a trusted person (your attorney-in-fact) the power to make health care decisions for you. You can also spell out what you want done if you become incapacitated. Of particular importance to many people is to make their desired provision for use (or, more commonly, non-use) of life-supporting procedures, where they are in a final and irreversible state. Usually, the document is worded so that it becomes effective only if you become incapacitated, as documented by a physician. "Health care decisions" usually include enforcing your written statement regarding whether you want life support technology to artificially prolong your life or you prefer a "natural death."

While the attorney-in-fact for health care is often the same person who serves as the attorney-in-fact for finances, this isn't mandatory. Some people choose different persons for each role.

Durable Power of Attorney for Health Care forms can be obtained from your state Medical Association, in many states, or from a nonprofit organization called Choice in Dying, 200 Varick St., New York, NY 10014. They are also contained in *WillMaker*, Nolo's computer will program.

3. Living Will

If you're concerned about being hooked up to life support systems, and other issues surrounding dying a natural death, you may want a "living will" as well as a durable power of attorney for health care. (Despite the confusingly similar names, living wills and living trusts are completely different animals.)

A living will is a document addressed to your doctors. In it you state your preferences about treatment, including life support systems. You may also, depending on state law, be able to name a "proxy"—a trusted relative or friend who can make certain health care decisions for you. The extent to which doctors must follow your instructions depends on your state's law and what you specify in the living will. Some states, for example, do not require a doctor to stop artificial feeding even if a patient's living will requested it. And in some states, living wills are effective only after you have been diagnosed with a terminal illness.

But even if not legally binding, your living will can serve as valuable evidence of your wishes if family, friends or doctors disagree about the treatment you should receive.

Many states have passed laws governing living wills or developed their own living will form. Up-to-date information about state requirements is available from *WillMaker*, (Nolo Press), including the specific form needed in your state. You can also get forms from Choice in Dying.

Reminder. Whatever arrangements you make concerning your wishes in case of incapacity, be sure to let your family know what your wishes are, what documents you have signed and where you keep them.

F. Long-Term Trusts to Control Property

In certain circumstances, you may want to dictate how your property is to be managed and distributed over many years. You may want to leave property to people who, for one reason or another, may not be able to manage it for themselves, even when they are over age 35. Or you may want to impose strict controls over property left to your spouse for his or her life, to be sure it remains intact to go eventually to your children from a former marriage.

Reminder. For a discussion of how to leave property to a minor or young adult, and have someone manage it until the beneficiary is older, see Chapter 9, "Property Left to Minor Children or Young Adults."

Long-term management. Not a do-it-yourself job. See an experienced lawyer if you want to create one of the property management trusts discussed in this section.

1. AB Trusts Used to Control Property

If you or your spouse have children from a previous marriage, you may want your current spouse to have some of your property during his or her life, but be sure that that property eventually goes to your children. One way to do this is to establish a special type of AB trust that limits the surviving spouse's use, and rights, to property in Trust A. The AB trust in this book gives the surviving spouse, as trustee of Trust A, maximum freedom over Trust A property. (See Chapter 5, "The Tax-Saving AB Trust.") Spouses in second or subsequent marriages often prefer more control over the surviving spouse's rights, to try to insure that their children will eventually receive the bulk of their property.

Example

Ilana and Harvey are both in their 50s. Ilana has a son from her first marriage. Harvey has two daughters from his. Ilana and Harvey purchase, equally, an $800,000 house. If one dies, each wants the other spouse to be able to live in the house for the remainder of his or her life. But after both have died, each wants his or her share of the house to go to the children of their first marriages. So Ilana and Harvey create an AB trust. Each spouse's A trust allows the surviving spouse full use of the house, but not the right to sell it and buy another one. Then half the house goes to Ilana's son, and the other half to Harvey's two daughters.

Many questions need to be resolved in setting up the trust.

- How strict should the controls on the surviving spouse be?

- Can the spouse sell the house to pay for health needs? For any needs?

- Should the spouse be the sole trustee, or is it better to have a child share that job or to have a child be the sole trustee?

- What reports and accountings must be given to the children?

Suppose a wife wants to allow her husband the right to stay in her home while he lives. How specifically does the right need to be pinned down in the trust? Can the husband sell the house and buy another? Can he rent it out? Suppose he needs to go to a nursing home—can the house then be sold? What happens to the profits of the sale? Who gets any income from trust property?

An AB trust intended to impose controls on trust property must be carefully drafted by a knowledgeable attorney. Inherently, you are dealing with possible conflicts—the basic concern, after all, is that the surviving spouse's desires and interests may be very different from, or directly conflict with, the desires and interests of the deceased spouse's children. To resolve these issues wisely, you need a trust geared to your desires and to the specific realities of your situation.

2. Spendthrift Trusts

If you want to leave property to an adult who just can't handle money, a "spendthrift trust," where an independent trustee can dole out the money little by little, is a good idea. A spendthrift trust keeps the property from being squandered by the beneficiary or seized by the beneficiary's creditors.

3. Trusts for Disabled Persons

A person with a serious physical or mental disability may not be able to handle property, no matter what his or her age. Often, the solution is to establish a trust with a competent adult as trustee to manage the trust property.

The trust should be carefully prepared by an expert familiar with federal and state law, so that the trust won't jeopardize the beneficiary's eligibility for government benefits.

A good resource here is *Planning for the Future: Providing a Meaningful Life for a Child With a Disability*, by Russell Grant and Joseph Fee (American Publishing Company).

4. Flexible Trusts

You may want the determination of how your property is spent after your death to be decided in the future by a successor trustee, not by you before you die. The usual way to do this is to create a "sprinkling trust," authorizing the trustee to decide how to spend trust money for several beneficiaries.

chapter 16

WILLS

I urge you to prepare a simple "back-up" will, even if you leave most, or even all, of your property by your living trust. Back-up will forms are contained in the Appendix.

A. Why Prepare a Back-Up Will?

It's always sensible to prepare a back-up will for one, or probably more, of the following reasons:

- **To name a personal guardian for your minor children.** If you have young children, you need a will to achieve the vital goal of nominating a personal guardian for them. In most states, you can't use your living trust to nominate a personal guardian. Also, in your will you can appoint a property guardian for your children to manage any of their property not otherwise legally supervised by an adult. Younger people with minor children, who don't have much property, may decide that because nominating a personal guardian is the primary thing they're worried about, a simple will is all the estate planning they currently need. (See Section B, below.)

- **To choose a beneficiary for suddenly-acquired property.** Anyone may end up acquiring valuable property at or shortly before death, such as a sudden gift, inheritance or lottery prize. Under the will forms in this book, that property will go to the residuary beneficiary of your will. You may well not get around to, or have time to, transfer the property to your trust. Therefore, it cannot be subject to your trust. And if you didn't have a will, the property would, under your state's "intestate succession" laws, go to your closest relatives.

- **To leave property not transferred by a probate-avoidance device.** If you don't get around to planning probate avoidance for all your property (by placing it in your living trust, for example), a will is a valuable back-up device. If you have a will, the property will go to who you want to have it (your residuary beneficiary), and not pass under the intestate succession laws.

- **To give away property someone left you that is still in probate.** If someone has left you property by will, and that property is still enmeshed in probate when you die, you can't arrange to transfer it by a probate-avoidance device. Since you don't have title to the property, you have no legal right to transfer it. But again, under your will, that property will go to your residuary beneficiary when the probate court releases it.

Disinheriting a child or spouse. If you want to disinherit a child or your spouse, you need to do so in your will. But before you decide to do this, re-read the materials in Chapter 8, "Choosing Your Beneficiaries," Section H, carefully. The law may restrict your choices.

- **To name your executor.** In your will, you name your executor (and alternate executor), the person with legal authority to supervise distribution of property left by your will and to represent your estate in probate court proceedings. It is a good idea to have an executor even if you have also set up a living trust and named a successor trustee to manage it when you die, because banks and other institutions are often reassured to know an executor exists.

- **For married couples, to avoid confusion in case of simultaneous death.** The will for a member of a couple provides that if both members "die simultaneously or under such circumstances as to render it difficult or impossible to determine who predeceased the other," the will writer is conclusively presumed to have outlived the other spouse. This clause works for each spouse, in his or her own will. How can that be, you may ask? Well, the official reason is that each will is interpreted independently from the other. The real reason is that it achieves a desired goal of preventing one spouse's property from going to another's estate if one only lives a few minutes or hours longer than the other.

B. What You Can Do in a Back-Up Will

The back-up will forms in this book enable you to:

- Make up to three specific gifts—for example, "I leave my piano to Julia Rhodes." You can leave property that you haven't transferred to your living trust—for example, your personal bank account or car—to whomever you choose.

    You can leave a gift to be shared among several beneficiaries (or alternate beneficiaries) in any percentages you choose. Before doing this in your will, be sure to review Chapter 8, "Choosing Your Beneficiaries," Section D.

- Name alternate beneficiaries for these specific gifts in case the primary beneficiary dies before you do.

- Name a residuary beneficiary and alternate residuary beneficiary to inherit any property subject to your will that is not specifically left to other named beneficiaries.

- Nominate a personal guardian and alternate for your minor children.

- Name a property guardian (who can be the same person as the personal guardian) to manage any of your minor children's property that isn't otherwise legally controlled by an adult. It's generally preferable to leave property to your minor children in children's trusts or under the Uniform Transfers to Minors Act rather than relying on a property guardian named in a will, which you name only as a back-up for property they may acquire from some other source. (See Chapter 9, "Property Left to Minor Children or Young Adults.")

- Appoint your executor. Normally, it's best to name the same person as your successor trustee and executor.

CHILDREN OMITTED FROM YOUR WILL

In a few states, children who are neither left something in your will nor expressly disinherited are entitled to claim a share of your estate. The legal term for children not mentioned in your will (in these states) is "pretermitted heirs." (See Chapter 8, "Choosing Your Beneficiaries," Section H.)

To ensure that no matter what state you live in, your will won't become ensnared in a lawsuit over whether or not a child is a pretermitted heir, simply list all your children in your will. The Nolo will forms state that if you didn't leave the child anything, it was intentional.

Children born or adopted after you sign your will. If you have a child after preparing your back-up will, prepare a new back-up will, naming that child and leaving him or her whatever property you choose.

You may decide that you need a more complicated will. For instance, perhaps you want to appoint different personal guardians for different minor children. Or you want to arrange for care of your pets or specifically forgive debts owed you. Some people want to use a "self-proving affidavit" (legal in most states) for their witnesses, which can make it easier to probate a will without a written statement or a court appearance by a witness. If you do want a more complicated will, consult *Nolo's Simple Will Book* or *WillMaker*, Nolo's computer will program.

C. Avoiding Conflicts Between Your Will and Living Trust

When you make both a living trust and a back-up will, pay attention to how the two work together. If your will and your trust document contain conflicting provisions, at the least you will create confusion among your inheritors, and at the worst, bitter disputes—maybe even a lawsuit—among friends and family.

Here are some guidelines:

- **Don't leave the same property in your living trust and will, even if it's to the same beneficiary.** If you transfer the property to your living trust and name a beneficiary in the trust document, that's all you need to do. Mentioning the property in your will raises the possibility of probate.

- **Name the same person to be executor of your will and successor trustee of your living trust.** There's one important exception: If you make a basic shared trust or AB trust, you'll probably name your spouse as executor of your will, but not as successor trustee—the successor trustee takes over only after both spouses have died. The surviving spouse, however, may want to revise her will after the death of the first spouse, to name her successor trustee to be her executor.

D. Pour-Over Wills

A "pour-over will" takes all the property you haven't transferred to your living trust and, at your death, leaves it ("pours it over") to that trust. Some lawyers urge all people who make living trusts to make pour-over wills, arguing that it's always best to send all your property through your living trust. There seems to be something about the name pour-over will that impresses people. The term sounds, well, sophisticated, like they're doing something really right. In fact, pour-over wills are not very desirable, in my opinion, for most people with a living trust.

1. When Not to Use a Pour-Over Will

Pour-over wills do not avoid probate. All property that is left through a will—any kind of will—must go through probate, unless the amount left is small enough to qualify for exemption from normal probate laws. Probate is most definitely not avoided simply because the beneficiary of a will is a living trust.

It's generally better to simply use a standard back-up will to take care of your left-over (non-living trust) property rather than a pour-over will. In the back-up will, you can name the people you want to get the will property, and skip the unnecessary extra step of pouring the property through the living trust after your death.

When used as a back-up will, a pour-over will actually has a disadvantage that standard wills don't: It forces the living trust to go on for months after your death, because the property left through the pour-over will must go through probate before it can be transferred to the trust. Usually, the property left in a living trust can be distributed to the beneficiaries, and the trust ended, within a few weeks after the person's death.

Example

Joy transfers her valuable property to her living trust. She also makes a pour-over will, which states that any property she owns at death goes to the living trust. When Joy dies, the property left through her will goes to the trust and is distributed to the residuary beneficiary of her living trust, her son Louis. The living trust must be kept going until probate of the will is finished, when property left by the will is poured over into the living trust. Normally, keeping the living trust ongoing for several months, or however long probate takes, would not require filing a trust tax return, since there's no income to this trust. Still, it's better to wind up a living trust as quickly as feasible.

If Joy had simply named Louis as the residuary beneficiary of a simple back-up will, the result would have been the same, but the process would have been simpler. The living trust would have been ended a few weeks after Joy's death. And after probate was finished, Louis would have received whatever property passed through Joy's will.

2. When You May Want a Pour-Over Will

There are, however, two situations in which you might want to use a pour-over will.

If you create an AB trust, a pour-over will can be desirable. The spouses want the maximum amount of property to eventually wind up in Trust A, the marital life estate trust. So each spouse writes a pour-over will, leaving his or her will property to their A trust. After a spouse dies, the other spouse should amend her or his will or prepare a new one, since there will no longer be a functional Trust A for the surviving spouse's property to go to.

Also, if you set up a child's subtrust for a young beneficiary in your living trust, you may want any property that child inherits through your will to go into the subtrust. Otherwise, you would create two trusts for the beneficiary: one in the will and one in your living trust.

Example

Jessica makes a living trust and leaves the bulk of her property to her 12-year-old son. She arranges, in the trust document, for any trust property her son inherits before the age of 30 to be kept in a subtrust, managed by Jessica's sister.

Jessica also makes a back-up will, in which she leaves everything to her son and again arranges for a subtrust to be set up if she should die before her son reaches age 30. So if Jessica dies before her son reaches 30, two separate subtrusts will be set up to manage property for him.

If Jessica used a pour-over will, any property her son inherited through the will would go into the subtrust created by her living trust. With only one subtrust, only half the paperwork of maintaining the subtrust is necessary, as compared to maintaining two separate subtrusts.

3. How to Create a Pour-Over Will

You can use the will forms in this book to create a pour-over will. To do so, you leave property subject to the will to your successor trustee, as trustee of your trust. A married person usually lists two people as successor trustee—first the surviving spouse (who is technically a continuing trustee) and then the person next in line.

Example

Nils, married to Mercedes, wants the property he leaves through his will to go to his living trust. In his will, he lists the beneficiary as "Mercedes Janson, trustee of the Nils and Mercedes Janson Living Trust, or, if she does not survive me, to Ingemar Janson, successor trustee of the Nils and Mercedes Janson Living Trust."

E. Filling in the Back-Up Will Form

Here are the steps necessary to prepare your own back-up will from a will form in the Appendix:

1. Select the correct form, depending on whether you are single (Form 10) or a member of a couple (Form 11).

As with the living trust forms, the will for a member of a couple is written in terms of a married couple, using the terms "husband" and "wife." If you are a member of an unmarried couple, please make the necessary word changes ("mate," "partner" or using each person's name, or whatever you feel works) in the will form, so that it makes sense for your situation.

2. Read through the will form carefully. There are a number of blanks to fill in. The information called for is identified below each blank. While most of this is self-explanatory, here is what you must fill in:

- Your name. This should be the form of the name you use to sign such documents as deeds, checks and loan applications. It needn't necessarily be the way your name appears on your birth or marriage certificate.

- Your city, county and state.

- The names of all your living children, and names of any children of a deceased child, if any.

- The names of the personal guardian, alternate personal guardian and property guardian and alternate property guardian for your minor children. You can name only one personal guardian and one property guardian for all your children.

- Up to three specific gifts. You do not have to make any specific gifts. You can simply leave all property subject to this will to your residuary beneficiary. If you leave some property to more than one beneficiary, or alternate beneficiaries, follow the instructions in Chapter 10, "Preparing Your Living Trust Document," Section D, for the wording of shared gifts. (Reminder: In Florida, you cannot leave your house to anyone but your spouse or your children.)

- The name of your residuary beneficiary and alternate residuary beneficiary. You can name more than one residuary beneficiary if you want. For example, many people list all their children.

- The names of your executor and alternate executor.

Do not sign or date your will yet. You do this when you complete your final will, with your witnesses.

3. Have the form typed, because a will with handwriting and typing combined is not valid. You may need to renumber the clauses if you omit items that don't apply to you. You do not need to initial each page; your signature at the end is all that is needed.

Don't use the form as your final will. Do not type the information required onto the form and attempt to use it as your final will. Courts are not used to wills like this. You want your will to look normal and unthreatening to a judge, which means typed, and with the fill-in-the-blank lines and instructions below these lines gone. So you can see how a final draft and a typed will should look, there are samples below of Form 10, a will for a single person.

Have the final draft of your will carefully typed (or printed out if you use a computer), double-spaced, on good 8-1/2" x 11" paper. Proofread it carefully and make sure it's letter-perfect. If you find mistakes, retype or print out the entire page. Don't ever make alterations on the face of your will by writing in words or crossing something out and initialing the change. It could make part or all of your will invalid.

4. Date and sign the will in front of three witnesses who do not stand to inherit anything from you. (Instructions are in Section F, below.).

F. Signing and Witnessing Your Will

To be valid, your will must be signed and dated in front of witnesses. You sign the will where the form provides. Then these witnesses must sign the will in your presence, and also in the presence of the other witnesses.

State laws vary as to how many witnesses you need, but three is enough in every state. Even if your state requires only two witnesses, three is better because it provides one more person to establish that your signature is valid, if that becomes necessary during probate.

Witnesses must be:

- Adults (18 or over) and of sound mind.

- People who won't inherit under the will. That means anyone who might inherit any gift through your will, including alternate residuary beneficiaries, cannot be a witness. But someone who will receive property only from your living trust can be a valid witness.

- People who should be easy to locate in the event of your death. This usually means people who aren't likely to move around a lot and (most of all) who are younger than you are.

Here's how to go about arranging for signing and witnessing your will:

- Have the three witnesses assemble in one place.

- Tell them that the paper you hold is your will. They don't need to know what's in it.

- Sign the signature page in the witnesses' presence. Use the exact spelling of your name as you typed in the heading.

- Have each witness sign the last page in the place indicated while the other witnesses are watching. The clause immediately preceding the witnesses' signatures states ("attests") that the events outlined just above have occurred.

The witnesses list the city, county and state of their residence (not where the will is signed). Listing the witnesses' addresses is not legally required, but can prove an aid in locating the witnesses later on, when the will becomes operational.

Get the details right. If a will doesn't comply with the technical requirements (say you had only one witness to your will), it cannot be validated by the probate court. It's not hard to do a will correctly. Double-check to be sure you've done so!

Sample Will Form, Ready to be Typed

WILL

of

Benjamin Werrin

_____

I, _____ Benjamin Werrin _____ , a resident of
your name

_____ Fairmont _____ , _____ Duchess _____ County, _____ New York _____ ,
city   county   state

declare that this is my will.

1. I revoke all wills and codicils that I have previously made.

2. I am not married.

3. I am the _____ father _____ of the _____ child _____ whose _____ name _____ is _____
mother/father   child/children   name(s)   is/are

Eric Werrin
_____

_____

_____

There are ___ living children of my deceased child _____ ,
name

whose names are:

_____

_____

_____

(B) If I fail to leave, by this will or otherwise, any property to any of the children listed above, my failure to do so is intentional.

(C) If at my death any of my children are minors, and a personal guardian is needed, I nominate

_____ to be appointed personal guardian
name

of my minor children. If _____ cannot serve as
name

personal guardian, I nominate _____ to be appointed
name

personal guardian.

(D) If at my death any of my children are minors, and a property guardian is needed,

I appoint _____ as property guardian for my minor children.
name

If _____ cannot serve as property guardian, I appoint

name

_____ as property guardian.

name

(E) I direct that no bond be required of any guardian.

4. (A) I leave the following specific gifts:

I leave _____ all my cameras _____

property described

to _____Sid Tropinsky_____, or if _____Sid Tropinsky_____

beneficiary's name   *beneficiary's name*

fails to survive me, to _____Nancy Werrin_____.

alternate beneficiary's name

I leave _____

property described

to _____, or if _____

beneficiary's name   *beneficiary's name*

fails to survive me, to _____.

alternate beneficiary's name

I leave _____

property described

to _____, or if _____

beneficiary's name   *beneficiary's name*

fails to survive me, to _____.

alternate beneficiary's name

(B) I leave all my other property subject to this will to

_____Eric Werrin_____, or if ___he___ ___fails___ to

residuary beneficiary's name   *he/she/they*   *fails/fail*

survive me, to _____Gil Nason_____.

alternate residuary beneficiary's name

5. (A) I nominate _____Gil Nason_____ to serve as executor of my will.

executor's name

If ___he_____ is unable to serve or continue serving as executor, I nominate

he/she

_____Nancy Werrin_____ to serve as executor.

alternate executor's name

(B) No bond shall be required of any executor.

I subscribe my name to this will this _____ day of _____, 19____, at

_____Fairmont_____, _____Duchess County_____, _____New York_____.

city   *county*   *state*

_____*Benjamin Werrin*_____

your signature

WITNESSES

On the date last written above, _____ Benjamin Werrin _____ declared to us, the
<u>your name</u>

undersigned, that this was _____ his _____ will, and requested us to act as witnesses to it.
<u>his/her</u>

_____ He _____ then signed this will in our presence, all of us being present at the same time. We now at
<u>He/She</u>

_____ his _____ request and in _____ his _____ presence, and in the presence of each other, have signed this
<u>his/her</u>   <u>his/her</u>

Will as witnesses.

We declare under penalty of perjury that the foregoing is true and correct.

_____
witness signature

_____, _____, _____
city   county   state

_____
witness signature

_____, _____, _____
city   county   state

_____
witness signature

_____, _____, _____
city   county   state

Final, Typed Will, Ready to be Signed and Witnessed

WILL

of

Benjamin Werrin

I, Benjamin Werrin, a resident of Fairmont, Duchess County, New York, declare that this is my will.

1. I revoke all wills and codicils that I have previously made.

2. I am not married.

3. I am the father of the child whose name is Eric Werrin.

4. (A) I make the following specific gifts:

I leave all my cameras to Sid Tropinsky, or if Sid Tropinsky fails to survive me, to Nancy Werrin.

(B) I leave all my other property subject to this will to Eric Werrin, or if he fails to survive me, to Gil Nason.

5. (A) I nominate Gil Nason to serve as executor of my will. If he is unable to serve or continue serving as executor, I nominate Nancy Werrin to serve as executor.

(B) No bond shall be required of any executor.

I subscribe my name to this will this _____ day of _____, 19____, at Fairmont, Duchess County, New York.

_____

WITNESSES

On the date last written above, Benjamin Werrin declared to us, the undersigned, that this was his will, and requested us to act as witnesses to it. He then signed this will in our presence, all of us being present at the same time. We now at his request and in his presence, and in the presence of each other, have signed such will as witnesses.

We declare under penalty of perjury that the foregoing is true and correct.

_____
witness signature

_____, _____, _____
city   county   state

_____
witness signature

_____, _____, _____
city   county   state

_____
witness signature

_____, _____, _____
city   county   state

chapter 17

IF YOU NEED EXPERT HELP

*M*any readers, if not the majority, will find the information in this book sufficient to prepare their own living trust and back-up will. However, readers who run into a snag of some kind may sensibly decide they need a lawyer's help. Throughout this book, I've indicated "red flags" that alert you to the need for professional advice, such as the necessity to make special plans for an incapacitated or disadvantaged beneficiary. And, of course, people with estates over $625,000 and couples with estates over $1,250,000 need an expert's help to review all their estate tax options and prepare the living trust best geared to their needs.

A. Hiring a Lawyer to Review Your Living Trust

Hiring a lawyer solely to review a living trust document you've prepared sounds like a good idea. It shouldn't cost much, and seems to offer a comforting security. Sadly, though, it may be difficult or even impossible to find a lawyer who will accept the job.

While this is unfortunate, I'm not willing to excoriate lawyers who won't review a do-it-yourself living trust. From their point of view, they are being asked to accept what can turn into a significant responsibility for what they regard as inadequate compensation, given their usual fees. Any prudent lawyer sees every client as a potential occasion for a malpractice claim, or at least, serious later hassles—a phone call four years down the line that begins, "We talked to you about our living trust, and now…." Many experienced lawyers want to avoid this kind of risk. Also, many lawyers feel that if they're only reviewing someone else's work, they simply don't get deeply enough into a situation to be sure of their opinions. All you can do here is to keep trying to find a sympathetic lawyer—or be prepared to pay more, enough so the lawyer can feel she has been paid adequately to review your living trust.

B. Working With an Expert

If you have decided you want legal help, the first consideration is what type of expert you should seek out. Questions about estate taxes may be better (and less expensively) answered by an experienced accountant than by a lawyer. Or if you're wondering what type of life insurance to buy, you may be better off talking to a financial planner. But for many sophisticated living trust issues, you'll need to see a lawyer.

1. What Type of Lawyer Do You Need?

The type of lawyer that is right for you depends on what your problem is. Before you talk to a lawyer, decide what kind of help you really need. Do you want someone to advise you on a complete estate plan or just to go over part of your trust? If you don't clearly tell the lawyer what you want, you may find yourself agreeing to turn over all your estate planning work.

If you've prepared a trust from this book, any good estate practice lawyer should be able to help you. Do make sure she's experienced with AB trusts, if you prepare that type of trust. If you have a more sophisticated trust problem—like a QTIP trust or generation-skipping trust (see Chapter 15, "A Living Trust as Part of Your Estate Plan," Section F)—it's important that you see an estate trust specialist, who'll probably cost more than a general practice estate lawyer.

If you hire an "expert," make sure that person really has the knowledge or expertise he or she claims. Many lawyers have recently discovered living trusts—or, more accurately, discovered their profit-making potential. Lawyers who know almost nothing about living trusts (it's easy to go through law school without ever hearing of one) have found that they can charge substantial fees—$900 to $1,500 is common—for a simple document. Some use computer programs to churn out trusts and may or may not take into account your specific needs.

It's also important that you feel a personal rapport with your lawyer. You want one who treats you as an equal. (Interestingly, the Latin root of the word "client" translates as "to hear, to obey.") When talking with a lawyer on the phone or at a first conference, ask specific questions that concern you. If the lawyer answers them clearly and concisely—explaining, but not talking down to you—fine. If he acts wise, but says little except to ask that the problem be placed in his hands (with the appropriate fee, of course), watch out. You are either talking with someone who doesn't know the answer and won't admit it (common), or someone who finds it impossible to let go of the "me expert, you peasant" way of looking at the world (even more common).

2. How to Choose a Lawyer

Finding a competent estate planning lawyer who charges a reasonable fee and respects your efforts to prepare your own living trust may not be easy. Here are some suggestions on how to go about the task.

a. Ask Friends and Business People

Personal recommendations are generally the best way to find a lawyer you'll like. If you have a close friend who's had a good experience with an estate planning lawyer, there's a good chance you'll work well with that lawyer too.

If friends can't help you, ask any business people you know for referrals. Anyone who owns a small business probably has a relationship with a lawyer. Ask around to find someone you know who is a satisfied client, and get the name of his lawyer. If that lawyer does not handle estate planning, she will likely know someone who does. And because of the continuing relationship with your business friend, the lawyer has an incentive to recommend someone who is competent.

Also ask people in any social or other organization in which you are involved. They may well know of a good lawyer whose attitudes are similar to yours. Senior citizens' centers and other groups that advise and assist older people may have a list of local lawyers who specialize in wills and estate planning and are well-regarded.

b. Look Into a Group Legal Plan

Some unions, employers and consumer groups offer group legal plans to their members or employees, who can obtain comprehensive legal assistance free or at low rates. If you are a member of such a plan, check with it first. Your problem may be covered free of charge. If it is, and you are satisfied that the lawyer you are referred to is knowledgeable in estate planning, this route is probably a good choice.

Some plans give you only a slight reduction in a lawyer's fee. In that case, you may be referred to a lawyer whose main virtue is the willingness to reduce fees in exchange for a high volume of referrals.

c. Check Out a Prepaid Legal Plan

For basic advice, you may want to consider joining a prepaid legal plan that offers advice, by phone or in person, at no extra charge. (Some of these plans throw in a free simple will, too.) Your initial membership fee may be reasonable, compared to the cost of hiring a lawyer by the hour, but there's no guarantee that the lawyers available through these plans are of the best caliber.

You should realize that the lawyer you see probably receives at most $2 or $3 a month for dealing with you. Why do lawyers agree to this minimal amount? They hope to find clients who will pay for extra legal services not covered by the monthly premium. The low basic fee means the lawyers have an incentive to complicate, rather than simplify, your problem. So if a plan lawyer recommends an expensive legal procedure, get a second opinion.

d. Legal Advice Over the Phone

As another alternative, consider getting legal advice in a relatively new form: over the phone. A group of lawyers in the Los Angeles area have formed a company, TeleLawyer, that offers legal advice for $3/minute ($180/ hour). It may sound expensive, but compared to the conventional way of buying legal advice from a lawyer, it can be a bargain.

TeleLawyer's staff includes lawyers who specialize in many different areas, including estate planning. You're charged only for the time you spend talking to the lawyer on the phone. So if you have a concrete question that can be answered fairly quickly, it won't cost much. If the lawyer can't answer your question, he or she will find out the answer and call you back.

TeleLawyer offers only advice. Its lawyers do not accept cases, and it does not give referrals to lawyers. All conversations are confidential.

To contact TeleLawyer, call 800-835-3529 (charged to your credit card) or 900-776-7000 (charged on your phone bill).

e.   Consult a Legal Clinic

Law firms with lots of small offices across the country, such as Hyatt Legal Services, trumpet their low initial consultation fees. It's true that a basic consultation is cheap, often about $50; anything beyond that isn't cheap at all. Generally, the rates average about the same as those charged by other local lawyers in general practice.

If you do consult a legal clinic, often the trick is to quickly extract the information you need and resist attempts to convince you that you need more services. If the lawyer you talk to is experienced in estate planning, however, and you're comfortable with the person and the service, it may be worthwhile. Unfortunately, most of these offices have extremely high lawyer turnover, so you may see a different lawyer every time you visit.

f.   Call an Attorney Referral Service

A lawyer referral service will give you the name of an attorney who practices in your area. Usually, you can get a referral to an attorney who claims to specialize in estate planning and will give you an initial consultation for a low fee.

Most county bar associations have referral services. In some states, independent referral services, run by or for groups of lawyers, also operate.

Unfortunately, few referral services screen the attorneys they list, which means those who participate may not be the most experienced or competent. Often, the lawyers who sign up with referral services are just starting out and need clients. It may be possible to find a skilled estate planning specialist through a referral service, but be sure to take the time to check out the credentials and experience of the person to whom you're referred.

g.   Living Trust Seminars

Newspapers, radio and TV are full of ads for free seminars on living trusts. Usually, these events are nothing more than elaborate pitches for paying a lawyer $1,000 to $1,500 to write a living trust. Is it worth it? Probably not. For most estates, the trust forms and instructions in this book are all you need.

Often these seminars are occasions for you to be cajoled by lawyers, financial planners and insurance agents to pay large sums of money to get your affairs in order before you die.

People are sold on the idea that much of their estate is likely to be gobbled up by estate taxes unless they set up trusts now to avoid some of the tax and buy life insurance to pay the rest. The problem is, most people don't have estates large enough to generate estate tax liability. And the seminar sponsors know it.

The sponsors try to sell:

- a lot of life insurance, to pay for supposed estate taxes, and

- their form AB trust to reduce estate taxes. (See Chapters 4 and 5.)

Be sure you need these alleged benefits before paying what will be a substantial amount to acquire them. Is your estate likely to be liable for estate taxes? What type of AB trust do you need? If your situation is more complex than what can be handled by using this book, you'll probably be better off paying the money to hire a good lawyer to draft a trust geared to your needs than paying too much for the standard form offered in these seminars.

C. Lawyer Fees

As you already know, lawyers are expensive. They charge fees usually ranging from $100 to $300 or more per hour. While fancy office trappings, dull suits and solemn faces are no guarantee (or even a good indication) that a particular lawyer will provide top-notch service in a style you will feel comfortable with, this conventional style almost always ensures that you will be charged at the upper end of the fee range. High fees and quality service don't necessarily go hand in hand. Indeed, the attorneys I think most highly of tend to charge moderate fees (for lawyers, that is), and seem to get along very nicely without stuffy law office trappings.

Depending on the area of the county where you live, generally, I feel that fees in the range of $100 to $200 per hour are reasonable in urban areas, given the average lawyer's overhead. In rural counties and small cities, $75 to $150 is more like it.

Be sure you've settled your fee arrangement—preferably in writing—at the start of your relationship. (In California, a written fee agreement is required by law if the bill is expected to be over $1,000.) In addition to the hourly fee, get a clear, written commitment from the lawyer stating how many hours your problem should take to handle.

D. Doing Your Own Legal Research

As an alternative to hiring a lawyer, you can explore doing your own legal research. This can work well for relatively simpler living trust questions, such as any specific state law about trust registration or a trustee's duty to manage trust property prudently.

If you decide you want to do your own research, how do you go about it? First, you need an introduction to how law libraries work. Since you can't hire your own law librarian, the best book explaining how nonlawyers can do their own legal work is *Legal Research: How to Find and Understand the Law*, by Steve Elias and Susan Levinkind (Nolo Press). It shows you, step-by-step, how to find answers in the law library. As far as I know, it's the only legal research book written specifically for non-professionals.

Next, locate a law library or a public library with a good law collection. In most counties, there's a law library in the main county courthouse, although quality varies widely. Most county law libraries are supported by tax dollars or by the fees paid to file court papers. The librarians are generally most helpful and courteous to nonlawyers who are venturing to do their own legal research. If the county library is not adequate, your best bet is a law school library. Those in state colleges and universities supported by tax dollars are almost always open to the public.

Many states have estate planning books prepared for practicing lawyers. These books contain specific clauses and forms for wills or trusts, and many other "hands on" materials. The best way to locate this type of book for your state is to ask the law librarian or search the library's computerized catalog by looking for the terms "estate planning," "wills" or "trusts."

Unfortunately, I cannot recommend doing your own research for "high end" living trust issues, especially regarding estate taxes. Drafting a QTIP or generation-skipping trust that complies with all federal regulations and achieves the goals you want is truly a complicated matter that requires considerable expertise. Remember you'll consider these types of trusts only if you have substantial assets. The risk that your trust won't be legally correct and therefore won't qualify for the tax breaks you want outweighs any possible savings gained by doing your own legal work.

LIVING TRUST RESEARCH BOOKS

In most states, you can find books on trusts written for the lawyers of your state.

In California, the Continuing Education of the Bar (CEB) publishes several useful estate planning books, including *Drafting California Revocable Inter Vivos Trusts* and *Estate Planning for the General Practitioner*.

Comparable books in New York are published by the Practicing Law Institute (PLI) and include *Use of Trusts in Estate Planning*, by Moore, and *Income Taxation of Estates and Trusts*, by Michaelson & Blattmaehr.

If you want to wade into the murk of estate tax issues, a standard resource is the CCH (Commerce Clearing House) *Estate and Gift Tax Reporter*, available in law libraries.

Glossary

AB trust. An estate tax-saving trust where one spouse leaves property in the trust, allowing the other spouse, during his or her lifetime, to use the income from the trust and authorizing limited rights to invade the trust principal. After the death of the surviving spouse, the trust property goes to the final beneficiaries.

Abstract of trust. A condensed version of a living trust, which leaves out the key parts of what property is in the trust and who are the beneficiaries. An Abstract of Trust is used to establish, to a financial organization or other institution, that a valid living trust has been established, without revealing specifics the grantor wants to keep private and confidential.

Acknowledgment. A statement in front of a person who is qualified to administer oaths (a Notary Public) that a document bearing a person's signature was actually signed by that person.

Administration of an estate. The court-supervised distribution of the probate estate of a deceased person. The person who manages the distribution is called the "executor" if there is a will. If there is no will, this person is called the "administrator." In some states, the person is called "personal representative" in either instance.

Adult. A person aged 18 or older.

Affidavit. A written statement signed under oath in front of a Notary Public.

Augmented estate. The property left by a will plus certain property transferred outside of the will by gifts, joint tenancies and living trusts. The augmented estate is calculated if a surviving spouse wants to claim his or her statutory share of the deceased spouse's property. In the states that use this concept, a surviving spouse is generally considered to be adequately provided for if he or she receives at least one-third of the augmented estate.

Basis. This is a tax term which has to do with the valuation of property for determining profit or loss on sale. To simplify to the basics, if you buy a house for $200,000, your tax basis is $200,000. If you later sell it for $350,000, your taxable profit is $150,000. *See also* **Stepped-up basis**.

Beneficiary. A person or organization who is legally entitled to receive property under a will or trust. A primary beneficiary is a person who directly and certainly will benefit from the will or trust. An alternate beneficiary is a person who inherits property if a primary beneficiary dies before the person who made the will or trust does. *See* **Residuary beneficiary** and **Final beneficiary**.

Bond. A document guaranteeing that a certain amount of money will be paid to those injured if a person occupying a position of trust does not carry out his or her legal and ethical responsibilities. Thus, if an executor, trustee or guardian who is bonded (covered by a bond) wrongfully deprives a beneficiary of his or her property (say by blowing it during a trip in Las Vegas), the bonding company will replace it, up to the limits of the bond.

Bypass trust. *See* **AB trust**.

Child's subtrust. A trust that is established by the terms of a trust form in this book. It comes into being only if, at the grantor's death, a young beneficiary hasn't yet reached the age the grantor specified in the trust document to receive his or her gift outright.

If the subtrust is set up, all trust property the young beneficiary is entitled to automatically goes into it. It will stay in trust until the beneficiary reaches the age specified by the grantor, or, if none is, up to 35. Then the beneficiary will receive the property outright.

Common law marriage. In a minority of states, couples may be considered married if they live together for a certain period of time and intend to be husband and wife.

Community property. Eight states follow a system of marital property ownership called "community property," and Wisconsin has a very similar "marital property" law. Very generally, all property acquired after marriage and before permanent separation is considered to belong equally to both spouses, except for gifts to and inheritances by one spouse, and, in some community property states, income from property owned by one spouse prior to marriage. Spouses can, however, enter into an agreement to the contrary.

A surviving spouse automatically owns one-half of all community property. The other spouse has no legal power to affect this.

Conservator. Someone appointed by a court to manage the affairs of a mentally incompetent person. In some states, this person is called a guardian.

Creditor. A person or institution to whom money is owed. A creditor may be the person who actually lent the money, or a lawyer or bill collector who is trying to collect the money for the original creditor.

Curtesy. *See* **Dower and curtesy**.

Custodian. A person named to care for property left to a minor under the Uniform Transfers to Minors Act. The custodian manages the property until the minor reaches the age at which state law says she must receive it. (In some states, the giver can specify, within limits, at what age the custodianship will end.)

The custodian has essentially the same powers as a child's subtrust trustee and may use the property for the minor's health, education and support. The custodian's authority and duties are clearly set out by state law (the Uniform Transfers to Minors Act). No court supervises the custodian.

Death taxes. Taxes levied on the property of a person who died. Federal death taxes are called estate taxes. State death taxes (if any) go by various names, including inheritance tax.

Debtor. A person who owes money.

Deceased spouse. With a shared living trust created by both spouses, the first spouse to die.

Decedent. A person who has died.

Deed. The legal document by which one person (or persons) transfers title (recorded ownership) to real estate.

Disclaimer trust. A trust where a beneficiary has the specific right to disclaim all or any portion of a gift left to him or her, so the gift goes to whomever is next entitled to receive it.

Domicile. The state, or country, where one has his or her primary home.

Donee. Someone who receives a gift.

Donor. Someone who gives a gift.

Dower and curtesy. The right of a widow or widower to receive or enjoy the use of a set portion of the deceased spouse's property (usually one-third to one-half) if the surviving spouse is not left at least that share. Dower refers to the title which a surviving wife gets, while curtesy refers to what a man receives. Until recently, these amounts differed in a number of states. However, states generally provide the same benefits regardless of sex.

Durable power of attorney. A power of attorney that remains effective even if the person who created it (called the "principal") becomes incapacitated. The person authorized to act (called the "attorney-in-fact") can make health care decisions and handle financial affairs of the principal.

Estate. Generally, all the property you own when you die. There are different kinds of estates: the taxable estate (property subject to estate taxation), the probate estate (property that must go through probate) or the net estate (the net value of the property).

Estate planning. Figuring out how to prosper when you're alive, die with the smallest taxable estate and probate estate possible and pass property to loved ones with a minimum of fuss and expense.

Estate taxes. Taxes imposed on property as it passes from the dead to the living. The federal government exempts at least $625,000 of property (depending on the year of death) and all property left to a surviving spouse. Taxes are imposed only on property actually owned at the time of death. So techniques designed to reduce taxes usually concentrate on the legal transfer of ownership of property while you are living, to minimize the amount of property owned at death.

Executor. The person named in a will to manage the deceased person's estate, deal with the probate court, collect assets and distribute them as the will specifies. In some states this person is called the "personal representative." If someone dies without a will, the probate court will appoint such a person, who is called the administrator of the estate.

Exemption trust. *See* **AB trust.**

Final beneficiary. The person(s) or institution(s) who receive the property in a marital life estate trust, after the life beneficiary of that trust dies.

Financial guardian. *See* **Property guardian.**

Funding a trust. Transferring ownership of property to a trust, in the name of the trustee.

Generation-skipping trust. An estate tax-saving trust, where the principal is left in trust for one's grandchildren, with one's children receiving only the trust income.

Gift. Any property given to another person or organization, either during the giver's lifetime, or by will or living trust after his or her death.

Gift tax. Tax on gifts made during a person's lifetime. Many gifts are exempt from tax: gifts to tax-exempt charities or the giver's spouse (if the recipient spouse is a U.S. citizen), and gifts of less than $10,000 to a single recipient in a calendar year.

Grantor. The person or persons who create a trust. Also called the "trustor," "settlor" or "creator."

Heirs. Persons who are entitled by state intestate law to inherit a deceased person's property if that person didn't make arrangements for what should happen to the property at his or her death.

Inherit. To receive property from one who dies.

Inheritance taxes. Taxes some states impose on property received by inheritors from a deceased's estate.

Inheritors. Persons or organizations who inherit property.

Instrument. Legalese for document; sometimes used to refer to the document that creates a living trust.

Inter vivos trust. Same as **Living trust.** ("Inter vivos" is Latin for "between the living.")

Intestate. Someone who dies without a will or other valid estate transfer device dies "intestate."

Intestate succession. The method by which property is distributed when a person fails to distribute it in a will or other estate transfer device. In such cases, the law of each state provides that the property be distributed in certain shares to the closest surviving relatives. In most states, these are a surviving spouse, children, parents, siblings, nieces and nephews, and next of kin, in that order. The intestate succession laws are also used in the event an heir is found to be pretermitted (not mentioned or otherwise provided for in the will).

Irrevocable trust. Means what it says. Once you create it, that's it. A trust that cannot be revoked by the person who created it once it's created. Unlike a revocable, probate-avoidance trust, it can't be amended or changed in any way.

Joint tenancy. A way to own jointly owned real or personal property. When two or more people own property as joint tenants, and one of the owners dies, the other owners automatically become owners of the deceased owner's share. Thus, if a parent and child own a house as joint tenants, and the parent dies, the child automatically becomes full owner. Because of this "right of survivorship," a joint tenancy interest in property does not go through probate, or, put another way, is not part of the probate estate. Instead it goes directly to the surviving joint tenant(s).

Liquid assets. Cash or assets that can readily be turned into cash.

Living trust. A trust set up while a person is alive and which remains under the control of that person until death. Also referred to as "inter vivos trust." Living trusts are an excellent way to minimize the value of property passing through probate. This is because they enable people (called "grantors") to specify that money or other property will pass directly to their beneficiaries after their death, free of probate, and yet allow the grantors to continue to control the property during their lifetime and even end the trust or change the beneficiaries if they wish.

Living trust with marital life estate. *See* **AB trust.**

Living will. A document, directed to physicians, in which you state that you do not want to have your life artificially prolonged by technological means.

Marital deduction. A deduction allowed by the federal estate tax law for all property passed to a surviving spouse who is a U.S. citizen. This deduction (which really acts like an exemption) allows anyone, even a billionaire, to pass his or her entire estate to a surviving spouse without any tax at all. Tax problems, however, are usually made worse by relying exclusively on the marital deduction.

Marriage. A specific status conferred on a couple by the state. In most states, it is necessary to file papers with a county clerk and have a marriage ceremony conducted by an authorized individual to be married.

In some states, however, couples may be considered married without a ceremony in certain circumstances. *See* **Common law marriage.**

Minor. In most states, persons under 18 years of age. All minors must be under the care of a competent adult (parent or guardian) unless they are "emancipated"—in the military, married or living independently with court permission. Property left to a minor must be handled by an adult until the minor becomes an adult under the laws of the state.

Mortgage. A document that makes a piece of real estate the security (collateral) for the payment of a debt. Most house buyers sign a mortgage when they buy; the bank lends money to buy the house, and the house serves as security for the debt. If the owners don't pay back the loan on time, the bank can seize the house and have it sold to pay off the loan.

Pay-on-death account. A simple bank account trust, revocable at any time before the death of the depositor. Also called a "Totten trust account" or "revocable trust account."

Personal guardian. An adult appointed or selected to care for a minor child in the event no biological or adoptive parent (legal parent) of the child is able to do so. If one legal parent is alive when the other dies, the child will automatically go to that parent, unless the best interests of the child require something else.

Personal property. All property other than land and buildings attached to land. Cars, bank accounts, wages, securities, a small business, furniture, insurance policies, jewelry, pets and season baseball tickets are all personal property.

Personal representative. *See* **Executor.**

Pour-over will. A will that "pours over" property into a trust. Property left through the will must go through probate before it goes into the trust.

Power of attorney. A legal document in which you authorize someone else to act for you. *See* **Durable power of attorney**.

Pretermitted heir. A child (or the child of a deceased child) who is either not named or (in some states) not provided for in a will. Most states presume that persons want their children to inherit. Accordingly, children, or the children of a child who has died, who are not mentioned or provided for in the will are entitled to a share of the estate.

Principal. Property owned by a trust, as distinguished from the income generated by that property.

Probate. The court proceeding in which: (1) the authenticity of your will (if any) is established, (2) your executor or administrator is appointed, (3) your debts and taxes are paid, (4) your heirs are identified and (5) your property in your probate estate is distributed according to your will (if there is a will).

Probate estate. All a decedent's property that passes through probate. Generally, this means all property owned at death less any property that has been placed in joint tenancy, a living trust, a bank account trust or in life insurance.

Probate fees. Fees paid from a decedent's property to an attorney or court during probate. Typically, fees take about 5% of the decedent's estate.

Property guardian. The person named in a will to care for property of a minor child not supervised by some other legal method, such as a minor's trust. Also called "the guardian of the minor's estate" or "financial guardian."

QTIP trust. A type of trust that allows a surviving spouse to postpone, until her death, paying estate taxes that were assessed on the death of the other spouse.

Quasi-community property. A rule that applies to married couples who have moved to Washington, Idaho or California. Laws in those states require all property acquired by people during their marriage in other states to be treated as community property at their death.

Real estate. Same as **Real property**.

Real property. All land and items attached to the land, such as buildings, houses, stationary mobile homes, fences and trees are real property or "real estate." All property that is not real property is personal property.

Recording. The process of filing a copy of a deed with the county land records office. Recording creates a public record of all changes in ownership of property in the state.

Residuary beneficiary. The residuary beneficiary of a trust for one person, or a basic shared trust created from this book, is that beneficiary who receives any trust property not otherwise given away by the trust document. The residuary beneficiary of a will is the beneficiary who receives any property the will writer owned that was not left to beneficiaries by the will or other method.

Residuary estate. Property that goes to the residuary beneficiary of a will or trust, after all specific gifts of property have been made.

Right of survivorship. The right of a surviving joint tenant to take ownership of a deceased joint tenant's share of the property.

Separate property. In states which have community property, all property that is not community property. *See* **Community property**.

Sprinkling trust. A trust that authorizes the trustee to decide how to distribute trust income or principal among different beneficiaries.

Stepped-up basis. The tax basis of inherited property is "stepped up" to the market value of the property at the decedent's death.

Subtrust. *See* **Child's subtrust**.

Successor trustee. The person (or institution) who takes over as trustee of a trust when the original trustee(s) have died or become incapacitated.

Surviving spouse. With a shared living trust created by both spouses, the living spouse after the other spouse dies.

Surviving spouse's trust. Where a couple has created an AB trust, the revocable living trust of the surviving spouse, after the other spouse has died.

Taking against the will. State law gives a surviving spouse the right to demand a certain share (in most states, one-third to one-half) of the deceased spouse's property. The surviving spouse can take that share instead of accepting whatever he or she inherited through the deceased spouse's will. If the surviving spouse decides to take the statutory share, it's called "taking against the will." *See* **Dower and curtesy**.

Tax basis. *See* **Basis**.

Taxable estate. The portion of an estate that is subject to federal or state estate taxes.

Tenancy by the entirety. A form of property ownership allowed in some states. It is similar to joint tenancy, but is allowed only for property owned by a husband and wife.

Tenancy in common. A way for co-owners to hold title to property that allows them maximum freedom to dispose of their interests by sale, gift or will. At a co-owner's death, his or her share goes to beneficiaries named in a will or trust or to the legal heirs, not to the other co-owners. Compare **Joint tenancy**.

Testamentary trust. A trust created by a will.

Testate. Someone who dies leaving a valid will or other valid property transfer devices dies "testate."

Testator. A person who makes a will, also called the will writer.

Title. A document that proves ownership of property.

Totten trust. *See* **Pay-on-death account**.

Trust. A legal arrangement under which one person or institution (called a "trustee") controls property given by another person (called a "grantor," "settlor" or "trustor") for the benefit of a third person (called a "beneficiary").

Trust corpus or res. Latin for the property transferred to a trust.

Trustee. The people or institutions who manage trust property under the terms of the trust document. With a revocable living trust created from the forms in this book, the creators of the trust (grantors) are the original trustees.

Trustee powers. The provisions in a trust document defining what the trustee may and may not do.

Uniform Transfers to Minors Act. A statute, adopted by most states, that provides a method for transferring property to minors and arranging for an adult to manage it until the child is older. *See* **Custodian**.

Will. A legal document in which a person directs what is to be done with his or her property after death. ☙

Appendix

Form 1: Basic Living Trust for One Person

Form 2: Basic Shared Living Trust

Form 3: AB Living Trust

Form 4: Witness Statement for a Florida Living Trust

Form 5: Assignment of Property to a Trust for One Person

Form 6: Assignment of Shared Property to a Trust for a Couple

Form 7: Amendment to Living Trust for One Person

Form 8: Amendment to Basic Shared Living Trust or AB Trust

Form 9: Revocation of Living Trust

Form 10: Basic Will for One Person

Form 11: Basic Will for a Member of a Couple

Form 12: Affidavit of Successor Trustee

Reminder

The circled numbers on the trust forms (①, ④, ⑦, etc.) refer to instructions in Chapter 10, "Preparing Your Living Trust Document," Section D, which explain what information you need to write on the blank lines. If you have any trouble completing a trust form or are puzzled by these numbers, please re-read Section D of Chapter 10.

Form 1: Basic Living Trust for One Person

The ①_____ Living Trust

your name (or name of trust, if different)

DECLARATION OF TRUST

I. TRUST NAME

This trust shall be known as The ①_____ Living Trust.

your name

II. TRUST PROPERTY

(A) Property Placed in Trust

①_____ , called the grantor or trustee, declares

your name

that _____ has set aside and holds in The ①_____

he/she your name

Living Trust all _____ interest in that property described in the attached Schedule A.②

his/her

The trust property shall be used for the benefit of the trust beneficiaries and shall be administered and distributed by the trustee in accordance with this Declaration of Trust.

(B) Additional or After-Acquired Property

The grantor may add property to the trust at any time.

III. RESERVED POWERS OF GRANTOR

(A) Amendment or Revocation

The grantor reserves the power to amend or revoke this trust at any time during _____ lifetime,

his/her

without notifying any beneficiary.

(B) Rights to Trust Property

Until the death of the grantor, all rights to all income, profits and control of the trust property shall be retained by the grantor.

(C) Homestead Rights

If the Grantor's principal residence is transferred to the trust, Grantor has the right to possess and occupy it for life, rent-free and without charge, except for taxes, insurance, maintenance and related costs and expenses. This right is intended to give Grantor a beneficial interest in the property and to ensure that Grantor does not lose eligibility for a state homestead tax exemption for which Grantor otherwise qualifies.

⑤(D) Incapacity of Grantor

If at any time, as certified in writing by a licensed physician, the grantor has become physically or mentally incapacitated, the successor trustee shall manage this trust. The successor trustee shall pay trust income at least annually to, or for the benefit of, the grantor and may also spend any amount of trust principal necessary in the trustee's discretion for the proper health care, support, maintenance, comfort or welfare of the grantor, in accordance with _____ accustomed manner of living, until the grantor, as certified by a licensed

his/her

physician, is again able to manage _____ own affairs, or until the grantor's death.

his/her

(E) Grantor's Death

After the death of the grantor, this trust becomes irrevocable. It may not be altered or amended in any respect, and may not be terminated except through distributions permitted by this Declaration of Trust.

IV. TRUSTEES

(A) Original Trustee

The trustee of The ① _____ Living Trust and all

your name

children's subtrusts created under this Declaration of Trust shall be ① _____.

(B) Successor Trustee

Upon the death of the trustee, or _____ incapacity as certified in writing by a licensed physician, the

his/her

successor trustee shall be ⑥ _____. If _____ is/are

name(s)   he/she/all of them

unable to serve or continue serving as successor trustee, the successor trustee shall be
⑥ _____.

name

[If you named more than one successor trustee, include ONE of the following two paragraphs here:]

Any of the successor trustees has full and independent authority to act for and represent the trust.

[or]

All of the successor trustees must consent, in writing, to any transaction involving the trust or trust property.

(C) Resignation of Trustee

Any trustee in office may resign at any time by signing a notice of resignation. The resignation must be delivered to the person or institution who is either named in this Declaration of Trust, or appointed by the trustee under Section IV, Paragraph (D), to next serve as trustee.

(D) Power to Appoint Successor Trustee

If all the successor trustees named in this Declaration of Trust cease to, or are unable to, serve as trustee, any trustee may appoint an additional successor trustee or trustees to serve in the order nominated. The appointment must be made in writing, signed by the trustee and notarized.

(E) Terminology

In this Declaration of Trust, the term "trustee" includes any successor trustee or successor trustees.

(F) Bond Waived

No bond shall be required of any trustee.

(G) Compensation

No trustee shall receive any compensation for serving as trustee, unless the trustee serves as a trustee of a child's subtrust created by this Declaration of Trust.

(H) Liability of Trustee

With respect to the exercise or non-exercise of discretionary powers granted by this Declaration of Trust, the trustee shall not be liable for actions taken in good faith.

V. BENEFICIARIES

Upon the death of the grantor, the property listed on Schedule A shall be distributed to the beneficiaries named in this section.

(A) Primary and Alternate Beneficiaries

1. ⑦ _____ shall be given

_____.
property identified

If _____ does not survive the grantor, that property shall be
beneficiary

given to _____.
alternate beneficiary

2. ⑦ _____ shall be given
beneficiary

_____.
property identified

If _____ does not survive the grantor, that property shall be
beneficiary

given to _____.
alternate beneficiary

3. ⑦ _____ shall be given

_____.
property identified

If _____ does not survive the grantor, that property shall be
beneficiary

given to _____.
alternate beneficiary

4. ⑦ _____ shall be given
beneficiary

_____.
property identified

If _____ does not survive the grantor, that property shall be
beneficiary

given to _____.
alternate beneficiary

5. ⑦ _____ shall be given
beneficiary

_____.
property identified

If _____ does not survive the grantor, that property shall be
beneficiary

given to _____.
alternate beneficiary

(B) Residuary Beneficiary

The residuary beneficiary of the trust shall be ⑧Ⓐ _____,
residuary beneficiary

who shall be given all trust property not specifically and validly disposed of by Section V, Paragraph (A). If

_____, does not survive the grantor, that property shall be given to
residuary beneficiary

⑧Ⓐ _____.
alternate residuary beneficiary

VI. DISTRIBUTION OF TRUST PROPERTY UPON DEATH OF GRANTOR

Upon the death of the grantor, the trustee shall distribute the trust property outright to the beneficiaries

named in Section V, Paragraphs (A) and (B), subject to any provision in this Declaration of Trust that creates

children's subtrusts or creates custodianships under the Uniform Transfers to Minors Act.

VII. TRUSTEE'S POWERS AND DUTIES

(A) Powers Under State Law

To carry out the provisions of The ① _____
your name

Living Trust , and any children's subtrusts created under this Declaration of Trust, the trustee shall have all

authority and powers allowed or conferred on a trustee under _____ law,
your state

subject to the trustee's fiduciary duty to the grantor and the beneficiaries.

(B) Specified Powers

The trustee's powers include, but are not limited to:

1. The power to sell trust property, and to borrow money and to encumber that property, specifically including trust real estate, by mortgage, deed of trust or other method.

2. The power to manage trust real estate as if the trustee were the absolute owner of it, including the power to lease (even if the lease term may extend beyond the period of any trust) or grant options to lease the property, to make repairs or alterations and to insure against loss.

3. The power to sell or grant options for the sale or exchange of any trust property, including stocks, bonds, debentures and any other form of security or security account, at public or private sale for cash or on credit.

4. The power to invest trust property in property of any kind, including but not limited to bonds, debentures, notes, mortgages and stocks.

5. The power to receive additional property from any source and add to any trust created by this Declaration of Trust.

6. The power to employ and pay reasonable fees to accountants, lawyers or investment experts for information or advice relating to the trust.

7. The power to deposit and hold trust funds in both interest-bearing and non-interest-bearing accounts.

8. The power to deposit funds in bank or other accounts uninsured by FDIC coverage.

9. The power to enter into electronic fund transfer or safe deposit arrangements with financial institutions.

10. The power to continue any business of the grantor.

11. The power to institute or defend legal actions concerning the trust or grantor's affairs.

12. The power to execute any document necessary to administer any child's subtrust created in this Declaration of Trust.

13. The power to diversify investments, including authority to decide that some or all of the trust property need not produce income.

(C) Payment by Trustee of the Grantor's Debts and Taxes

The grantor's debts and death taxes shall be paid by the trustee. The trustee shall pay these from the following trust property:

_____

_____

_____.

If the property specified above is insufficient to pay all the grantor's debts and death taxes, the trustee shall determine how such debts and death taxes shall be paid from trust property.

VIII. GENERAL ADMINISTRATIVE PROVISIONS

(A) Controlling Law

The validity of The ① _____ Living Trust shall
your name

be governed by the laws of _____.
your state

(B) Severability

If any provision of this Declaration of Trust is ruled unenforceable, the remaining provisions shall nevertheless remain in effect.

(C) Amendments

The term "Declaration of Trust" includes any provisions added by amendments.

(D) Accountings

No accountings or reports shall be required of the trustee.

IX. CHILDREN'S SUBTRUSTS

All trust property left to any of the minor or young adult beneficiaries listed below in Section IX, Paragraph (A), shall be retained in trust for each such beneficiary in a separate subtrust of this

① _____ Living Trust. Each subtrust may be identified
your name

and referred to by adding the name of that subtrust's beneficiary to the name of this trust. The following terms apply to each subtrust:

(A) Subtrust Beneficiaries and Age Limits

A subtrust shall end when the beneficiary of that subtrust, listed below, becomes 35, except as otherwise specified in this section:

⑩Subtrust for   Shall end at age

_____   _____

_____   _____

_____   _____

_____   _____

_____   _____

(B) Powers and Duties of Subtrust Trustee

1. Until a child's subtrust ends, the trustee may distribute to or use for the benefit of the beneficiary as much of the net income or principal of the child's subtrust as the trustee deems necessary for the beneficiary's health, support, maintenance or education. Education includes, but is not limited to, college, graduate, postgraduate and vocational studies, and reasonably related living expenses.

2. In deciding whether to make a distribution to the beneficiary, the trustee may take into account the beneficiary's other income, resources and sources of support.

3. Any subtrust income that is not distributed to a beneficiary by the trustee shall be accumulated and added to the principal of the subtrust for that beneficiary.

4. The trustee of a child's subtrust is not required to make any accounting or report to the subtrust beneficiary.

(C) Assignment of Interest of Beneficiary Prohibited

The interests of the beneficiary of a child's subtrust shall not be transferable by voluntary or involuntary assignment or by operation of law before actual receipt by the beneficiary. These interests shall be free from the claims of creditors and from attachments, execution, bankruptcy or other legal process to the fullest extent permitted by law.

(D) Compensation of Trustee

Any trustee of a child's subtrust created under this Declaration of Trust shall be entitled to reasonable compensation out of the subtrust assets for ordinary and extraordinary services, and for all services in connection with the termination of any subtrust.

(E) Termination of Subtrusts

A child's subtrust shall end when any of the following events occurs:

1. The beneficiary reaches the age specified in Section IX, Paragraph (A). If the subtrust ends for this reason, the remaining principal and accumulated income of the subtrust shall be given outright to the beneficiary.

2. The beneficiary dies. If the subtrust ends for this reason, the subtrust property shall pass to the beneficiary's heirs.

3. The trustee distributes all subtrust property under the provisions of this Declaration of Trust.

X. CUSTODIANSHIPS UNDER THE UNIFORM TRANSFERS TO MINORS ACT

    1. All property ⑪ _____ becomes entitled to
_{beneficiary}

under this trust document shall be given to _____ as
_{custodian's name}

custodian for _____ under the _____
_{beneficiary}   _{state}

Uniform Transfers to Minors Act, until _____ reaches age _____.
_{beneficiary}

    2. All property ⑪ _____ becomes entitled to
_{beneficiary}

under this trust document shall be given to _____ as
_{custodian's name}

custodian for _____ under the _____
_{beneficiary}   _{state}

Uniform Transfers to Minors Act, until _____ reaches age _____.
_{beneficiary}

    3. All property ⑪ _____ becomes entitled to
_{beneficiary}

under this trust document shall be given to _____ as
_{custodian's name}

custodian for _____ under the _____
_{beneficiary}   _{state}

Uniform Transfers to Minors Act, until _____ reaches age _____.
_{beneficiary}

Certification by Grantor

    I certify that I have read this Declaration of Trust and that it correctly states the terms and conditions under which the trust property is to be held, managed and disposed of by the trustee and I approve the Declaration of Trust.

Dated: _____

_____

Grantor and Trustee

NOTARY'S ACKNOWLEDGMENT

State of _____

County of _____

On _____, 19_____, before me, _____,

a notary public in and for said state, personally appeared _____,

personally known to me (or proved to me on the basis of satisfactory evidence) to be the person whose name is

subscribed to the within Declaration of Trust, and acknowledged to me that he/she executed the same in his/her

authorized capacity and that by his/her signature on the instrument he/she executed the Declaration of Trust.

_____

Signature of Notary   [SEAL]

SCHEDULE A②

All the grantor's interest in the following property:

Form 2: Basic Shared Living Trust

The ①_____ Living Trust

your name (or name of trust, if different)

DECLARATION OF TRUST

I. TRUST NAME

This trust shall be known as The ①_____

your names

Living Trust.

II. TRUST PROPERTY

(A) Property Placed in Trust

①_____ , called the grantors

your names

or trustees, declare that they have set aside and hold in The ①_____

your names

Living Trust all their interest in the property described in the attached Schedules A, B and C.②

The trust property shall be used for the benefit of the trust beneficiaries, and shall be administered and

distributed by the trustees in accordance with this Declaration of Trust.

(B) Rights Retained by Grantors

As long as both grantors are alive, both grantors retain all rights to all income, profits and control of the

trust property listed on Schedule A of The ①_____

your names

Living Trust.

(1) As long as _____ is alive, she shall retain all

wife's name

rights to all income, profits and control of her separate property listed on Schedule B of The

①_____ Living Trust.

your names

(2) As long as _____ is alive, he shall retain all

husband's name

rights to all income, profits and control of his separate property listed on Schedule C of The

①_____ Living Trust.

your names

(C) Additional or After-Acquired Property

Either grantor, or both, may add property to the trust at any time.

(D) Character of Property Placed in Trust

While both grantors are alive, property transferred to this trust shall retain its original character. If the trust is revoked, the trustee shall distribute the trust property to the grantors based on the same ownership rights they had before the property was transferred to the trust.

Specifically:

1. Shared Property

All trust property listed on Schedule A:

④ _____
identify the character of shared property listed in Schedule A

_____

_____

_____

_____.

2. Separate Property

The trust property listed on Schedule B shall retain its character as the separate property of

_____. The trust property listed on
wife's name

Schedule C shall retain its character as the separate property of _____.
husband's name

[Make appropriate deletions if wife and/or husband has no separate property.]

(E) Revocation

As long as both grantors live, either grantor may revoke The

① _____ Living Trust at any time
your names

by writing given to the other grantor. No beneficiary need be given any notice of revocation.

(F) Amendment

As long as both grantors live, The ① _____
your names

Living Trust may be altered, amended or modified only by a writing signed by both grantors.

(G) Homestead Rights

If the Grantors' principal residence is transferred to the trust, Grantors have the right to possess and occupy it for life, rent-free and without charge, except for taxes, insurance, maintenance and related costs and expenses. This right is intended to give Grantors a beneficial interest in the property and to ensure that the Grantors, or either of them, do not lose eligibility for a state homestead tax exemption for which either Grantor otherwise qualifies.

III. TRUSTEES

(A) Original Trustees

The trustees of The ① _____ Living Trust and
your names

any other trusts or children's subtrusts created under this Declaration of Trust shall be

① _____. Either trustee may act for, and represent, the
your names

trust in any transaction.

(B) Trustee on Death or Incapacity of Original Trustee

Upon the death or incapacity, as certified in writing by a licensed physician, of

_____ or
wife's name

_____, the other spouse shall serve as sole trustee
husband's name

of this trust and any children's subtrusts created under this Declaration of Trust.

(C) Trustee's Responsibility

The trustee in office shall serve as trustee of all trusts created under this Declaration of Trust, including all children's subtrusts.

(D) Terminology

In this Declaration of Trust, the term "trustee" includes any successor trustee or trustees. The singular "trustee" also includes the plural.

(E) Successor Trustee

Upon the death or incapacity of the surviving spouse, or the incapacity of both spouses, the successor

trustee shall be ⑥ _____. If _____ is/are unable to
name(s)   he/she/all of them

serve or to continue serving as successor trustee, the next successor trustee shall be

⑥ _____.

[If you named more than one successor trustee, include ONE of the following two paragraphs here:]

Any of the successor trustees has full and independent authority to act for and represent the trust.

[or]

All of the successor trustees must consent, in writing, to any transaction involving the trust or trust property.

(F) Resignation of Trustee

Any trustee in office may resign at any time by signing a notice of resignation. The resignation must be delivered to the person or institution who is either named in this Declaration of Trust, or appointed by the trustee under Section III, Paragraph (G), to next serve as trustee.

(G) Power to Appoint Successor Trustee

If all the successor trustees named in this Declaration of Trust cease to, or are unable to, serve as trustee, any trustee may appoint an additional successor trustee or trustees to serve in the order nominated. The appointment must be made in writing, signed by the trustee and notarized.

(H) Bond Waived

No bond shall be required of any trustee.

(I) Compensation

No trustee shall receive any compensation for serving as trustee, unless the trustee serves as a trustee of a child's subtrust created by this Declaration of Trust.

(J) Liability of Trustee

With respect to the exercise or non-exercise of discretionary powers granted by this Declaration of Trust, the trustee shall not be liable for actions taken in good faith.

IV. BENEFICIARIES

(A) Husband's Primary and Alternate Beneficiaries

Upon the death of _____, trust property
husband's name

owned by _____, as his share of the trust property
husband's name

listed on Schedule A and any separate property listed on Schedule C shall be distributed as specified to the beneficiaries named in this section.

1. Husband's Specific Beneficiaries

a. ⑦ _____ shall be given

beneficiary's name(s)

_____ .

property identified

If _____ does not survive _____ ,

beneficiary · husband's name

that property shall be given to _____ .

alternate beneficiary

b. ⑦ _____ shall be given

beneficiary's name(s)

_____ .

property identified

If _____ does not survive _____ ,

beneficiary · husband's name

that property shall be given to _____ .

alternate beneficiary

c. ⑦ _____ shall be given

beneficiary's name(s)

_____ .

property identified

If _____ does not survive _____ ,

beneficiary · husband's name

that property shall be given to _____ .

alternate beneficiary

d. ⑦ _____ shall be given

beneficiary's name(s)

_____ .

property identified

If _____ does not survive _____ ,

beneficiary · husband's name

that property shall be given to _____ .

alternate beneficiary

e. ⑦ _____ shall be given

beneficiary's name(s)

_____ .

property identified

If _____ does not survive _____ ,

beneficiary · husband's name

that property shall be given to _____ .

alternate beneficiary

2. Husband's Residuary Beneficiary

The residuary beneficiary of any trust property owned by _____
husband's name

as his share of the trust property listed on Schedule A or any separate property listed on Schedule C, and not

specifically and validly disposed of by Section IV, Paragraph (A)1, shall be

(7A) _____. If _____
residuary beneficiary   residuary beneficiary

does not survive _____, that property shall be given to
husband's name

(7A) _____.
alternate residuary beneficiary

(B) Wife's Primary and Alternate Beneficiaries

Upon the death of _____, trust property
wife's name

owned by _____, as her share of the trust property
wife's name

listed on Schedule A and any separate property listed on Schedule B shall be distributed as specified to the

beneficiaries named in this section.

1. Wife's Specific Beneficiaries

a. (7)_____ shall be given
beneficiary's name(s)

_____.
property identified

If _____ does not survive _____ ,
beneficiary   wife's name

that property shall be given to _____ .
alternate beneficiary

b. (7)_____ shall be given
beneficiary's name(s)

_____.
property identified

If _____ does not survive _____ ,
beneficiary   wife's name

that property shall be given to _____ .
alternate beneficiary

c. (7)_____ shall be given
beneficiary's name(s)

_____.
property identified

If _____ does not survive _____ ,
beneficiary   wife's name

that property shall be given to _____ .
alternate beneficiary

d. ⑦_____ shall be given
beneficiary's name(s)

_____.
property identified

If _____ does not survive _____ ,
beneficiary   wife's name

that property shall be given to _____ .
alternate beneficiary

e. ⑦_____ shall be given
beneficiary's name(s)

_____.
property identified

If _____ does not survive _____ ,
beneficiary   wife's name

that property shall be given to _____ .
alternate beneficiary

2. Wife's Residuary Beneficiary

The residuary beneficiary of any trust property owned by _____
wife's name

as her share of the trust property listed on Schedule A or any separate property listed on Schedule B, and not

specifically and validly disposed of by Section IV, Paragraph (B)1, shall be

⑧Ⓐ_____. If _____
residuary beneficiary   residuary beneficiary

does not survive _____, that property shall be given to
wife's name

⑧Ⓐ_____.
alternate residuary beneficiary

V. ADMINISTRATION OF TRUST PROPERTY

(A) Terminology

The first grantor to die shall be called the "deceased spouse." The living grantor shall be called the

"surviving spouse."

(B) Division and Distribution of Trust Property on Death of Grantor

1. Upon the death of the deceased spouse, the trustee shall divide the property of The

①_____ Living Trust listed on Schedules A, B and C
your names

into two separate trusts, Trust 1 and Trust 2. The trustee shall serve as trustee of Trust 1 and Trust 2.

2. Trust 1 shall contain all the property of The ①_____
your names

Living Trust owned by the deceased spouse at the time it was transferred to the trust, plus accumulated income, appreciation in value and the like attributable to the ownership interest of the deceased spouse and his or her share of any property acquired in the trust's name, EXCEPT trust property left by the terms of this trust to the surviving spouse. Trust 1 becomes irrevocable at the death of the deceased spouse. The trustee shall distribute the property in Trust 1 to the beneficiaries named by the deceased spouse in Section IV of this Declaration of Trust, subject to any provision of this Declaration of Trust that creates children's subtrusts or creates custodianships under the Uniform Transfers to Minors Act.

3. Trust 2 shall contain all the property of The ①_____
your names

Living Trust owned by the surviving spouse at the time it was transferred to the trust, plus accumulated income, appreciation in value and the like attributable to the ownership interest of the surviving spouse and any trust property left by the deceased spouse to the surviving spouse.

4. The trustee shall have exclusive authority to determine the paperwork and recordkeeping necessary to establish Trust 1 and Trust 2.

(C) Property Left to The Surviving Spouse

Any trust property left by the deceased spouse to the surviving spouse shall remain in the surviving spouse's revocable trust, Trust 2, without necessity of a formal transfer to that trust.

(D) Administration of Trust 2

1. Rights Retained by Surviving Spouse

Until the death of the surviving spouse, all rights to all income, profits and control of property in Trust 2 shall be retained by or distributed to the surviving spouse.

2. Revocation

The surviving spouse may amend or revoke Trust 2 at any time during his or her lifetime, without notifying any beneficiary.

3. Distribution of Property in Trust 2

Upon the death of the surviving spouse, Trust 2 becomes irrevocable, and the property in Trust 2 shall be distributed to the beneficiaries listed in Section IV, subject to any provision of this Declaration of Trust that creates children's subtrusts or creates custodianships under the Uniform Transfers to Minors Act.

VI. INCAPACITY

(A) Incapacity of Both Grantors

⑤ If both grantors of The ① _____ Living

your names

Trust become physically or mentally incapacitated, as certified in writing by a licensed physician, the successor

trustee shall manage The ① _____ Living Trust, and shall

your names

pay trust income at least annually to, or for the benefit of, the grantors and may also spend any amount of trust

income or trust principal necessary, in the successor trustee's discretion, for the proper health care, support,

maintenance, comfort and welfare of the grantors, in accordance with their accustomed standard of living, until a

licensed physician certifies that the grantors, or either of them, are again able to manage their own affairs, or until

their deaths.

⑤(B) Incapacity of Surviving Spouse

If, after the death of the deceased spouse, the surviving spouse becomes physically or mentally

incapacitated, as certified in writing by a licensed physician, the successor trustee shall manage Trust 2, and pay

trust income at least annually to, or for the benefit of, the surviving spouse and may also spend any amount of the

trust principal necessary in the successor trustee's discretion, for the proper health care, support, maintenance,

comfort and welfare of the surviving spouse, in accordance with his or her accustomed standard of living, until a

licensed physician certifies that the surviving spouse is again able to manage his or her own affairs, or until his or

her death.

VII. SIMULTANEOUS DEATH

If both grantors should die simultaneously, or under such circumstances as to render it difficult or

impossible to determine who predeceased the other, it shall be conclusively presumed that both died at the same

moment, and neither shall be presumed to have survived the other for purposes of this living trust.

VIII. TRUSTEE'S POWERS AND DUTIES

(A) Powers Under State Law

To carry out the provisions of this Declaration of Trust, and to manage the trust property of The

① _____ Living Trust, Trust 1, Trust 2 and any child's

your names

subtrust created under this Declaration of Trust, the trustee shall have all authority and power allowed or conferred under _____ law, subject to the trustee's fiduciary duty to the grantors

your state

and the beneficiaries.

(B) Specified Powers

The trustee's powers include, but are not limited to:

1. The power to sell trust property, and to borrow money and to encumber property, specifically including trust real estate, by mortgage, deed of trust or other method.

2. The power to manage trust real estate as if the trustee were the absolute owner of it, including the power to lease (even if the lease term may extend beyond the period of any trust) or grant options to lease the property, to make repairs or alterations and to insure against loss.

3. The power to sell or grant options for the sale or exchange of any trust property, including stocks, bonds, debentures and any other form of security or security account, at public or private sale for cash or on credit.

4. The power to invest trust property in property of any kind, including but not limited to bonds, debentures, notes, mortgages and stocks.

5. The power to receive additional property from any source and add to any trust created by this Declaration of Trust.

6. The power to employ and pay reasonable fees to accountants, lawyers or investment experts for information or advice relating to the trust.

7. The power to deposit and hold trust funds in both interest-bearing and non-interest-bearing accounts.

8. The power to deposit funds in bank or other accounts uninsured by FDIC coverage.

9. The power to enter into electronic fund transfer or safe deposit arrangements with financial institutions.

10. The power to continue any business of either grantor.

11. The power to institute or defend legal actions concerning the trust or grantor's affairs.

12. The power to execute any document necessary to administer any trust created in this Declaration of Trust.

13. The power to diversify investments, including authority to decide that some or all of the trust property need not produce income.

(C) Payment by the Trustee of the Grantors' Debts and Taxes

1. Wife's Debts and Taxes

_____'s debts and death taxes shall be paid
wife's name

by the trustee. The trustee shall pay these from the following trust property:

⑨ _____

_____

_____.

2. Husband's Debts and Taxes

_____'s debts and death taxes shall be paid
husband's name

by the trustee. The trustee shall pay these from the following trust property:

⑨ _____

_____

_____.

3. If Specified Property Insufficient

If the property specified above is insufficient to pay all a grantor's debts and death taxes, the trustee shall

determine how such debts and death taxes shall be paid from that grantor's trust property.

IX. GENERAL ADMINISTRATIVE PROVISIONS

(A) Controlling Law

The validity of The ① _____ Living Trust and
your names

construction of its provisions shall be governed by the laws of _____.
your state

(B) Severability

If any provision of this Declaration of Trust is ruled unenforceable, the remaining provisions shall

nevertheless remain in effect.

(C) Amendments

The term "Declaration of Trust" includes any provisions added by valid amendment.

(D) Accountings

No accountings or reports shall be required of the trustee.

X. CHILDREN'S SUBTRUSTS

All trust property left to any of the minor or young adult beneficiaries listed below in Section X, Paragraph (A), shall be retained in trust for each such beneficiary in a separate subtrust of this

① _____ Living Trust. Each subtrust may be identified
        your names

and referred to by adding the name of that subtrust's beneficiary to the name of this trust. The following terms apply to each subtrust:

(A) Subtrust Beneficiaries and Age Limits

A subtrust shall end when the beneficiary of that subtrust, listed below, becomes 35, except as otherwise specified in this section:

⑩ Subtrust for   Shall end at age

_____   _____

_____   _____

_____   _____

_____   _____

_____   _____

(B) Powers and Duties of Subtrust Trustee

1. Until a child's subtrust ends, the trustee may distribute to or use for the benefit of the beneficiary as much of the net income or principal of the child's subtrust as the trustee deems necessary for the beneficiary's health, support, maintenance or education. Education includes, but is not limited to, college, graduate, postgraduate and vocational studies, and reasonably related living expenses.

2. In deciding whether to make a distribution to the beneficiary, the trustee may take into account the beneficiary's other income, resources and sources of support.

3. Any subtrust income that is not distributed to a beneficiary by the trustee shall be accumulated and added to the principal of the subtrust for that beneficiary.

4. The trustee of a child's subtrust is not required to make any accounting or report to the subtrust beneficiary.

(C) Assignment of Interest of Beneficiary Prohibited

The interests of the beneficiary of a child's subtrust shall not be transferable by voluntary or involuntary assignment or by operation of law before actual receipt by the beneficiary. These interests shall be free from the claims of creditors and from attachments, execution, bankruptcy or other legal process to the fullest extent permitted by law.

(D) Compensation of Trustee

Any trustee of a child's subtrust created under this Declaration of Trust shall be entitled to reasonable compensation without court approval out of the subtrust assets for ordinary and extraordinary services, and for all services in connection with the termination of any subtrust.

(E) Termination of Subtrusts

A child's subtrust shall end when any of the following events occurs:

1. The beneficiary reaches the age specified in Section X, Paragraph (A). If the subtrust ends for this reason, the remaining principal and accumulated income of the subtrust shall be given outright to the beneficiary.

2. The beneficiary dies. If the subtrust ends for this reason, the subtrust property shall pass to the beneficiary's heirs.

3. The trustee distributes all subtrust property under the provisions of this Declaration of Trust.

XI. CUSTODIANSHIPS UNDER THE UNIFORM TRANSFERS TO MINORS ACT

1. All property ⑪_____ becomes entitled to
beneficiary

under this trust document shall be given to _____ as
custodian's name

custodian for _____ under the _____
beneficiary   state

Uniform Transfers to Minors Act, until _____ reaches age _____.
beneficiary

2. All property ⑪_____ becomes entitled to
beneficiary

under this trust document shall be given to _____ as
custodian's name

custodian for _____ under the _____
beneficiary   state

Uniform Transfers to Minors Act, until _____ reaches age _____.
beneficiary

3. All property ⑪_____ becomes entitled to

beneficiary

under this trust document shall be given to _____ as

custodian's name

custodian for _____ under the _____

beneficiary   state

Uniform Transfers to Minors Act, until _____ reaches age _____.

beneficiary

Certification by Grantors

We certify that we have read this Declaration of Trust and that it correctly states the terms and conditions under which the trust property is to be held, managed and disposed of by the trustees and we approve the Declaration of Trust.

Dated: _____

_____

Grantor and Trustee

_____

Grantor and Trustee

NOTARY'S ACKNOWLEDGMENT

State of _____

County of _____

On _____, 19_____, before me, _____,

a notary public in and for said state, personally appeared _____

_____, personally known to me (or proved to me on the basis of

satisfactory evidence) to be the persons whose names are subscribed to the within Declaration of Trust, and

acknowledged to me that they executed the same in their authorized capacities and that by their signatures on the

instrument they executed the Declaration of Trust.

_____

Signature of Notary   [SEAL]

SCHEDULE A ③

SHARED PROPERTY PLACED IN TRUST

SCHEDULE B

WIFE'S SEPARATE PROPERTY PLACED IN TRUST

All Wife's interest in the following property:

SCHEDULE C

HUSBAND'S SEPARATE PROPERTY PLACED IN TRUST

All Husband's interest in the following property:

Form 3: AB Living Trust

The ①_____ AB Living Trust.
your name (or name of trust, if different)

DECLARATION OF TRUST

I. TRUST NAME

This trust shall be known as The ①_____
your names

Living Trust.

II. TRUST PROPERTY

(A) Property Placed in Trust

①_____, called the grantors or
your names

trustees, declare that they have set aside and hold in The ①_____
your names

Living Trust all their interest in the property described in the attached Schedules A, B and C.②

The trust property shall be used for the benefit of the trust beneficiaries and shall be administered and

distributed by the trustees in accordance with this Declaration of Trust.

(B) Rights Retained by Grantors

As long as both grantors are alive, both grantors retain all rights to all income, profits and control of the

trust property listed on Schedule A of The ①_____ Living Trust.
your names

(1) As long as _____ is alive, she shall retain all rights to all income,
wife's name

profits and control of her separate property listed on Schedule B of The

①_____ Living Trust.
your names

(2) As long as _____ is alive, he shall retain all rights to all income,
husband's name

profits and control of his separate property listed on Schedule C of The

①_____ Living Trust.
your names

-1-

(C) Additional or After-Acquired Property

Either grantor, or both, may add property to the trust at any time.

(D) Character of Property Placed in Trust

While both grantors are alive, property transferred to this trust shall retain its original character. If the trust is revoked, the trustee shall distribute the trust property to the grantors based on the same ownership rights they had before the property was transferred to the trust, as specified below.

1. Shared Property

All trust property listed on Schedule A:

④ _____
identify the character of shared property listed in Schedule A

_____

_____

_____

_____.

2. Separate Property

The trust property listed on Schedule B shall retain its character as the separate property of

_____. The trust property listed on Schedule C
wife's name

shall retain its character as the separate property of _____.
husband's name

[Make appropriate deletions if wife and/or husband has no separate property.]

(E) Revocation

As long as both grantors live, either grantor may revoke The ① _____
your names

Living Trust at any time by writing given to the other grantor. No beneficiary need be given any notice of revocation. After the death of a spouse, the surviving spouse can amend his or her continuing revocable living trust, Trust 2, as defined in Section V, Paragraph (B).

(F) Amendment

As long as both grantors live, The ① _____
your names

Living Trust may be altered, amended or modified only by a writing signed by both grantors.

After the death of a spouse, the surviving spouse can amend his or her revocable living trust, Trust B, The Surviving Spouse's Trust, as defined in Section V.

(G) Homestead Rights

If the Grantors' principal residence is transferred to the trust, Grantors have the right to possess and occupy it for life, rent-free and without charge, except for taxes, insurance, maintenance and related costs and expenses. This right is intended to give Grantors a beneficial interest in the property and to ensure that the Grantors, or either of them, do not lose eligibility for a state homestead tax exemption for which either Grantor otherwise qualifies.

III. TRUSTEES

(A) Original Trustees

The trustees of The ① _____
your names

Living Trust and any other trusts or childrens subtrusts created under this Declaration of Trust shall be

① _____ .
your names

Either trustee may act for, and represent, the trust, in any transaction.

(B) Trustee on Death or Incapacity of Original Trustee

Upon the death or incapacity, as certified in writing by a licensed physician, of

_____ or _____ ,
wife's name   husband's name

the other spouse shall serve as sole trustee of this trust and all trusts and any child's subtrusts created under this Declaration of Trust.

(C) Trustee's Responsibility

The trustee in office shall serve as trustee of this trust and all trusts and any child's subtrusts created under this Declaration of Trust.

(D) Terminology

In this Declaration of Trust, the term "trustee" includes any successor trustee or trustees. The singular "trustee" also includes the plural.

(E) Successor Trustee

⑤Upon the death or incapacity of the surviving spouse, or the incapacity of both spouses, the successor trustee shall be ⑥_____. If _____

name(s)   he/she/all of them

is/are unable to serve or to continue serving as successor trustee, the next successor trustee shall be ⑥_____.

name

[If you named more than one successor trustee, include ONE of the following two paragraphs here:]

Any of the successor trustees has full and independent authority to act for and represent the trust.

[or]

All of the successor trustees must consent, in writing, to any transaction involving the trust or trust property.

(F) Resignation of Trustee

Any trustee in office may resign at any time by signing a notice of resignation. The resignation must be delivered to the person or institution who is either named in this Declaration of Trust, or appointed by the trustee under Section III, Paragraph (G), to next serve as the trustee.

(G) Power to Appoint Successor Trustee

If all the successor trustees named in this Declaration of Trust cease to, or are unable to, serve as trustee, any trustee may appoint an additional successor trustee or trustees to serve in the order nominated. The appointment must be made in writing, signed by the trustee and notarized.

(H) Bond Waived

No bond shall be required of any trustee.

(I) Compensation

No trustee shall receive any compensation for serving as trustee, unless the trustee serves as a trustee of an A trust or child's subtrust created by this Declaration of Trust.

(J) Liability of Trustee

With respect to the exercise or non-exercise of discretionary powers granted by this Declaration of Trust, the trustee shall not be liable for actions taken in good faith.

IV. BENEFICIARIES

(A) Wife's Specific and Alternate Beneficiaries

Upon the death of _____, trust property
wife's name

owned by _____, as her share of the trust property
wife's name

listed on Schedule A and any separate property listed on Schedule B shall be distributed as specified to the

beneficiaries named in this section.

⑦1. _____ shall be given
beneficiary's name(s)

_____ .
property identified

If _____ does not survive _____ ,
beneficiary   wife's name

that property shall be given to _____ .
alternate beneficiary

⑦2. _____ shall be given
beneficiary's name(s)

_____ .
property identified

If _____ does not survive _____ ,
beneficiary   wife's name

that property shall be given to _____ .
alternate beneficiary

⑦3. _____ shall be given
beneficiary's name(s)

_____ .
property identified

If _____ does not survive _____ ,
beneficiary   wife's name

that property shall be given to _____ .
alternate beneficiary

(B) Husband's Specific and Alternate Beneficiaries

Upon the death of _____, trust property owned by
husband's name

_____, as his share of the trust property listed on Schedule A and
husband's name

any separate property listed on Schedule C shall be distributed as specified to the beneficiaries named in this

section.

⑦1. _____ shall be given
beneficiary's name(s)

_____.
property identified

If _____ does not survive _____ ,
beneficiary   husband's name

that property shall be given to _____ .
alternate beneficiary

⑦2. _____ shall be given
beneficiary's name(s)

_____.
property identified

If _____ does not survive _____ ,
beneficiary   husband's name

that property shall be given to _____ .
alternate beneficiary

⑦3. _____ shall be given
beneficiary's name(s)

_____.
property identified

If _____ does not survive _____ ,
beneficiary   husband's name

that property shall be given to _____ .
alternate beneficiary

(C) Remaining Trust Property

Except as provided by Section IV, Paragraph (A) or (B), all other trust property of the deceased spouse shall be transferred to, and administered as part of, Trust A, The Marital Life Estate Trust, defined in Section V.

V. CREATION OF TRUST A, THE MARITAL LIFE ESTATE TRUST, ON DEATH OF DECEASED SPOUSE

(A) Terminology

1. The first grantor to die shall be called the "deceased spouse." The living grantor shall then be called the "surviving spouse."

2. The "trust property of the deceased spouse" shall consist of all property of The

① _____ Living Trust owned by the deceased spouse
your names

at the time it was transferred to the trust, plus accumulated income, appreciation in value and the like attributable to the ownership interest of the deceased spouse, and his or her share of all property acquired in the trust's name.

3. The "trust property of the surviving spouse" shall consist of all property of The

① _____ Living Trust owned by the surviving spouse at
your names

the time it was transferred to the trust, plus accumulated income, appreciation in value and the like, attributable to

the ownership interest of the surviving spouse, and his or her share of all property acquired in the trust's name.

(B) Division of Trust Property on Death of Deceased Spouse

1. Upon the death of the deceased spouse, the trustee shall divide the property of The

① _____ Living Trust listed on Schedules A, B and C
your names

into two separate trusts, Trust A and Trust B.

2. All trust assets of the deceased spouse, as defined in Section V, Paragraph (A)2, shall be placed in a

trust known as Trust A, the Marital Life Estate Trust, after making any specific gifts provided for in Section IV,

Paragraph (A) or (B), subject to any provision in this Declaration of Trust that creates childrens' subtrusts or

creates custodianship under the Uniform Transfers to Minors Act.

3. The trustee shall place all trust assets of the surviving spouse, as defined in Section V, Paragraph (A)3,

in a trust known as Trust B (The Surviving Spouse's Trust).

4. Physical segregation of the assets of The ① _____
your names

 Living Trust is not required to divide that trust's property into Trust A and Trust B. The trustee shall exclusively

determine what records, documents and actions are required to establish and maintain Trust A and Trust B.

(C) Administration of Trust A

All property held in Trust A shall be administered as follows:

1. Upon the death of the deceased spouse, Trust A shall be irrevocable.

2. The life beneficiary of Trust A shall be the surviving spouse.

3. If _____ is the deceased spouse, the final
wife's name

beneficiaries of Trust A shall be:

⑦Ⓑ _____

_____

_____

_____

If _____ is the deceased spouse, the alternate final beneficiaries of
   wife's name

Trust A shall be:

(7B)_____

_____

_____

_____

4. If _____ is the deceased spouse, the final beneficiaries
   husband's name

of Trust A shall be:

(7B)_____

_____

_____

_____

If _____ is the deceased spouse, the alternate final beneficiaries of
   husband's name

Trust A shall be:

(7B)_____

_____

_____

_____

5. After the deceased spouse's death, the trustee shall pay to or spend for the benefit of the surviving spouse the net income of Trust A in quarter-annual or more frequent installments. The trustee shall also pay to or spend for the benefit of the surviving spouse any sums from the principal of Trust A necessary for the surviving spouse's health, education, support and maintenance, in his or her accustomed manner of living.

6. (12) No accounting of Trust A shall be required of the trustee, except that the final beneficiaries shall be provided with copies of the annual federal income tax return.

7. The trustee shall be entitled to reasonable compensation from assets of Trust A for services rendered managing Trust A, without court approval.

8. Upon the death of the life beneficiary, the trustee shall distribute the property of Trust A to the final beneficiary or beneficiaries.

VI. TRUST B: THE SURVIVING SPOUSE'S TRUST

(A) Creation of Trust B, The Surviving Spouse's Trust

Upon the death of the deceased spouse, all trust property owned by the surviving spouse, as defined in Section V, Paragraph (A)3, shall be held in Trust B, The Surviving Spouse's Trust.

(B) Administration of Trust B

Until the death of the surviving spouse, the surviving spouse retains all rights to all income, profits and control of the property in Trust B. The surviving spouse may amend or revoke Trust B at any time during his or her lifetime, without notifying any beneficiary.

(C) Distribution of Property in Trust B

1. Upon the death of the surviving spouse, Trust B becomes irrevocable.

2. The trustee shall first distribute any specific gifts of the surviving spouse to the beneficiaries named in Section IV, Paragraph (A) or (B). The trustee shall then distribute all remaining property of Trust B to his or her final, or alternate final, beneficiaries, as named in Section V, Paragraph (C)3 or (C)4.

3. All distributions under Section VI, Paragraph (C), are subject to any provision in this Declaration of Trust that creates children's subtrusts or creates custodianships under the Uniform Transfers to Minors Act.

VII. INCAPACITY

(A) Incapacity of Both Grantors

⑤ If both grantors of The ①_____
your names

Living Trust become physically or mentally incapacitated, as certified in writing by a licensed physician, the successor trustee shall manage The ①_____
your names

Living Trust, and pay trust income at least annually to, or for the benefit of, the grantors and may also spend any amount of trust principal necessary in the successor trustee's discretion, for the health, education, support and maintenance of the grantors, in accordance with their accustomed standard of living, until a licensed physician certifies that the grantors, or either of them, are again able to manage their own affairs, or until their deaths.

⑤(B) Incapacity of Surviving Spouse

If, after the death of the deceased spouse, the surviving spouse becomes physically or mentally incapacitated, as certified in writing by a licensed physician, the successor trustee shall:

1. Manage Trust B and pay trust income at least annually to, or for the benefit of, the surviving spouse, and may also spend any amount of that trust's principal necessary in the successor trustee's discretion, for the proper health, education, support and maintenance of the surviving spouse, in accordance with his or her accustomed standard of living, until a licensed physician certifies that the surviving spouse is again able to manage his or her own affairs, or until his or her death.

Any income in excess of amounts spent for the benefit of the surviving spouse shall be accumulated and added to the property of Trust B.

2. Manage Trust B, under the terms of this Declaration of Trust, until a licensed physician certifies that the surviving spouse is again able to manage his or her own affairs and is able to serve as trustee of that trust, or until the death of the surviving spouse.

VIII. SIMULTANEOUS DEATH

If both grantors should die simultaneously, or under such circumstances as to render it difficult or impossible to determine who predeceased the other, it shall be conclusively presumed that both died at the same moment, and neither shall be presumed to have survived the other for purposes of this living trust.

IX. TRUSTEE'S POWERS AND DUTIES

(A) Powers Under State Law

To carry out the provisions of this Declaration of Trust and to manage the trust property of The

① _____ Living Trust, Trust A and

your names

Trust B, and any child's subtrust created under this Declaration of Trust, the trustee shall

have all authority and power allowed or conferred under _____ law, subject to the

your state

trustee's fiduciary duty to the grantors and the beneficiaries.

(B) Specified Powers

The trustee's powers include, but are not limited to:

1. The power to sell trust property, and to borrow money and to encumber property, specifically including trust real estate, by mortgage, deed of trust or other method.

2. The power to manage trust real estate as if the trustee were the absolute owner of it, including the power to lease (even if the lease term may extend beyond the period of any trust) or grant options to lease the property, to make repairs or alterations and to insure against loss.

3. The power to sell or grant options for the sale or exchange of any trust property, including stocks, bonds, debentures and any other form of security or security account, at public or private sale for cash or on credit.

4. The power to invest trust property in property of any kind, including but not limited to bonds, debentures, notes, mortgages and stocks.

5. The power to receive additional property from any source and add to any trust created by this Declaration of Trust.

6. The power to employ and pay reasonable fees to accountants, lawyers or investment experts for information or advice relating to the trust.

7. The power to deposit and hold trust funds in both interest-bearing and non-interest-bearing accounts.

8. The power to deposit funds in bank or other accounts uninsured by FDIC coverage.

9. The power to enter into electronic fund transfer or safe deposit arrangements with financial institutions.

10. The power to continue any business of either grantor.

11. The power to institute or defend legal actions concerning the trust or the grantors' affairs.

12. The power to execute any documents necessary to administer any trust created in this Declaration of Trust.

13. The power to diversify investments, including authority to decide that some or all of the trust property need not produce income.

(C) Payment by the Trustee of the Grantors' Debts and Taxes

1. Wife's Debts and Taxes

_____'s debts and death taxes shall be paid
                                 wife's name

by the trustee. The trustee shall pay these from the following trust property: ⑨_____

_____

_____.

2. Husband's Debts and Taxes

_____'s debts and death taxes shall be paid
husband's name

by the trustee. The trustee shall pay these from the following trust property: ⑨_____

_____

_____.

3. If Specified Property Insufficient

If the property specified above is insufficient to pay all a grantor's debts and death taxes, the trustee shall

determine how such debts and death taxes shall be paid from that grantor's trust property, except as limited by any

law, or IRS regulation, controlling the property in Trust A.

X. GENERAL ADMINISTRATIVE PROVISIONS

(A) Controlling Law

The validity of The ①_____ Living Trust and
your names

construction of its provisions shall be governed by the laws of _____.
your state

(B) Severability

If any provision of this Declaration of Trust is ruled unenforceable, the remaining provisions shall

nevertheless remain in effect.

(C) Amendments

The term "Declaration of Trust" includes any provisions added by valid amendment.

XI. CHILDREN'S SUBTRUSTS

All trust property left to any of the minor or young adult beneficiaries listed below in Section XI,

Paragraph (A), shall be retained in trust for each such beneficiary in a separate subtrust of this

①_____ Living Trust.
your names

Each subtrust may be identified and referred to by adding the name of that subtrust's beneficiary to the name of this

trust. The following terms apply to each subtrust:

(A) Subtrust Beneficiaries and Age Limits

A subtrust shall end when the beneficiary of that subtrust, listed below, becomes 35, except as otherwise specified in this section:

⑩Subtrust for   Shall end at age

_____   _____

_____   _____

_____   _____

_____   _____

_____   _____

(B) Powers and Duties of Subtrust Trustee

1. Until a child's subtrust ends, the trustee may distribute to or use for the benefit of the beneficiary as much of the net income or principal of the child's subtrust as the trustee deems necessary for the beneficiary's health, support, maintenance or education. Education includes, but is not limited to, college, graduate, postgraduate and vocational studies, and reasonably related living expenses.

2. In deciding whether to make a distribution to the beneficiary, the trustee may take into account the beneficiary's other income, resources and sources of support.

3. Any subtrust income that is not distributed to a beneficiary by the trustee shall be accumulated and added to the principal of the subtrust for that beneficiary.

4. The trustee of a child's subtrust is not required to make any accounting or report to the subtrust beneficiary.

(C) Assignment of Interest of Beneficiary Prohibited

The interests of the beneficiary of a child's subtrust shall not be transferable by voluntary or involuntary assignment or by operation of law before actual receipt by the beneficiary. These interests shall be free from the claims of creditors and from attachments, execution, bankruptcy or other legal process to the fullest extent permitted by law.

(D) Compensation of Trustee

Any trustee of a child's subtrust created under this Declaration of Trust shall be entitled to reasonable compensation without court approval out of the subtrust assets for ordinary and extraordinary services, and for all services in connection with the termination of any subtrust.

(E) Termination of Subtrusts

A child's subtrust shall end when any of the following events occurs:

1. The beneficiary reaches the age specified in Section XI, Paragraph (A). If the subtrust ends for this reason, the remaining principal and accumulated income of the subtrust shall be given outright to the beneficiary.

2. The beneficiary dies. If the subtrust ends for this reason, the subtrust property shall pass to the beneficiary's heirs.

3. The trustee distributes all subtrust property under the provisions of this Declaration of Trust.

XII. CUSTODIANSHIPS UNDER THE UNIFORM TRANSFERS TO MINORS ACT

1. All property ⑪ _____ becomes entitled to

　　　　　　　　　　　　　　　　　beneficiary

under this trust document shall be given to _____ as

　　　　　　　　　　　　　　　　custodian's name

custodian for _____ under the _____

　　　　　　beneficiary　　　　　　　　　　　　　　　　state

Uniform Transfers to Minors Act, until _____ reaches age _____ .

　　　　　　　　　　　　　beneficiary

2. All property ⑪ _____ becomes entitled to

　　　　　　　　　　　　　　　　　beneficiary

under this trust document shall be given to _____ as

　　　　　　　　　　　　　　　　custodian's name

custodian for _____ under the _____

　　　　　　beneficiary　　　　　　　　　　　　　　　　state

Uniform Transfers to Minors Act, until _____ reaches age _____ .

　　　　　　　　　　　　　beneficiary

3. All property ⑪ _____ becomes entitled to

　　　　　　　　　　　　　　　　　beneficiary

under this trust document shall be given to _____ as

　　　　　　　　　　　　　　　　custodian's name

custodian for _____ under the _____

　　　　　　beneficiary　　　　　　　　　　　　　　　　state

Uniform Transfers to Minors Act, until _____ reaches age _____ .

　　　　　　　　　　　　　beneficiary

Certification by Grantors

We certify that we have read this Declaration of Trust and that it correctly states the terms and conditions under which the trust property is to be held, managed and disposed of by the trustees and we approve the Declaration of Trust.

Dated: _____

_____

Grantor and Trustee

_____

Grantor and Trustee

NOTARY'S ACKNOWLEDGMENT

State of _____

County of _____

On _____, 19_____, before me, _____,

a notary public in and for said state, personally appeared _____

_____, personally known to me (or proved to me on the basis of

satisfactory evidence) to be the persons whose names are subscribed to the within Declaration of Trust, and

acknowledged to me that they executed the same in their authorized capacities and that by their signatures on the

instrument they executed the Declaration of Trust.

_____

Signature of Notary   [SEAL]

SCHEDULE A ③

SHARED PROPERTY PLACED IN TRUST

SCHEDULE B

WIFE'S SEPARATE PROPERTY PLACED IN TRUST

All Wife's interest in the following property:

SCHEDULE C

HUSBAND'S SEPARATE PROPERTY PLACED IN TRUST

All Husband's interest in the following property:

Form 4: Witness Statement for a Florida Living Trust

STATEMENT OF WITNESS

On this _____ day of _____, 19___ ,

_____ declared to me, the undersigned, that this
your name(s)

Declaration of Trust was _____ living trust and requested me to act as witnesses to it.
his/her/their

_____ then signed this living trust in my presence. I now
your name(s)

at _____ request, in _____ presence, subscribe my name as witness and declare I understand this
his/her/their   his/her/their

to be _____ living trust.
his/her/their

I declare under penalty of perjury that the foregoing is true and correct, this _____ day of

_____, 19_____ .

_____

witness's signature

_____

witness's typed name

_____, _____, _____

city   county   state

Form 5: Assignment of Property to a Trust for One Person

ASSIGNMENT OF PROPERTY

I, _____, as grantor, hereby assign and transfer all my

your name

rights, title and interest in the following property _____

_____

_____ to

_____, as trustee of the _____

your name   your name

Living Trust, dated _____, 19_____.

Executed at _____, _____, on

city   state

_____, 19_____.

date

_____

Grantor

Form 6: Assignment of Shared Property to a Trust for a Couple

ASSIGNMENT OF PROPERTY

We, _____,
<small>your names</small>

as grantors, hereby assign and transfer all our rights, title and interest in the following property

_____

_____

_____ to

_____, as trustees of
<small>your names</small>

the _____ Living Trust,
<small>your names</small>

dated _____, 19_____.

    Executed at _____, _____, on
<small>city   state</small>

_____, 19_____.
<small>date</small>

_____
Grantor

_____
Grantor

Form 7: Amendment to Living Trust for One Person

AMENDMENT TO LIVING TRUST

This Amendment to The ① _____ Living Trust

your name

dated _____, 19_____, is made this _____ day of _____, 19_____,

date Declaration of Trust signed

by _____, the grantor and trustee of the trust. Under the

your name

power of amendment reserved to the grantor by Section III, Paragraph (A), of the trust, the grantor amends the

trust as follows:

    1. The following is added to the Declaration of Trust:

_____

_____

    2. The following is deleted from the Declaration of Trust:

_____

_____

    [Repeat as needed]

    In all other respects, the Declaration of Trust as executed on _____, 19_____,

by the grantor is hereby affirmed.

    Executed at _____, _____, on

city   state

_____, 19_____.

date

_____

Grantor and Trustee

NOTARY'S ACKNOWLEDGMENT

State of _____

County of _____

On _____, 19_____, before me, _____,

a notary public in and for said state, personally appeared _____,

personally known to me (or proved to me on the basis of satisfactory evidence) to be the person whose name is

subscribed to the within Amendment of Trust, and acknowledged to me that he/she executed the same in his/her

authorized capacity and that by his/her signature on the instrument he/she executed the Amendment of Trust.

_____
Signature of Notary   [SEAL]

Form 8: Amendment to Basic Shared Living Trust or AB Trust

AMENDMENT TO LIVING TRUST

This Amendment to The ① _____ Living Trust
your names

dated _____, 19____, is made this ____ day of _____, 19____,
date Declaration of Trust signed

by _____,
your names

the grantors and trustees of the trust. Under the power of amendment reserved to the grantors by Section II,

Paragraph (F), of the Declaration of Trust, the grantors amend the trust as follows:

    1. The following is added to the Declaration of Trust:

_____

_____

    2. The following is deleted from the Declaration of Trust:

_____

_____

    [Repeat as needed]

    In all other respects, the Declaration of Trust as executed on _____, 19____,

by the grantors is hereby affirmed.

    Executed at _____, _____, on
                           city   state

_____, 19____.
date

_____

Grantor and Trustee

_____

Grantor and Trustee

-1-

NOTARY'S ACKNOWLEDGMENT

State of _____

County of _____

On _____, 19_____, before me, _____,

a notary public in and for said state, personally appeared _____

_____, personally known to me (or proved to me on the basis of

satisfactory evidence) to be the persons whose names are subscribed to the within Declaration of Trust, and

acknowledged to me that they executed the same in their authorized capacities and that by their signatures on the

instrument they executed the Declaration of Trust.

_____

Signature of Notary   [SEAL]

Form 9: Revocation

REVOCATION OF LIVING TRUST

On _____, 19___, _____ created
your name(s)

a revocable living trust, called "The _____
your name(s)

Living Trust," with _____ as the grantor(s) and
your name(s)

trustee(s). Under the terms of the trust, the grantor(s) reserved to _____ the full
himself/herself/themselves

power to revoke the trust.

According to the terms of the Declaration of Trust, and the laws of the State of _____,
your state

the grantor(s) hereby revoke the Declaration of Trust and state that the trust is completely revoked. All property of

The _____ Living Trust shall be returned to the grantor(s)
your name(s)

and legally owned by _____ as defined in the Declaration of Trust.
him/her/them

Dated: _____

_____
your signatures

_____

Notary's Acknowledgment

State of _____

County of _____

On _____, 19_____, before me, _____,

a notary public in and for said state, personally appeared _____

_____, personally known to me (or proved to me on the basis of

satisfactory evidence) to be the person(s) whose name(s) is/are subscribed to the within instrument, and

acknowledged to me that he/she/they executed the same in his/her/their authorized capacity(ies) and that by his/

her/their signature(s) on the instrument the person(s), or the entity upon behalf of which the person(s) acted,

executed the Declaration of Trust.

_____
Signature of Notary   [SEAL]

Form 10: Basic Will for One Person

WILL

of

_____
your name

I, _____, a resident of
your name

_____, _____ County, _____,
city   county   state

declare that this is my will.

1. I revoke all wills and codicils that I have previously made.

2. I am not married.

3. (A) I am the _____ of the _____ whose _____ _____
mother/father   child/children   name(s)   is/are

_____

_____

_____

_____

_____.

There are ___ living children of my deceased child _____,
name

whose names are:

_____

_____

_____.

(B) If I fail to leave, by this will or otherwise, any property to any of the children listed above, my failure to do so is intentional.

(C) If at my death any of my children are minors, and a personal guardian is needed, I nominate

_____ to be appointed personal guardian
name

of my minor children. If _____ cannot serve as
name

personal guardian, I nominate _____ to be appointed
name

personal guardian.

(D) If at my death any of my children are minors, and a property guardian is needed,

I appoint _____ as property guardian for my minor children.

name

If _____ cannot serve as property guardian, I appoint

name

_____ as property guardian.

name

(E) I direct that no bond be required of any guardian.

4. (A) I make the following specific gifts:

I leave _____

property described

to _____, or if _____

beneficiary's name   beneficiary's name

fails to survive me, to _____.

alternate beneficiary's name

I leave _____

property described

to _____, or if _____

beneficiary's name   beneficiary's name

fails to survive me, to _____.

alternate beneficiary's name

I leave _____

property described

to _____, or if _____

beneficiary's name   beneficiary's name

fails to survive me, to _____.

alternate beneficiary's name

(B) I leave all my other property subject to this will to

_____, or if _____ fails to

residuary beneficiary's name   he/she

survive me, to _____.

alternate residuary beneficiary's name

5. (A) I nominate _____ to serve as executor of my will.

executor's name

If _____ is unable to serve or continue serving as executor, I nominate

he/she

_____ to serve as executor.

alternate executor's name

(B) No bond shall be required of any executor.

I subscribe my name to this will this _____ day of _____, 19____, at

_____, _____, _____.

city   county   state

_____

your signature

WITNESSES

On the date last written above, _____ declared to us, the
your name

undersigned, that this was _____ will, and requested us to act as witnesses to it. _____ then
his/her   He/She

signed this will in our presence, all of us being present at the same time. We now at _____ request
his/her

and in _____ presence, and in the presence of each other, have signed this will as witnesses.
his/her

We declare under penalty of perjury that the foregoing is true and correct.

_____
witness signature

_____
witness printed name

_____, _____, _____
city   county   state

_____
witness signature

_____
witness printed name

_____, _____, _____
city   county   state

_____
witness signature

_____
witness printed name

_____, _____, _____
city   county   state

Form 11: Basic Will for a Member of a Couple

WILL

of

_____
your name

I, _____, a resident of
your name

_____, _____ County, _____,
city   county   state

declare that this is my will.

    1. I revoke all wills and codicils that I have previously made.

    2. I am married to _____.
name

    3. (A) I am the _____ of the _____ whose _____ _____
mother/father   child/children   name(s)   is/are

_____

_____

_____

_____

_____.

    There are ___ living children of my deceased child _____,
name

whose names are:

_____

_____

_____.

     (B) If I fail to leave, by this will or otherwise, any property to any of the children listed above, my failure to do so is intentional.

     (C) If at my death any of my children are minors, and a personal guardian is needed, I nominate

_____ to be appointed personal guardian
name

of my minor children. If _____ cannot serve as
name

personal guardian, I nominate _____ to be appointed
name

personal guardian.

(D) If at my death any of my children are minors, and a property guardian is needed,

I appoint _____ as property guardian for my minor children.
name

If _____ cannot serve as property guardian, I appoint
name

_____ as property guardian.
name

(E) I direct that no bond be required of any guardian.

4. (A) I make the following specific gifts:

I leave _____
property described

to _____, or if _____
beneficiary's name   beneficiary's name

fails to survive me, to _____.
alternate beneficiary's name

I leave _____
property described

to _____, or if _____
beneficiary's name   beneficiary's name

fails to survive me, to _____.
alternate beneficiary's name

I leave _____
property described

to _____, or if _____
beneficiary's name   beneficiary's name

fails to survive me, to _____.
alternate beneficiary's name

(B) I leave all my other property subject to this will to

_____, or if _____ fails to
residuary beneficiary's name   he/she

survive me, to _____.
alternate residuary beneficiary's name

5. (A) I nominate _____ to serve as executor of my will.
executor's name

If _____ is unable to serve or continue serving as executor, I nominate
he/she

_____ to serve as executor.
alternate executor's name

(B) No bond shall be required of any executor.

6. If my spouse and I should die simultaneously, or under such circumstances as to render it difficult or impossible to determine who predeceased the other, I shall be conclusively presumed to have survived my spouse for purposes of this will.

I subscribe my name to this will this _____ day of _____, 19____, at

_____, _____, _____.
    city   county   state

_____
        your signature

WITNESSES

On the date last written above, _____ declared to us, the
               your name

undersigned, that this was _____ will, and requested us to act as witnesses to it. _____ then
          his/her   He/She

signed this will in our presence, all of us being present at the same time. We now at _____ request and
                               his/her

presence, and in the presence of each other, have signed this will as witnesses.

We declare under penalty of perjury that the foregoing is true and correct.

_____
witness signature

_____
witness printed name

_____, _____, _____
city   county   state

_____
witness signature

_____
witness printed name

_____, _____, _____
city   county   state

_____
witness signature

_____
witness printed name

_____, _____, _____
city   county   state

Form 12: Affidavit of Successor Trustee

AFFIDAVIT OF ASSUMPTION OF DUTIES BY SUCCESSOR TRUSTEE

State of _____, County of _____.
                state   county

_____, of legal age, first being duly sworn, declares:
             successor trustee's name

On _____, 19____, _____ created
         date   name(s) of grantor(s)

the _____ Living Trust.
          name(s) of grantor(s)

On _____, 19____, _____ died, as
         date   grantor's name

established in the attached certified copy of the Certificate of Death.

[for a shared or AB trust, add:]

On _____, 19____, _____ died, as
         date   second grantor's name

established in the attached certified copy of the Certificate of Death.

The Declaration of Trust creating the _____ Living Trust
                              grantor(s) name(s)

provides that upon the death of the grantors, I, _____,
                                  successor trustee's name

become the trustee of the trust.

I hereby accept the office of trustee of the trust, and am now acting as trustee of the trust.

Dated: _____

_____
Successor Trustee

NOTARY'S ACKNOWLEDGMENT

State of _____

County of _____

On _____, 19_____, before me, _____,

a notary public in and for said state, personally appeared _____

_____, personally known to me (or proved to me on the basis of

satisfactory evidence) to be the person(s) whose name(s) is/are subscribed to the within instrument, and

acknowledged to me that he/she/they executed the same in his/her/their authorized capacity(ies) and that by his/

her/their signature(s) on the instrument the person(s), or the entity upon behalf of which the person(s) acted,

executed the instrument.

_____

Signature of Notary   [SEAL]

Index

CATALOG

...more from Nolo Press

🖳 Book with disk

	EDITION	PRICE	CODE
Sexual Harassment on the Job	2nd	$18.95	HARS
Trademark: How to Name Your Business & Product	2nd	$29.95	TRD
Workers' Comp for Employers	2nd	$29.95	CNTRL
Your Rights in the Workplace	2nd	$15.95	YRW

CONSUMER

	EDITION	PRICE	CODE
Fed Up With the Legal System: What's Wrong & How to Fix It	2nd	$9.95	LEG
Glossary of Insurance Terms	5th	$14.95	GLINT
How to Insure Your Car	1st	$12.95	INCAR
How to Win Your Personal Injury Claim	1st	$24.95	PICL
Nolo's Pocket Guide to California Law	4th	$10.95	CLAW
Nolo's Pocket Guide to Consumer Rights	2nd	$12.95	CAG
The Over 50 Insurance Survival Guide	1st	$16.95	OVER50
True Odds: How Risk Affects Your Everyday Life	1st	$19.95	TROD
What Do You Mean It's Not Covered?	1st	$19.95	COVER

ESTATE PLANNING & PROBATE

	EDITION	PRICE	CODE
How to Probate an Estate (California Edition)	8th	$34.95	PAE
Make Your Own Living Trust	2nd	$19.95	LITR
Nolo's Simple Will Book	2nd	$17.95	SWIL
Plan Your Estate	3rd	$24.95	NEST
The Quick and Legal Will Book	1st	$15.95	QUIC
Nolo's Law Form Kit: Wills	1st	$14.95	KWL

FAMILY MATTERS

	EDITION	PRICE	CODE
A Legal Guide for Lesbian and Gay Couples	8th	$24.95	LG
Child Custody: Building Agreements That Work	1st	$24.95	CUST
Divorce & Money: How to Make the Best Financial Decisions During Divorce	2nd	$21.95	DIMO
How to Adopt Your Stepchild in California	4th	$22.95	ADOP
How to Do Your Own Divorce in California	21st	$21.95	CDIV
How to Do Your Own Divorce in Texas	6th	$19.95	TDIV
How to Raise or Lower Child Support in California	3rd	$18.95	CHLD
Nolo's Pocket Guide to Family Law	4th	$14.95	FLD
Practical Divorce Solutions	1st	$14.95	PDS
The Guardianship Book (California Edition)	2nd	$24.95	GB
The Living Together Kit	7th	$24.95	LTK

GOING TO COURT

	EDITION	PRICE	CODE
Collect Your Court Judgment (California Edition	2nd	$19.95	JUDG
Everybody's Guide to Municipal Court (California Edition)	1st	$29.95	MUNI

▣ Book with disk

	EDITION	PRICE	CODE
Everybody's Guide to Small Claims Court (California Edition) 12th		$18.95	CSCC
Everybody's Guide to Small Claims Court (National Edition) 6th		$18.95	NSCC
Fight Your Ticket ... and Win! (California Edition) 6th		$19.95	FYT
How to Change Your Name (California Edition) 6th		$24.95	NAME
Represent Yourself in Court: How to Prepare & Try a Winning Case 1st		$29.95	RYC
The Criminal Records Book (California Edition) 5th		$21.95	CRIM

HOMEOWNERS, LANDLORDS & TENANTS

	EDITION	PRICE	CODE
Dog Law 2nd		$12.95	DOG
▣ Every Landlord's Legal Guide (National Edition) 1st		$29.95	ELLI
For Sale by Owner (California Edition) 2nd		$24.95	FSBO
Homestead Your House (California Edition) 8th		$9.95	HOME
How to Buy a House in California 3rd		$24.95	BHCA
Neighbor Law: Fences, Trees, Boundaries & Noise 2nd		$16.95	NEI
Safe Homes, Safe Neighborhoods: Stopping Crime Where You Live 1st		$14.95	SAFE
Tenants' Rights (California Edition) 12th		$18.95	CTEN
The Deeds Book (California Edition) 3rd		$16.95	DEED
The Landlord's Law Book, Vol. 1: Rights & Responsibilities (California Edition) 5th		$34.95	LBRT
The Landlord's Law Book, Vol. 2: Evictions (California Edition) 5th		$34.95	LBEV

HUMOR

	EDITION	PRICE	CODE
29 Reasons Not to Go to Law School 1st		$9.95	29R
Poetic Justice 1st		$9.95	PJ

IMMIGRATION

	EDITION	PRICE	CODE
How to Become a United States Citizen 5th		$14.95	CIT
How to Get a Green Card: Legal Ways to Stay in the U.S.A. 2nd		$24.95	GRN
U.S. Immigration Made Easy 5th		$39.95	IMEZ

MONEY MATTERS

	EDITION	PRICE	CODE
Building Your Nest Egg With Your 401(k) 1st		$16.95	EGG
Chapter 13 Bankruptcy: Repay Your Debts 1st		$29.95	CH13
How to File for Bankruptcy 5th		$25.95	HFB
Money Troubles: Legal Strategies to Cope With Your Debts 3rd		$18.95	MT
Nolo's Law Form Kit: Personal Bankruptcy 1st		$14.95	KBNK
Nolo's Law Form Kit: Rebuild Your Credit 1st		$14.95	KCRD
Simple Contracts for Personal Use 2nd		$16.95	CONT
Smart Ways to Save Money During and After Divorce 1st		$14.95	SAVMO
Stand Up to the IRS 2nd		$21.95	SIRS

▣ Book with disk

PATENTS AND COPYRIGHTS

RESEARCH & REFERENCE

SENIORS

SOFTWARE

ORDER FORM

Code	Quantity	Title	Unit price	Total

Subtotal	
California residents add Sales Tax	
Basic Shipping ($5 for 1 item; $6 for 2-3 items, $7 for 4 or more)	
UPS RUSH delivery $7–any size order*	
TOTAL	

Name

Address

(UPS to street address, Priority Mail to P.O. boxes)   * Delivered in 3 business days from receipt of order. S.F. Bay area use regular shipping.

FOR FASTER SERVICE, USE YOUR CREDIT CARD AND OUR TOLL-FREE NUMBERS

Order 24 hours a day	1-800-992-6656
Fax your order	1-800-645-0895
e-mail	NoloInfo@nolopress.com
General Information	1-510-549-1976
Customer Service	1-800-728-3555, Mon.-Sat. 9am-5pm, PST

METHOD OF PAYMENT

☐ Check enclosed
☐ VISA   ☐ MasterCard   ☐ Discover Card   ☐ American Express

Account #   Expiration Date

Authorizing Signature

Daytime Phone

Prices subject to change.

Visit our store
If you live in the Bay Area, be sure to visit the Nolo Press Bookstore on the corner of 9th and Parker Streets in West Berkeley. You'll find our complete line of books and software, all at a discount. We also have t-shirts, posters and a selection of business and legal self-help books from other publishers. Open every day.

NOLO PRESS 950 PARKER ST., BERKELEY, CA 94710

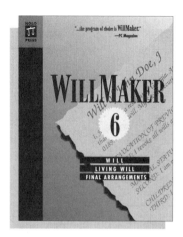
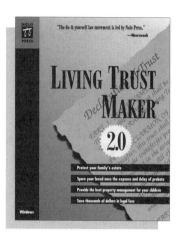

Take 2 minutes & Get a 2-year NOLO *News* subscription free!*

CALL
1-800-992-6656

FAX
1-800-645-0895

E-MAIL
NOLOSUB@NOLOPRESS.com

OR MAIL US THIS POSTAGE-PAID REGISTRATION CARD

*U.S. ADDRESSES ONLY.
TWO YEAR INTERNATIONAL SUBSCRIPTIONS:
CANADA & MEXICO $10.00;
ALL OTHER FOREIGN ADDRESSES $20.00.

With our quarterly magazine, the **NOLO** *News*, you'll

- **Learn** about important legal changes that affect you
- **Find out first** about new Nolo products
- **Keep current** with practical articles on everyday law
- **Get answers** to your legal questions in *Ask Auntie Nolo's* advice column

- **Save money** with special Subscriber Only discounts
- **Tickle your funny bone** with our famous *Lawyer Joke* column.

It only takes 2 minutes to reserve your free 2-year subscription or to extend your **NOLO** *News* subscription.

REGISTRATION CARD

NAME _____ DATE _____

ADDRESS _____

_____ PHONE NUMBER _____

CITY _____ STATE _____ ZIP _____

WHERE DID YOU HEAR ABOUT THIS BOOK? _____

WHERE DID YOU PURCHASE THIS PRODUCT? _____

DID YOU CONSULT A LAWYER? (PLEASE CIRCLE ONE)   YES   NO   NOT APPLICABLE

DID YOU FIND THIS BOOK HELPFUL?   (VERY)   5   4   3   2   1   (NOT AT ALL)

SUGGESTIONS FOR IMPROVING THIS PRODUCT _____

WAS IT EASY TO USE?   (VERY EASY)   5   4   3   2   1   (VERY DIFFICULT)

DO YOU OWN A COMPUTER? IF SO, WHICH FORMAT? (PLEASE CIRCLE ONE)   WINDOWS   DOS   MAC

LITR 2.0

Nolo helps lay people perform legal tasks without the aid—or fees—of lawyers."

—USA TODAY

[Nolo books are ..."written in plain language, free of legal mumbo jumbo, and spiced with witty personal observations."

—ASSOCIATED PRESS

"...Nolo publications...guide people simply through the how, when, where and why of law."

—WASHINGTON POST

"Increasingly, people who are not lawyers are performing tasks usually regarded as legal work... And consumers, using books like Nolo's, do routine legal work themselves."

—NEW YORK TIMES

"...All of [Nolo's] books are easy-to-understand, are updated regularly, provide pull-out forms...and are often quite moving in their sense of compassion for the struggles of the lay reader."

—SAN FRANCISCO CHRONICLE